WOODROW WILSON
AND THE REIMAGINING
OF EASTERN EUROPE

WOODROW WILSON AND THE REIMAGINING OF EASTERN EUROPE

Larry Wolff

STANFORD UNIVERSITY PRESS
Stanford, California

STANFORD UNIVERSITY PRESS
Stanford, California

© 2020 by the Board of Trustees of the Leland Stanford Junior University.
All rights reserved.

No part of this book may be reproduced or transmitted in any form or by any means, electronic or mechanical, including photocopying and recording, or in any information storage or retrieval system without the prior written permission of Stanford University Press.

Printed in the United States of America on acid-free, archival-quality paper

Library of Congress Cataloging-in-Publication Data

Names: Wolff, Larry, author.
Title: Woodrow Wilson and the reimagining of Eastern Europe / Larry Wolff.
Description: Stanford, California : Stanford University Press, [2020] | Includes bibliographical references and index.
Identifiers: LCCN 2019019235 (print) | LCCN 2019021634 (ebook) | ISBN 9781503611184 (cloth : alk. paper) | ISBN 9781503611191 (pbk. : alk. paper) | ISBN 9781503611207 (ebook)
Subjects: LCSH: Wilson, Woodrow, 1856–1924. | Europe, Eastern—Foreign relations—United States. | United States—Foreign relations—Europe, Eastern. | Self-determination, National—Europe, Eastern—History—20th century. | Europe, Eastern—Boundaries—History—20th century. | World War, 1914–1918—Territorial questions—Europe, Eastern. | United States—Foreign relations—1913–1921.
Classification: LCC DJK45.U6 (ebook) | LCC DJK45.U6 W65 2020 (print) | DDC 327.7304709/041—dc23
LC record available at https://lccn.loc.gov/2019019235

Cover design: Kevin Barrett Kane

Cover image: 1939 Postcard of Woodrow Wilson by Arthur Szyk, Polish American Fraternity, NY World's Fair. Printed by Drukarnia Narodowa, Krakow.

Typeset by Kevin Barrett Kane in 10/15 Sabon LT Pro

For ORLANDO,
*who wrote the high school musical
about Woodrow Wilson
and the Paris Peace Conference*

Now this is the Law of the Jungle—as old and as true as the sky;
And the Wolf that shall keep it may prosper, but the Wolf that shall break it must die.
As the creeper that girdles the tree-trunk, the Law runneth forward and back—
For the strength of the Pack is the Wolf, and the strength of the Wolf is the Pack.
Wash daily from nose-tip to tail-tip; drink deeply, but never too deep;
And remember the night is for hunting, and forget not the day is for sleep.
—Rudyard Kipling, *The Jungle Book*

TINTIN: May I ask you a question? I read in a brochure about Syldavia that if your king loses his sceptre he will be forced to abdicate. Is that true?

POLICE CAPTAIN: As a matter of fact it is . . .
But how does this concern you?
—Hergé, *King Ottokar's Sceptre*

"Diplomacy? The wiliest diplomat is absolutely helpless in our hands."
—Gilbert and Sullivan, *Princess Ida*

If I were not a little mad and generally silly
I should give you my advice upon the subject, willy-nilly;
I should show you in a moment how to grapple with the question,
And you'd really be astonished at the force of my suggestion.
—Gilbert and Sullivan, *Ruddigore*

"You ought to be brave for two reasons: the first is that you are a Gascon, and the second is that you are my son. Never fear quarrels, but seek adventures."
—Alexandre Dumas, *The Three Musketeers*

"His Super-Ego was insatiable."
—Sigmund Freud on Woodrow Wilson

Contents

Acknowledgments ix

Introduction
1

1. Wilson's Eastern Question
and the End of the Ottoman Empire
15

2. "This War of Emancipation":
The Wilsonian Deliverance
of the Habsburg Peoples
56

3. Wilsonian Friendship: Personal Sympathy
and Geopolitical Transformation
115

4. National Majorities and National Minorities
in Wilson's Eastern Europe
168

CONCLUSION:
The Dynamics of Wilsonian Mental Mapping
228

Notes 249
Index 271

Acknowledgments

The subject of Woodrow Wilson's Eastern Europe has been a challenging foray into the twentieth century for me, though the theme is closely related to my earlier work, in the book *Inventing Eastern Europe*, about how the philosophes of the Enlightenment in the eighteenth century came to see Europe divided into an east and a west. Just as Voltaire and Rousseau philosophized about Eastern Europe from afar without ever setting eyes on any of its lands, so Wilson transformed Eastern Europe at the Paris Peace Conference without ever visiting the region. Like Voltaire in the eighteenth century, Wilson in the twentieth century took powerful possession of Eastern Europe in his own mind and registered its contours and meanings through the imagery of mental mapping.

I had the opportunity to reflect on these issues in 2015 at a conference on mental mapping at Södertörn University in Stockholm, and I am most grateful to Norbert Götz and Rolf Petri who guided the proceedings. Rolf has been an important friend and colleague of mine over many years now, from Stockholm and Berlin to Venice and Mestre and the beaches of Pesaro, and he has helped me think through many historical issues, from nostalgia to ideology.

I lived a large part of my life in the twentieth century and now find myself reading my way back into it as a historian. My colleagues in European history at New York University who work on the twentieth century have discussed with me some of the relevant issues, and in this respect I would especially like to thank Stefanos Geroulanos, Stephen Gross, Molly Nolan, Guy Ortolano, Ruth Ben-Ghiat, and Peter Baldwin. For thinking about the twentieth century, I would never neglect to mention the inspirational intellectual companionship of my late, great colleague

ACKNOWLEDGMENTS

Tony Judt. I'm further grateful to a wonderful cohort of graduate students who have challenged me over the past decade to think long and hard with them about twentieth-century Europe: Madigan Fichter, James Robertson, Filip Erdeljac, Petro Nungovitch, Joanna Curtis, Kyle Shybunko, Rosie Johnston, and Katie David. Woodrow Wilson is, of course, also a subject in American history, which I approach from a Europeanist's perspective, and I'm lucky to have had at NYU inspirational colleagues in American history, especially Tom Bender and Linda Gordon, who have even been reciprocally engaged with Eastern Europe in different fashions. I have been inspired by very original recent discussions of Woodrow Wilson and the peace settlement by Erez Manela, Leonard Smith, Trygve Throntveit, and my friend Adam Tooze. Marisa Bellack at the *Washington Post* published the essay that became the first installment of this book.

I first presented some of my material on Wilson and national plebiscites at the 2016 NYU conference on referendums, and was grateful for comments from Sara Hobolt, Istvan Rev, Joan-Pau Rubiés, and Jacques Rupnik. I was very pleased to get to outline some of my thoughts about Wilson at the NYU conference on the end of the Habsburg and Ottoman empires, in a concluding panel discussion that included my friends Molly Greene, Krishan Kumar, Zvi Ben-Dor, and Holly Case. Zvi has been a great friend and colleague for twelve years now, and I'm grateful to him for many things, including the opportunity to think about a sharper focus on the year 1919.

It has meant a lot to me, while completing this project, to have my friend Philipp Ther (along with his saxophone) as a visitor at NYU. Furthermore, as a visitor at the Remarque Institute, my friend Maria Tatar helped me to focus on the figure of Erich Maria Remarque and the issues of World War I. At Remarque in recent years I've been grateful for the assistance and support of Samantha Paul, while at the Center for European and Mediterranean Studies I have felt lucky to be working once again with Mikhala Stein Kotlyar, with whom I worked in Cambridge so many years back. It was many years before that that my dear friend Peter Stansky, at Stanford, first introduced me to Gladstone and the Bulgarian horrors, which turned out to be essential for thinking about Wilson and Eastern Europe in this book.

ACKNOWLEDGMENTS

I'm always grateful to my provost, my colleague, my friend Katy Fleming, who actually took the time (while running the whole university) to co-teach a course with me, covering some of the Mediterranean and East European issues that were relevant to Woodrow Wilson. My colleague Elisabeth Bronfen has further inspired me to think about issues of twentieth-century culture, and, indeed, without her support and collaboration I would never have lectured at Bayreuth on Richard Wagner and Bugs Bunny. I've worked on Wilson at NYU Shanghai during January term for the past seven years, and Joanna Waley-Cohen, the provost there, has been a great friend and colleague. My Boston friend Jim Cronin has helped me plan out a series of events focused on the twentieth and twenty-first centuries, even as the Red Sox won another World Series and the Patriots won another Super Bowl.

My father's untiring intellectual curiosity about Woodrow Wilson has encouraged me from the start. He is the only person I know who can reliably recite the list of American presidents chronologically, forwards and backwards. Both my father and my mother have given me loving support in all my endeavors, and I can never thank them enough. Perri Klass believed that I could make this project work, and it was so much fun to be writing this book with her on Cape Cod in our little unit in Deck 2. My son Anatol gave me both the encouragement and the PDFs that I needed to work on this project in its final stages from Shanghai, while my daughter Josephine offered every other sort of disciplinary coaching. Of my son Orlando, what can I say? He wrote the high school musical about Woodrow Wilson and the Paris Peace Conference!

WOODROW WILSON
AND THE REIMAGINING
OF EASTERN EUROPE

Introduction

"You are the foster-father of a chiefless land," the famous Polish pianist and national leader Ignacy Jan Paderewski wrote to U.S. President Woodrow Wilson in October 1917, six months after the United States entered World War I.[1] In August 1918 Tomáš Garrigue Masaryk, who was soon to become Czechoslovakia's first president, wrote to Wilson: "Your name, Mr. President, as you have no doubt read, is openly cheered in the streets of Prague—our nation will forever be grateful to you and to the people of the United States."[2] It would be difficult to overestimate either the enthusiasm for Woodrow Wilson in Eastern Europe during and after World War I or his huge impact on the political transformation embodied in the peace settlement at Versailles, which gave Eastern Europe its twentieth-century form on the map as a system of interlocking national states. Neither Czechoslovakia nor Yugoslavia still exist today, but they survived under changing political regimes across the twentieth century, from the end of World War I to the end of the Cold War, falling apart only in the 1990s. They were created in significant part thanks to Wilson's advocacy, while the reconstitution of Poland on the map of Europe—after more than a century of geopolitical nonexistence following the country's eighteenth-century partition by Russia, Prussia, and Austria—found its most potent political affirmation in Wilson's Fourteen Points speech of January 1918, which, in Point Thirteen, called for the creation of an independent Polish state of "territories inhabited by indisputably Polish populations."

The Versailles settlement in Europe, as shaped by Wilson's commitment to correlating nationality and sovereignty, was full of flaws (like the impossibility of applying the word "indisputably") that became increasingly apparent already during the interwar years, especially when targeted by Nazi Germany in the 1930s. Yet Wilson's impact on the modern political structuring of Eastern Europe was perhaps his most enduring international legacy. Even Stalin, though he absorbed the Baltic states of Lithuania, Latvia, and Estonia, allowed the Wilsonian creations of Yugoslavia and Czechoslovakia to continue to exist, such that Cold War Eastern Europe, from Bulgaria to Poland, largely resembled interwar Eastern Europe as it appeared on the map, albeit with very different political regimes. For this reason, it is striking that, while almost every aspect of Wilson's political and international legacy has come up for academic revision in recent years, his policy toward Eastern Europe has remained relatively unreconsidered over the past half century. This is all the more surprising for the fact that Eastern Europe itself has undergone tremendous transformations over the last generation, since the end of the Cold War, suggesting the importance of critically reconsidering the historical contingency of twentieth-century borders.

Wilson, elected in 1912, was one of the most academically and intellectually distinguished American presidents. With a Ph.D. in political science from Johns Hopkins University, he became professor of jurisprudence and political economy at Princeton in 1890, subsequently serving as president of the university from 1902 until 1910, when he was elected governor of New Jersey. His was a rapid political ascent, in which he won the presidency of the United States only two years later as a Democrat, defeating the Republican incumbent president, William Howard Taft, and the former president Theodore Roosevelt in a three-way race. "Our duty is to cleanse, to reconsider, to restore, to correct the evil without impairing the good, to purify and humanize every process of our common life," Wilson declared in his first inaugural address of 1913, burning with Progressive Era idealism. "The Nation has been deeply stirred, stirred by a solemn passion, stirred by the knowledge of wrong, of ideals lost, of government too often debauched and made an instrument of evil. The feelings with which we face this new age of right and opportunity sweep across our heartstrings like some air out of God's own presence."[3] The son of a Presbyterian minister, Wilson possessed a sense of righteousness that often presumed to mediate between the passions of the people and the presence of the deity. Harold Nicolson, as a member of the British delegation at the Paris Peace Conference, scathingly claimed that "the defects of Wilson's character, his rigidity and spiritual arrogance, became pathologically enhanced after his arrival in Europe," and "his mind was illumined only by the incense of his own self-worship; God-worship; People-worship." Historian Jill Lepore has also noted that he was a true believer in the "virtually limitless" executive power of the presidency.[4] Wilson's righteousness, to be sure, was accompanied by a sense of obstinate pride, which became a tragic flaw when he refused to compromise over the details of the Treaty of Versailles and the League of Nations in order to satisfy his critics in the U.S. Senate. Ultimately, the Senate refused to approve the settlement that Wilson had so feverishly negotiated in Paris.

Theodore Roosevelt, also a Progressive, once commented that "Wilson is merely a less virile *me*." With his long face and large ears, poor vision, and troubled digestion, Wilson's self-confidence was founded on his intellectual qualities. He could relate to ordinary Americans as a baseball fan, and enjoyed a low-brow fondness for limericks, even composing one on the subject of his own homeliness, beginning thus:

> For beauty I am not a star,
> There are others more perfect by far . . .

Yet, in spite of such personal modesty, when asked if he ever thought he was wrong about anything, he would confidently reply, "Not in matters where I have qualified myself to speak."[5] Eastern Europe was to become one of those matters on which he felt qualified to speak.

Wilson's political life was conditioned by complex intellectual underpinnings, and his ideas, including his ideas about Eastern Europe, merit close and subtle consideration. Just as in domestic politics he was closely associated with the ideals of the Progressive movement, so in international politics he himself elaborated a framework of principles that defined what it meant to be diplomatically progressive. His fierce focus on the principle of national self-determination was intended as a democratic vindication of the rights of small nations—especially in Eastern Europe—against large empires like Austria-Hungary and Ottoman Turkey. Already in 1915, before America's entry into the war, Masaryk had lectured in London on "The Problem of Small Nations in the European Crisis"—and Wilson, in 1918 and 1919, would not only embrace Masaryk as a personal friend and sympathetic associate, but would also become the advocate of small nations, including Masaryk's Czechoslovakia.

The Versailles settlement in Eastern Europe has been generally understood, ever since 1919, as a purposeful, though sometimes confused, attempt to apply Wilson's abstract, high-minded principle of national self-determination to the messy reality of the geopolitical and ethnographic map. Wilson's political approach to the Paris Peace Conference in 1919 was far from strictly theoretical, however, and his approach to the remaking of Europe may best be understood as the intersection of his international principles with a rapidly developed and highly colored mental mapping of the region of Eastern Europe. Mental mapping is the approach to geography that considers the subjective, psychological, and cultural aspects of how individuals and communities understand the places and spaces on the map.[6] Mental maps—not just the graphic and material maps on the wall but also the imagistic, impressionistic, idiosyncratic maps in the human mind—shaped the perspectives of the peacemakers who gathered in Paris in 1919, disposing of territories that, for the most part, they had never actually visited. Wilson went to Europe for the first time when he sailed in December 1918, and he was, moreover, the first sitting U.S. president ever to visit Europe. He came to know Paris and visited both London and Rome, but he never set eyes on the Czech, Polish, Hungarian, or South Slavic lands whose political futures he so notably determined. In his reimagining of the map of Eastern Europe, he followed the historical precedent of eighteenth-century philosophes like Voltaire and Rousseau, who invented Eastern Europe by articulating its coherence as a distinctive region: they were fascinated by Eastern Europe but never visited it in person.

Wilson's personal knowledge of and interest in Eastern Europe was very limited before America entered World War I. The Habsburg ambassador to Washington during the early years of the war, Konstantin Dumba, later commented truculently in his memoirs about Wilson's "utter ignorance of facts and of geography." Wilson's *History of the American*

People, published in 1902 at the height of mass immigration to America from the lands of Eastern Europe, had contained derogatory remarks about immigrants, including "men of the meaner sort of Hungary and Poland, men out of the ranks where there was neither skill nor intelligence." Ten years later, in the presidential election of 1912, this passage was publicized by his political opponents, and Wilson had to apologize to immigrant voters.[7] Immigrants from the partitioned Polish lands were the largest contingent from Eastern Europe who came to the United States during the decades preceding World War I, and every national community in the region was represented among the arrivals to the United States. Most of them would have some national stake in the postwar peace settlement.

Wilson attempted to create contacts and acquire information about Eastern Europe during the war, and in September 1917, his most important adviser and confidant, Colonel Edward House, established "The Inquiry"—a team of academics and intellectuals dedicated to the task of gathering, digesting, and summarizing for Wilson's benefit the relevant information on lands and peoples that had rarely loomed large on the agenda of American foreign policy. A subgroup of these scholars, under the guidance of Archibald Cary Coolidge of the Harvard History Department, was the very first coordinated American team of experts concerning Eastern Europe and, eventually, determined the future of its postwar academic study in the United States. Coolidge's academic team would not only make their presence felt in Paris at the time of the peace conference but would actually do what Wilson never did: travel to some of the eastern scenes that occupied the deliberations of the statesmen in Paris. Wilson's mental map was partly shaped by these American observers and scholars, but also partly by his own eastern contacts, whether leaders like Paderewski and Masaryk, whom he met in America during the war, or others whom he met in Paris, from plaintive Carpathian goatherds to Queen Marie of Romania. There was also a deeper background of American cultural prejudices and preconceptions concerning the lands of Eastern Europe, sometimes mediated by communities of American immigrants from the region, and Wilson's vision of Eastern Europe was conditioned by those more general cultural imaginings.

INTRODUCTION

In 1919, the journalist Walter Lippmann, who was a member of The Inquiry, published a study of the peace settlement that had only just been signed, and noted that its weakness was located geographically in Eastern Europe: "No one who knows anything of the internal conditions of the new states of eastern Europe can for a moment imagine that they will survive squeezed in between gigantic revolutions in both Germany and Russia. Those new states are fragments of destroyed empires, and each contains within itself problems that have all the seeds of disorder."[8] Certainly, when the moment arrived in the 1930s and 1940s, Nazi Germany and Stalinist Russia would set out to destroy Wilson's Eastern Europe. Prophecy aside, however, Lippmann very accurately noted that the peace settlement had constituted "new states of eastern Europe," and that they were produced from "fragments of destroyed empires." This book will consider how those fragments were reshuffled in Wilson's conception of Eastern Europe, his mental mapping of the region, and translated into a new geopolitical cartography: an Eastern Europe that was framed and "squeezed" by Germany and Russia, but did not actually include them. Accordingly, Germany and Russia will stand largely outside the central arena of this book, which nevertheless acknowledges their undeniable significance for implicitly defining—and, eventually, undoing—Wilson's Eastern Europe.

Wilson had no sympathy for the Russian tsarist empire, and in March 1917—the month of his second inauguration—following the February Revolution in Russia, America promptly recognized the provisional government of Alexander Kerensky. Thus, by the time America entered the war in April, there was no question of an alliance with the tsar. Furthermore, the tsarist government's secret agreement with Britain and France in 1915, to obtain Constantinople and the Dardanelles as spoils of war, represented precisely the sort of imperial aggrandizement that Wilson denounced and sought to reform. With Lenin in power following the Bolshevik Revolution of October 1917, Wilson was again ideologically unsympathetic, as before toward the tsarist government, and in the Fourteen Points speech of January 1918, he preferred to envision an implicitly democratic future for Russia that would allow for "the independent determination of her own political development . . . under institutions of her own choosing." This was, in fact, the language that Wilson would employ to describe the new states of Eastern Europe, as recognized by the peace conference, but Bolshevik Russia remained unrepresented at the conference and excluded from Wilson's postwar conception of democratic polities under the auspices of the League of Nations.

Lenin also challenged Wilson with a rival conception of self-determination, first formulated in 1914, and then rearticulated in November 1917, emancipating the nationalities of the Russian empire with a "Declaration of the Rights of the Peoples of Russia," allowing for their "free self-determination" and even the possibility of their independence. Indeed, Arthur Herman has suggested that Wilson's Fourteen Points speech in January was partly a response to Lenin's appeal to self-determination in November.[9] Although aware of the Slavic affinity between Russia and some of the peoples of Eastern Europe—and worried at the peace conference that Russian influence might lead to "the formation of a Slavic bloc hostile to western Europe"—Wilson never thought of Bolshevik Russia as part of the new system of states that he sought to create in Eastern Europe.[10] There was perhaps an element of self-fulfilling prophecy in the emergence of the Leninist Comintern (the Communist International) in 1919 as the rival international organization to the Wilsonian League of Nations, each with its own vision of a new postwar world order. Lenin supposedly dismissed the League of Nations as a "thieves' kitchen."

This book presents four thematic chapters on Woodrow Wilson and Eastern Europe. The first chapter on Wilson and the Ottoman empire argues that the president's longest-standing preconception about Eastern Europe was simply liberal hatred of the Ottoman empire, dating back to his university years in the 1870s, the decade of the Ottoman Eastern Crisis. It was the moral rhetoric of the British prime minister William Gladstone in the 1870s, his denunciation of alleged Ottoman atrocities in Bosnia and Bulgaria, that was later echoed in Wilson's wartime approach to the Ottoman empire and his sympathy for Ottoman subject peoples.

The second chapter considers Wilson and the Habsburg monarchy, and argues that the Ottoman case became Wilson's anti-imperial model for approaching Austria-Hungary in what gradually evolved into a spirit of moral outrage. The commitment to the abolition of that empire came very late in Wilson's wartime leadership, but thoroughly shaped his conduct at the Paris Peace Conference. What has not been generally appreciated about Wilson's Habsburg policy is the force of the Ottoman analogy and example, but also, and even more strikingly, the president's evolving conception of the war as one of emancipation, specifically with reference to the "enslaved" peoples of Austria-Hungary. Wilson was born in Virginia, and lived through the Civil War as a child of the Confederacy. His first wife Ellen, who died as First Lady in 1914, was from Georgia, and his second wife Edith, whom he married in 1915, was a fellow Virginian. The segregation of the federal government was carried out during the Wilson presidency, canceling the legacy of Reconstruction and reneging on the Fourteenth Amendment's promise of citizenship rights for all and equality before the law in the United States. Wilson, however, somewhat awkwardly came to terms with Lincoln during World War I, when he conceived of the war as a war of emancipation. The legacy of Lincoln's Civil War was partly adapted and partly displaced by political concern over a new war on behalf of different "enslaved" populations, this time in Eastern Europe.

The third chapter addresses the mosaic of individual friendships and sentimental sympathies that influenced Wilson personally from the time that he brought America into the war in 1917. Some of these were new personal acquaintances—like Paderewski and Masaryk—who were quickly elevated to the status of new friends and then became metonymic emblems of his friendship for their entire nations. Wilson remade the map of Eastern Europe at the Paris Peace Conference, but it was a map that had been already sentimentally colored with his serendipitous accumulation of personal sympathies. His commitment to a new map, based on the new political principles of self-determination, rested upon the theoretical pursuit of a geopolitical tabula rasa in which the defeat of the Central Powers canceled the mappings of the past. Most notably it was the abolition of the Habsburg and Ottoman empires which made it possible to reimagine the map of Eastern Europe.

The fourth and final chapter follows the Wilsonian principle of self-determination, even as the president, learning more and more about the lands and peoples of Eastern Europe, came to appreciate the contradictions of principle when confronted with more information about regional ethnography. The creation of new states based on national predominance inevitably left some parts of the population outside the privileged governing group that defined the national state. A new Polish state would also govern over the Ukrainians of Eastern Galicia; a new Czechoslovak state would also govern over the Germans of the Sudetenland. These circumstances pointed to the provocative concept of the "national minority" which gradually emerged from the Wilsonian principle of self-determination, partly destabilizing the postwar settlement by creating a whole new logic of minority politics.

Wilson was initially regarded as a messianic figure in Europe—and most especially in Eastern Europe—for his promise of a new international politics based on a new map. The president partly subscribed to this sense of his own messianic mission, while never doubting that he was attempting to apply a set of moral principles to foreign policy in pursuit of a systematically structured peace settlement. Yet Wilson's political consciousness was shaped as much by irrational fantasy as by logical principle, and it is no coincidence that Sigmund Freud (born a subject of the Habsburg monarchy) participated in one of the earliest efforts to compose a biographical account of Wilson, co-authored by Freud and William Bullitt in the 1930s, and highlighting the devastating effects of Wilson's supposedly overwhelming Oedipus Complex.[11] Freud, whose sons served in the Habsburg army during the war, was not inclined to admire Wilson and wielded the intellectual weapons of psychoanalysis to critical effect. Without necessarily conceding the claims of psychoanalysis to define Wilson's legacy, it is nevertheless crucial to understand the aspects of fantasy that went into Wilson's imagining of Eastern Europe—the lands that he never visited but politically transformed—and the ways in which unsystematic, emotional, and even irrational aspects of mental mapping shaped the application of his supposedly rigorous principles.

On January 5, 1918, three days before Wilson's famous Fourteen Points speech, the president and Colonel House met in the morning and, according to House, "got down to work at half past ten and finished remaking the map of the world."[12] It was a hyperbolic remark, of course, but the two men made it come partly true over the next year and a half, when, at the Paris Peace Conference, they did dramatically remake the map of Eastern

Europe. That Wilsonian reimagining of Eastern Europe was based on fantasy as well as principle, impressions as well as investigations, prejudice as well as research, but, unquestionably, there has never been another American president who was so curious, so passionate, and so engaged concerning Eastern Europe. Wilson's remaking of the map—working together in Paris with British Prime Minister David Lloyd George and French Prime Minister Georges Clemenceau—represented the culmination of a long tradition of engagement with Eastern Europe, dating back to the Enlightenment. Wilson aspired to a certain intellectual and political mastery of the region, following in an American idiom from the Enlightenment's intellectual invention of Eastern Europe and the Victorian political preoccupation with the Polish Question and the Eastern Question.[13]

The details of Wilsonian policy toward Eastern Europe were first presented as history in Victor Mamatey's *The United States and East Central Europe, 1914–1918: A Study in Wilsonian Diplomacy and Propaganda*, published in 1957, which remained perhaps the principal study for half a century. Mamatey, born in the United States in 1917, during the Wilson presidency, was educated in Bratislava and Prague in Wilsonian interwar Czechoslovakia. He thus stood in relatively close historical proximity to the Wilsonian moment itself, and one might have expected more extensive revisionist work in the succeeding generations. Yet Eastern Europe has remained oddly absent from the agenda of issues that historians have recently highlighted in writing about Wilson. Erez Manela's pioneering work *The Wilsonian Moment*, published in 2007, showed that Wilson's impact was not limited to Europe, but extended to Egypt, India, China, and Korea—and there has been some implicit presumption that his European significance was already studied and well understood.[14]

Important recent works on Wilson's international impact, such as Lloyd Ambrosius's *Woodrow Wilson and American Internationalism*, Trygve Throntveit's *Power without Victory: Woodrow Wilson and the American Internationalist Experiment*, and Manfred Berg's *Woodrow Wilson: Amerika und die Neuordnung der Welt*—all published in 2017—subtly reconsider the principles of Wilsonian policy, but without excavating the details of the settlement of Eastern Europe. The same is true of Patricia O'Toole's biographical account, *The Moralist: Woodrow Wilson and the World He Made*, published in 2018.¹⁵ Neither Paderewski nor Masaryk is listed in the index of any of these works.

In 2018, two very comprehensive German centennial studies of the Versailles settlement were published by Eckart Conze and Jörn Leonhard, respectively, the former with a chapter on "Old Empires and New States," covering Eastern Europe, and the latter with a section on "State Formation and Sovereignty in East Central Europe and Southeastern Europe"—though in both cases the particular role of Woodrow Wilson with regard to Eastern Europe is somewhat understated. Leonhard's emphasis on sovereignty is echoed and elaborated in Leonard Smith's 2018 book *Sovereignty at the Paris Peace Conference of 1919*. Smith observes that the hallmark of the peace conference was its assumption of the right to assign postwar sovereignty, notably with regard to the emergence of new states in Eastern Europe.¹⁶

Eric Yellin's *Racism in the Nation's Service: Government Workers and the Color Line* (2013) and other research on Wilson's domestic policy has shown clearly that his progressivism did not extend to African Americans.¹⁷ Even at Princeton, where Wilson has long been considered to be the most celebrated university president, it has been recently debated whether his name should be removed from campus institutions and buildings. Eastern Europe, by contrast, is the region where Wilson's name and image have been ceremoniously reestablished in recent decades. After the creation of Czechoslovakia in 1918, Prague's main train station (originally named for the Habsburg emperor Franz Joseph) was renamed for Woodrow Wilson, and in the 1920s, a fourteen-foot bronze statue of Wilson was erected in front of the station, with the inscription: "The world must be made safe for democracy." When the Nazis occupied Prague during World War II, they demolished the statue and removed Wilson's name from the train station, which for decades, through the postwar communist period, was simply known as the "Prague Main Station." After the communist regime collapsed in the Velvet Revolution of 1989, led by Václav Havel, the Prague street dubbed *Vítězného února* ("Victorious February"), commemorating the communist seizure of power in February 1948, was renamed *Wilsonova*.¹⁸ Finally, in 2011, a new statue of Wilson was put up at the train station in place of the old one, with Havel present for its unveiling.

INTRODUCTION

Bratislava, now the Slovak capital, was briefly rechristened "Wilsonovo Mesto" or "Wilson City" in 1918–19 by those who resisted their country's incorporation into Czechoslovakia. In Warsaw, the Polish capital, there was a major square named for Wilson—Plac Wilsona—to mark his role in restoring Polish independence, and, though it was renamed for the revolutionary Paris Commune during Poland's communist period, it is once more Plac Wilsona today in post-communist Poland. The Danish American sculptor Gutzon Borglum, who created the presidential monument at Mount Rushmore, South Dakota, and the Confederacy monument at Stone Mountain, Georgia, also sculpted a Woodrow Wilson monument for Wilson Park in Poznań, Poland, unveiled in 1931. In Zagreb, Croatia, the University Square became Woodrow Wilson Square in 1919, celebrating his role in the creation of the Yugoslav state. It was, predictably, renamed for Tito after World War II, and today it is Republic of Croatia Square.[19] The persistence—and sometimes the subversion—of Wilson's legacy and memory in Eastern Europe across the twentieth century points to the importance of an academic reconsideration of his complex relation to the region.

In the early months of 1919, while Wilson presided at the Paris Peace Conference, one of the most famous contemporary performing artists from Eastern Europe was going gradually insane and recording his mental breakdown in a diary. Vaslav Nijinsky, Polish by identity and descent, born in Ukraine, trained as a Russian dancer, and famous for revolutionizing modern ballet with the Ballets Russes under the guidance of his lover Sergei Diaghilev, documented in his diary his fascination with Woodrow Wilson. Nijinsky believed that Wilson alone could stop the war (though the war was actually already over) and save the world: "Wilson wants to stop the war, but people do not understand him. Wilson is not a dancer. Wilson is god in politics. I am Wilson."[20] Nijinsky, only thirty and already a legend, was at the end of his sensational career; he had choreographed and starred in *The Afternoon of a Faun* in 1912, simulating masturbation on stage in Paris the same year that Wilson was elected president in the United Sates. In 1913, Nijinsky choreographed Stravinsky's *Rite of Spring* to create a spectacularly controversial revolutionary landmark of cultural modernism—and six years later, as he was about to be declared

12

incurably insane, he identified with Wilson: "I am Wilson." If the *Rite of Spring* celebrated the worship of a pagan deity through human sacrifice and sexual abandon, six years later Wilson was the deity: "Wilson is god in politics."

Punning with hostile intensity on "Pederewski" (Paderewski) and pederasty, while declaring himself ambivalently a Pole—"I am a Pole through my mother and father, but I am Russian because I was brought up there"—Nijinsky set up an implicit opposition between Diaghilev and Wilson ("Diaghilev does not want love for everyone, Diaghilev wants love for himself") and worried anxiously that someone would try to assassinate the American president: "I want Wilson to achieve his aims, because his aims

FIGURE 1. On July 4, 1931, a statue of Wilson was unveiled in the Polish city of Poznań. The statue was funded by Ignacy Jan Paderewski, and the sculptor was Gutzon Borglum, who also designed the Mount Rushmore monument in South Dakota. Borglum, standing in front of his statue, traveled to Poland for the unveiling in 1931.

are nearer to truth. I feel Wilson's death. I am afraid he might get a bullet through the head."[21] That the madness of Nijinsky involved such close identification with Wilson suggests some of the ways that the American president dominated the consciousness of Eastern Europe in 1919. Wilson would not achieve his aims—because the U.S. Senate rejected the treaty of Versailles. Neither would he be shot in the head, but he did suffer a stroke that same year, severely disabling him during what remained of his presidency. Yet, America's engagement in the war and Wilson's presence at the Paris Peace Conference definitively transformed both the geopolitical map of Eastern Europe and the whole world's awareness of that region, making his own individual mental mapping into a template for Europe in the twentieth century. The map of Eastern Europe today still reflects Wilson's problematic preoccupation with delineating an interlocking complex of national states, and its origins can be traced in the intellectual history of Wilson's writings and thoughts as they emerged from the cultural context of mental mapping during and after World War I.

I

Wilson's Eastern Question and the End of the Ottoman Empire

Woodrow Wilson and William Gladstone

"That is Gladstone, the greatest statesman that ever lived," the adolescent Woodrow Wilson supposedly said, pointing to a portrait. "I intend to be a statesman too." This story, which is sometimes attributed to Wilson's childhood, but more usually to the age of sixteen, gives his American political destiny an interestingly transatlantic dimension. The figure of Gladstone offered the young Wilson a role model for thinking about morality and Christianity in relation to political liberalism, and Sigmund Freud and William Bullitt, in their psychoanalytic study of Wilson, did not hesitate to signal the fixation on Gladstone as an Oedipal displacement of admiration for Wilson's domineeringly pious Presbyterian minister father.[1] If Wilson was, in fact, politically attuned to Gladstone's career from the age of sixteen—that is, from 1872—the young American would have been just old enough to appreciate the most dramatic phase of Gladstone's career in the 1870s, his political comeback in 1876, with the denunciation of Ottoman rule in southeastern Europe in the pamphlet *The Bulgarian Horrors and the Question of the East*. With the Liberal Party in opposition, Gladstone condemned his political archrival Tory Prime Minister Benjamin Disraeli for supporting the Ottoman government against Russia, and the Ottoman oppression of Christian Slavs became a key issue in British politics from 1876 right up to Gladstone's assault on Disraeli during the Midlothian election campaign in 1879 and 1880.[2] These were precisely the years of Wilson's undergraduate study of history and politics at Princeton, and the Gladstonian demand, in the name of oppressed Slavic populations, for a moral foreign policy would later become important to Wilson's political future as a statesman.

Wilson's surviving papers from these early years suggest that he was enthusiastically following Gladstone's Midlothian campaign and deeply sympathetic to Christians living under Muslim Turkish rule. Wilson was notably hostile to Disraeli, "the now exalted Jew," and commented on his "charlatanry" and lack of principle.[3] At the height of the Eastern Crisis in 1876, as Gladstone denounced Ottoman atrocities in Bulgaria, Disraeli prepared to send the Royal Navy to Constantinople to support the Ottomans against Russia. Around the same time, the twenty-year-old Wilson read an article about Disraeli in the *British Quarterly Review* by the twenty-four-year-old Herbert Asquith, a future Liberal prime minister of Great Britain, who was already fiercely partisan in his excoriation of Disraeli:

> We believe that Mr. Disraeli's influence on English politics has been almost unmixedly bad. From first to last he has fought for his own hand, and we are unable to trace in the windings of his erratic course any connecting clue of principle. We do not accuse him of deliberate treachery to his convictions, because in our opinion his ill-assorted stock of many-coloured theories never deserved so honourable a name. The man who has never known what it is to believe is secure from the imputation of apostasy. But we do charge him with pretending to the high title of statesman, without that faith in a governing idea, that allegiance to a worthy cause, that serious sincerity of purpose, that single-minded and self-forgetful fervour, which alone dignify public life and make the profession of politics respectable.[4]

Asquith's article, attacking Disraeli for his lack of principles and convictions, strikingly anticipated the evolution of Wilson's mature political perspective, and reading Asquith in 1876, at the height of the Eastern Crisis, occurred at a formative moment for Wilson. Much later, at Versailles, he would define himself as the supreme statesman of principles, convictions, and sincerity of purpose in international affairs, in defiance of the world of Disraelian self-interest and opportunism. Both his allies and his enemies would recognize a Gladstonian "single-minded and self-forgetful fervour" as the hallmark of his statesmanship. In 1881, the twenty-five-year-old Wilson noted the death of Disraeli with no "sniffles."[5]

The establishment of the new states of Poland, Czechoslovakia, and Yugoslavia on the postwar map of Europe is closely associated with Wilson's principle of self-determination at the Paris Peace Conference, which also vindicated the dissection of the Habsburg monarchy into national components. The negotiation of a treaty with Turkey came last in Paris, after the treaty with Germany at Versailles, with Austria at Saint-Germain, with Bulgaria at Neuilly, and with Hungary at Trianon. The United States did not participate either in the Treaty of Sèvres with Turkey in August 1920 or in its revision by the Treaty of Lausanne in July 1923, by which time Wilson was long out of office, entirely removed from international affairs, and approaching his death in February 1924. In January 1918, however, Wilson's interest in the Ottoman empire was very much present in the Fourteen Points as Point Twelve, which advocated the "autonomous development" of the nationalities under Ottoman rule and the opening of the Dardanelles to international shipping.[6] Point Eleven addressed relations among the formerly Ottoman Balkan states, which had interested Gladstone half a century before. Later, at the peace conference, Wilson was surprisingly open to the possibility of exercising an American mandate over Constantinople and the Bosphorus straits, though this was ruled out first by the American Senate rejecting the entire Wilsonian project and then by the Turkish military, led by Mustafa Kemal Pasha (later known as Atatürk), affirming Turkish sovereignty. Still, Gladstone's righteous eagerness to expel the Turks altogether from Europe was not only echoed by Wilson in Paris in the most explicit fashion, but also amplified by the improbable vision of an American mandate in Constantinople.

■ ■ ■

"A veritable hornet's nest"
In the eighteenth century Voltaire had suggested to Russia's empress Catherine the Great that expelling the Ottoman empire from Europe would constitute a kind of redemption of European civilization. He wrote to Catherine in 1768, at the outbreak of the Russian-Ottoman war, denouncing the Ottomans for their "barbarism," and affirming that "if ever the Turks should be chased from Europe, it will be by the Russians."[7] Gladstone,

more than a hundred years later, made this into an issue in an electoral campaign, demanding "the extinction of the Turkish executive power in Bulgaria"—and in Bosnia too—as a matter of Christian moral principle. In the famous peroration of his "Bulgarian Horrors" pamphlet he exclaimed:

> Let the Turks now carry away their abuses in the only possible manner, namely by carrying off themselves. Their Zaptiehs and their Mudirs, their Bimbashis and their Yuzbachis, their Kaimakams and their Pashas, one and all, bag and baggage, shall, I hope, clear out from the province they have desolated and profaned. This thorough riddance, this most blessed deliverance, is the only reparation we can make to the memory of those heaps on heaps of dead; to the violated purity alike of matron, of maiden, and of child; to the civilisation which has been affronted and shamed; to the laws of God or, if you like, of Allah; to the moral sense of mankind at large.[8]

Gladstone's moral outrage, rhetorically reinforced by the enumeration of names that were meant to sound alien and barbaric to the British public ("their Bimbashis and their Yuzbachis"), would become part of the legacy of modern liberalism. Wilson, who would have no hesitations about speaking for "the moral sense of mankind," certainly appreciated the basic elements of this Turcophobe legacy. "Wilson's anti-Ottoman feelings seem to have affected his judgments on the Ottoman Empire throughout the peace conference," the Turkish historian Nevzat Uyanik suggests.[9]

Colonel House's diary from December 18, 1912, right after Wilson's election as president, though before his inauguration, recounts a somewhat cryptic retort from the president-elect to the proposal of sending Henry Morgenthau as U.S. ambassador to the sultan in Istanbul. Wilson commented, "There ain't going to be no Turkey."[10] Morgenthau himself objected to the posting on the grounds that Jews "were so strongly opposed to having any position made a distinctly Jewish one or having the impression continued that Turkey was the only country where a Jew would be received as our country's representative"—but he accepted the embassy and served in Istanbul until 1916. There Morgenthau became a notable voice of protest against the genocidal Armenian massacres of 1915, attempting to seize the attention of Wilson in Washington and the broader American public.

In 1915, echoing Gladstone's denunciation of "Bulgarian Horrors," Morgenthau created a Committee on Armenian Atrocities, and in October 1916, in the midst of his reelection campaign, Wilson spoke in Cincinnati on behalf of peoples "who have no political standing in Europe, like the Armenians, like the people of Poland—like all those peoples who seem caught between the forces of this terrible struggle and seem likely to be crushed almost out of existence."[11] The United States had not yet entered the war, but Wilson was addressing the possibility of providing war relief. He was not unaware of the feelings of voting Polish-Americans, and the equation of Poles and Armenians as wartime victims allowed Wilson to extend his Gladstonian moral outrage from the Ottoman sphere to the wider domain of oppressed peoples throughout Eastern Europe.

In September 1914, just after the outbreak of the war, British Prime Minister Herbert Asquith spoke in Dublin and cited Gladstone's belief that "the greatest triumph of our time will be the enthronement of the idea of public right as the governing idea of European politics." Back in 1876, during the Eastern Crisis the young Asquith was being read in the *British Quarterly Review* by the young Wilson, both of them anti-Ottoman and anti-Disraeli Gladstonians. In 1914, they were the mature leaders of their respective nations, and Asquith's Dublin speech proposed principles that would also become increasingly important to Wilson: "the definite repudiation of militarism as the governing factor in the relations of states," but also the preservation of "the independent existence and the free development of the smaller nationalities—each with a corporate consciousness of its own." These were to include "Belgium, Holland, Switzerland and the Scandinavian countries, Greece and the Balkan states" (though not necessarily the nationalities of the Habsburg monarchy or the Ottoman empire) and were to be "recognized as having exactly as good a title as their more powerful neighbors . . . to a place in the sun."[12] In May 1916, Colonel House quoted this speech, including the acknowledgment of Gladstone, in a message to Wilson, with suggestions for incorporating this material into one of Wilson's own speeches.[13] While Wilson sometimes accepted suggestions, he generally wrote his own speeches, and his words therefore offer a relatively clear sense of his own intellectual perspective.

In October 1916 in Cincinnati, when Wilson cited the Poles and the Armenians (neither of whom was acknowledged in Asquith's list of small nationalities), the American president elaborated his own view of the importance of small nations in international affairs: "Why, there come into my office in Washington men of these bloods, who say to me, 'Mr President, we are not trying to draw this government into taking sides in any way, but people of our own blood, people whom we love, are dying of mere neglect and starvation. Can you not find some way by which we can help them?'"[14] Wilson, with the United States still neutral, was focused on the problem of how to provide war relief to suffering civilians, many of them related to American immigrant communities.

The spirit of Gladstonian outrage and sympathy would eventually shape Wilson's whole approach to war aims and peace negotiations, and already in 1916, in Cincinnati, he declared himself with passion:

> Our heart goes out to these helpless people who are being crushed and whom we would like to save. America does not believe in the rights of small nations merely because they are small, does not believe in the rights of small nations merely because we are big and they are helpless and the big ought not to impose upon the helpless. But we believe in them because, when we think of the sufferings of mankind, we forget where political boundaries lie, and say, "These people are of the flesh and blood of mankind, and America is made up out of the peoples of the world." What a fine future of distinction and glory is open for a people who, by instinctive sympathy, can interpret and stand for the rights of men everywhere.[15]

With Christian emphasis on the sufferings of mankind and charity toward the helpless, Wilson reframed Gladstonian righteousness in international affairs by adding a peculiarly American twist, the "instinctive sympathy" that derived from America's own immigrant society.

> Here is the great melting pot, as we have told ourselves, in which the varied stocks of the world are melted together and united in a single magical compound out of which is to grow the spirit and the power of a new nation. The singular thing about the United States is that it has

not the kind of national consciousness which impels a people to take advantage of some other people in the world. It is shot through with all the sympathies of all the nations of mankind.[16]

These sympathies could range universally as long as the United States remained neutral, but, once America entered the war in 1917, Wilson would have to adjust his sympathies to fit the wartime alliances.

Before America entered the war, Wilson attempted to play a mediating role in pursuit of peace in Europe, and in December 1916 he called upon the belligerent states to specify their war aims. The Anglo-French response in January insisted on "the liberation of Italians, of Slavs, of Roumanians and of Tcheco-Slovaques from foreign domination; the enfranchisement of populations subject to the bloody tyranny of the Turks; the expulsion from Europe of the Ottoman Empire decidedly alien to western civilization."[17] This program of liberation not only implicitly infringed upon the sovereignty of the Habsburg monarchy but was explicitly committed to the destruction of the Ottoman empire in Europe—though little enough remained of Ottoman Europe after the Balkan Wars of 1912–13, really just eastern Thrace and Constantinople on the European side of the Bosphorus.

Arthur Balfour, wartime British foreign secretary under Prime Minister David Lloyd George, wanted the British ambassador in Washington, DC, to discuss the issue of the Ottoman empire in Europe forcefully with Wilson: "It has been argued indeed that the expulsion of the Turks from Europe forms no proper or logical part of this general scheme. The maintenance of the Turkish Empire was during many generations regarded by statesmen of world-wide authority as essential to the maintenance of European peace. Why, it is asked, should the cause of peace be now associated with a complete reversal of this traditional policy?"[18] Balfour's reversal, or rather the displacement of the traditional Disraelian perspective by the Gladstonian perspective on Turkey, was attributed to Turkey's "barbarous" conduct, and especially to the Armenian massacres: "A Turkish government controlled, subsidized and supported by Germany has been guilty of massacres in Armenia and Syria more horrible than any recorded in the history even of those unhappy countries. Evidently the interests of peace and the claims of nationality alike require that Turkish rule over alien races shall if possible be brought to an end; and we may hope that the expulsion of Turkey from Europe will contribute as much to the cause of peace as the restoration of Alsace Lorraine to France."[19] It was, furthermore, the "Balfour Declaration" of November 1917 that proposed to create a Jewish homeland out of Ottoman Palestine. Britain and France were, of course, at war with the Ottoman empire, and had suffered huge casualties when they attempted (and failed) to capture Constantinople and the Bosphorus straits in the Gallipoli campaign of 1915.

Wilson, while maintaining a neutral public stance, was privately as hostile as Balfour to Turkey. Colonel House's diary records a discussion with the president in January 1917 about what sorts of peace terms Wilson might endorse: "We thought that since Germany and Russia had agreed to free Poland that should be put in. We naturally agreed upon Belgium and Serbia being restored. Alsace and Lorraine we were not quite certain of, but we agreed that Turkey should cease to exist."[20] It was by far the most bluntly absolute verdict on international affairs that the two men produced, and they went so far as to imagine the dire consequences: "The question was raised as to what would happen to our Ambassador at Constantinople when this speech was made, and whether he would be promptly executed or be permitted to flee the country."[21] There was perhaps a hint of a jocular tone here, as Wilson and House imagined the barbarous Turks acting in the comic opera spirit of Mozart's Osmin, the easily enraged overseer in Mozart's *Abduction from the Seraglio*, or Gilbert and Sullivan's Mikado, seeking punishments to fit the crime. The Ottomans were almost humorously conceived as barbarously bloodthirsty, undertaking the immediate execution of the American ambassador—Morgenthau's successor, Abram Isaac Elkus, in this inevitably Jewish posting.

In the end, Wilson's speech in Congress presented the principle "that no right anywhere exists to hand peoples about from sovereignty to sovereignty as if they were property," illustrated only by "a single example, that statesmen everywhere are agreed that there should be a united independent and autonomous Poland."[22] The notion that Turkey must "cease to exist" went unmentioned, and Elkus in Istanbul remained happily unharmed—though he would be recalled later in 1917. House, discussing a possible peace with the German ambassador Count Johann Heinrich von Bernstorff, commented to Wilson, "I was surprised to hear how easily he took to the general proposition of eliminating Turkey." This was clearly a fundamental part of the Wilsonian peace package. Bernstorff was less amenable in correspondence with Secretary of State Robert Lansing, rejecting the purported Allied intention "to dismember and dishonor Germany, Austria-Hungary, Turkey, and Bulgaria," and, more specifically, "to destroy Austria-Hungary and to annihilate Turkey."[23] The annihilation of Turkey was rejected by Germany when it was perceived as part of a broader framework of intended dismemberments.

The United States declared war on Germany in April 1917 and on Austria-Hungary in December 1917, but it never declared war on the Ottoman empire. Wilson's persistent Turcophobia nevertheless shaped his sense of the war and the peace, both during the period of American neutrality and after America's entry into the war. In August 1917, the Belgian diplomat, Baron Ludovic Moncheur, met with Wilson to discuss the war, and reported on the conversation to his prime minister, Count Charles de Broqueville :

> Wilson spoke incidentally of the question of the Near East. "Turkey, that mass of different races, is a veritable hornet's nest which keeps Europe always in alarm. It is necessary to find a remedy there, but the solution of the problem has not yet been found." The President did not want to formulate his opinion on the opportunity which might come to expel the Turks from Europe, but he said that, in all events, the Straits ought to become an international [water]way.[24]

The notion of a mixed population forming a "hornet's nest" was very much the opposite of his American ideal of the "melting pot" with its magical powers of national synthesis. Not formally at war with Turkey, Wilson discreetly kept the "solution" to himself, but his mental mapping of Eastern Europe was strongly negative in its view of the Ottoman empire, and as he came to look more deeply into the matter of mixed populations during the coming years, his vision of Eastern Europe as a whole would be shaped by a broader application of the imagery of the Turkish hornet's nest.

• • •

"The indescribable agonies of being governed by the Turk"

In October 1917 Wilson told Colonel House "that he was not willing that anyone should go abroad to represent him excepting me"—that only House knew the president's mind. They forged that unity of mind as they discussed the various fronts of the war. "We spoke of the Italian campaign and the campaign in Asia Minor, and the partition or non-partition of Turkey," House noted. Wilson's anxiety about Turkey at this moment was not just morally Gladstonian, but also strategic, for he feared that a negotiated peace might leave Germany "impregnable in both Austria and Turkey and her dream of Mittel-Europa would be realized."[25] That is, the asymmetrical alliances by which Germany actually dominated the Habsburg and Ottoman empires would enable Germany to control markets from Bohemia and Hungary to Romania, Bulgaria, and the Middle East. Friedrich Naumann's influential book *Mitteleuropa*, outlining German economic interests in central Europe, was published in 1915 (and in English, as *Central Europe*, in 1917), and Wilson had very rapidly accepted its message as the key to understanding Germany's war aims. German influence in Turkey was supposed to facilitate the domination of Europe, and this now became the strategic reason for Wilson's contemplation of a speech about "the partition or non-partition of Turkey." House wrote in his diary:

> He [Wilson] thought he should say that Turkey should become effaced, and that the disposition of it should be left to the peace conference. Without advising that I thought it advisable to make such a speech now, I added that if it was made, it should be stated that Turkey must not be partitioned among the belligerents, but must become autonomous in its several parts according to racial lines. He accepted this . . .[26]

This conversation outlined much of the Wilsonian program for the future peace, a settlement focused on achieving autonomy for national communities, rather than seizing territorial spoils through partition to satisfy the appetite of the victors. Wilson believed that Turkey should be effaced; House emphasized that there were different approaches to effacement. The "mass of different races" that made up the Ottoman "hornet's nest" might become the basis for reimagining (but not partitioning) the empire as autonomous component parts. This would, furthermore, quickly become the principle for reconstituting the Habsburg monarchy, also to be reimagined on the basis of national autonomy.

In November 1916, Morgenthau, now back in New York, wrote to Wilson anxiously about Germany's "permeation of Turkey and the Balkans," closely related to economic anxieties about Mittel-Europa. Yet, though it was Germany that actively permeated passive Turkey, it was somehow Turkey, according to Morgenthau, that functioned as the corruptive agent.

> It can easily be shown that Turkey was the cancer in the life of the world, and, not being properly treated, has now grown into the greatest cancer of Central Europe. If the Turks have, for four hundred and fifty years, constantly endangered the peace of Europe, what will happen to the world if Germany and Turkey now assume the role of tyrant and trouble-maker together?[27]

This model suggested that while Germany might economically and militarily dominate Turkey, it was Turkey that morally infected Germany and Europe by its cancerous spirit of tyranny. Ultimately, the two evil empires converged in spirit, according to Morgenthau, such that "in Turkey we see the evil spirit of Germany at its worst—culminating at last in the greatest crime of all ages," namely, the massacre of the Armenians.[28]

On December 4, Wilson delivered his State of the Union speech to Congress with an emphasis on international politics and the ambition of the Germans: "They have established a power over other lands and peoples than their own—over the great Empire of Austria-Hungary, over hitherto free Balkan states, over Turkey, and within Asia—which must be relinquished." Wilson therefore concluded that a prospective peace would have to "deliver the peoples of Austria-Hungary, the peoples of the Balkans, and the peoples of Turkey, alike in Europe and in Asia, from the impudent and alien dominion of the Prussian military and commercial autocracy."[29] It was an unusual formulation, inasmuch as it called for Turkish subject peoples to be delivered from German imperial domination, not from Turkish sultanic despotism.

Although Wilson's State of the Union speech still insisted that "we do not wish in any way to impair or to rearrange the Austro-Hungarian Empire," and that "it is no affair of ours what they do with their own life, either industrially or politically," he took a more interfering line with respect to the peoples of the Ottoman empire: "We shall hope to secure for the peoples of the Balkan peninsula and for the people of the Turkish Empire the right and opportunity to make their own lives safe, their own fortunes secure against oppression or injustice and from the dictation of foreign courts or parties."[30] Thus, at the end of 1917, even before embracing autonomy for the Habsburg peoples, Wilson urged a sort of autonomous self-determination ("the right and opportunity to make their own lives safe") for the Ottoman peoples. He did so, however, on the unexpected principle that they were being tyrannized by the German government and economy. Such reasoning would become completely redirected over the course of the coming years, and at the peace conference, as both the Ottoman and Habsburg peoples were eventually seen as in need of emancipation from the tyranny of their own Ottoman and Habsburg governments.

In the following weeks, leading up to Wilson's all-important Fourteen Points speech in Congress on January 8, 1918, Colonel House's think tank "The Inquiry" presented the preliminary results of its research on a prospective peace settlement. The Inquiry was chaired by the philosopher Sidney Edward Mezes, president of the City College of New York (and Colonel House's brother-in-law), working closely with the lawyer David Hunter Miller, the young journalist Walter Lippmann, and the Harvard historian Archibald Cary Coolidge (a direct descendant of Thomas Jefferson), who also brought to the project his academic protégés Robert Howard Lord and Robert Kerner, young experts on Eastern Europe. Coolidge was particularly interested in the Ottoman empire, had visited Constantinople in the 1890s ("I saw the Sultan going to mosque") and even dedicated himself for some years to the project of writing a biography (never completed) of the sixteenth-century sultan Suleiman the Magnificent.[31] In November 1917, Coolidge corresponded with a British authority on Turkey, writing, "I have travelled a little in the East myself and have lectured at Harvard on the Eastern Question." Coolidge also wrote to Mezes, "I can throw myself heart and soul into Balkan and Turkish questions. It will be useful to me that I have given a course on the Eastern Question on and off for the last twenty years."[32] The Inquiry would thus incorporate Coolidge's academic Ottoman interests.

In 1917, Harvard University Press published a slender volume of academic essays on peace settlements of the nineteenth century, including one by Coolidge titled "Claimants to Constantinople" and another by his student Lord on the Ottoman implications of the Congress of Berlin. These essays derived from a forum at the American Historical Association meeting in Cincinnati in December 2016 and looked toward a future peace settlement of the ongoing war. Lord considered the Congress of Berlin a failure, because it had not managed to dismantle the Ottoman empire entirely and replace it with new national states: "the ignoring of the desires of the Serb race for national unity; the bestowal upon Austria of Bosnia . . . [and] the restoration of nearly half of what it had lost to a government which was admittedly the disgrace of Europe." The propping up of the disgraceful Ottoman empire was blamed—in a Gladstonian spirit that would have gratified Wilson—entirely on the Turcophile Disraeli.[33] Coolidge, in "Claimants on Constantinople," traced the rivalry between Russian strategic and German economic designs on the Ottoman capital, and looked to a postwar scenario in which Constantinople might conceivably function as a post-Ottoman free city state. Coolidge himself believed that such a free state would be sabotaged by Russian and German competition for influence, but considered the fate of Constantinople to be crucial to the outcome of the war: "Never in all its long history, save perhaps when it fell into the hands of the Turks in 1453, has the fate of Constantinople meant more to the world than it does in the present struggle."[34] This grandiose affirmation seemed to assume that the city would not continue to serve as the Ottoman capital after the war, that the empire itself might cease to exist, and that the dilemma of political succession would require the installation of as yet undetermined foreign authorities. Coolidge's framing of the problem of "Claimants to Constantinople" pointed toward the eventual articulation of the Wilsonian possibility of an American mandate.

The Inquiry's memorandum on war aims, prepared in December 1917 and discussed by Wilson and House on January 4, 1918, advised the president that "it is necessary to free the subject races of the Turkish empire from oppression and misrule," and "this implies at the very least autonomy for Armenia and the protection of Palestine, Syria, Mesopotamia, and Arabia by the civilized nations." Turkey's war debt to Germany was to be canceled, in order to make the country independent, "freed from intermeddling and enabled to develop institutions adapted to the genius of her own people." Thus emancipated from debt, and relieved of the government of numerous provinces, Turkey might "be given a new start, considerably reduced in size, without power to misgovern alien races."[35] The Inquiry already looked beyond the Ottoman empire to a new and modern Turkey, imperially effaced but nationally reconceived, and surgically separated now from the "alien races" who had been previously subject to misgovernment.

This vision of the Ottoman empire was not fundamentally Gladstonian, inasmuch as it was minimally concerned with driving the Turks from Europe. The Balkan Wars had, to a considerable extent, achieved that end in 1912 and 1913, and The Inquiry dealt with "The Balkans" separately from "Turkey"—while entertaining proposals to rearrange the geopolitical outcome of those earlier wars. Ottoman Salonika became Greek Thessaloniki in 1913, but The Inquiry considered that it might alternatively serve as a Serbian port. Ottoman Albania declared independence in 1912, for fear of being consumed by the Balkan Wars, but The Inquiry considered the possibility of abolishing it altogether and partitioning it among its neighbors.[36] The Inquiry's academic spirit of freewheeling hypothetical geopolitics contributed to the Wilsonian readiness to operate transformatively upon the map of Eastern Europe.

Wilson's Fourteen Points speech eventually summed up the Turkish issues in a single sentence under Point Twelve: "The Turkish portion of the present Ottoman Empire should be assured a secure sovereignty, but the other nationalities which are now under Turkish rule should be assured an undoubted security of life and an absolutely unmolested opportunity of autonomous development, and the Dardanelles should be permanently opened as a free passage to the ships and commerce of all nations under international guarantees." Wilson's notes show that it was he who penciled in the term "Ottoman" empire on an original text that referenced "the Turkish portion of the present Turkish empire," thus clarifying the relation of the empire as a whole to its national components. Furthermore, it was his emendation that added the "opportunity of autonomous development" for all "other nationalities" of the empire. This had the effect of aligning Point Twelve on the Ottoman empire quite clearly with Point Ten on the Habsburg monarchy: "The peoples of Austria-Hungary, whose place among the nations we wish to see safeguarded and assured, should be accorded the freest opportunity to autonomous development."[37] At this moment the Habsburg monarchy was still to be "safeguarded and assured," while the Ottoman empire was already targeted by Wilson for effacement, if not abolition, but the program of "autonomous development" according to the principle of nationality seemed to iron out the difference between those two ultimate ends.

Following the Fourteen Points speech, Wilson engaged in secret peace discussions with the Habsburg emperor Karl, mediated by the Austrian ambassador in Madrid, Prince Karl Emil von Fürstenberg, and the Austrian foreign minister in Vienna, Count Ottokar Czernin. The ultimate purpose would have been to secure a separate peace with Austria, leaving Germany isolated, but Wilson was now particularly determined that this separate peace should conform to the principles of the Fourteen Points. Those points created an alignment of geopolitical concerns in Eastern Europe: Point Ten, the peoples of Austria-Hungary; Point Eleven, the Balkan states; Point Twelve, the Ottoman empire; Point Thirteen, Poland.

In the query that Wilson sent to Emperor Karl (communicated by telegram to Vienna from Madrid on March 5, 1918), the president articulated the connections and relations that made these separate points into one single geopolitical problem. The president asked that the emperor supply a positive program for resolving national tensions across the region:

> Most especially should I like to know how His Majesty proposes to end the dispute in the Balkans and to satisfy the national aspirations of the Slav peoples who are so closely related to masses of his own subjects, and what solution he would suggest for the Adriatic coast? What definite concessions to Italy he would regard as just and what in his opinion is the best method of removing the rivalries and antagonisms of the

> Balkan States which have only been increased by the war, and who is to protect the non-Turkish peoples subject to Turkish rule?[38]

Here "the Balkans" served as an ethnographic link between related Slavic peoples of the Habsburg monarchy and the non-Turkish subjects of the Ottoman empire, thus generalizing the ethnographic issues that had been earlier represented in separate points.

This same sense of regional connections and relations was evident in the appeal by the Serbian Minister Ljubomir Mihailović in Washington to U.S. Secretary of State Lansing, urging that the United States declare war against Turkey and Bulgaria (the allies of Germany and Austria), which was also being urged in the Senate by the Mormon Senator William Henry King of Utah. According to Mihailović such a declaration would encourage the Serbian army by demonstrating that America would "take part in the solution of the Balkan question," and would simultaneously exercise "great influence upon the people in Austria-Hungary," encouraging their "revolutionary spirit" and compromising the Habsburg military effort.[39] As in Wilson's query to Emperor Karl, the problem of Turkey was inextricably related to the Balkans and therefore to the peoples of Austria-Hungary. Wilson's idea of the Ottoman empire thus continued to shape his evolving view of nationalities and autonomies in the broader region of Eastern Europe.

The question of America's possible declaration of war on Turkey was still being discussed up until the final months of the war. In August 1918, Wilson took a week's vacation from Washington, DC, and spent it with House at his vacation home on the Massachusetts shore, north of Boston, near Manchester-by-the-Sea. There they also hosted William Wiseman of British Intelligence, who reported to the British Foreign Office by telegram at the end of August. Balfour's secretary Eric Drummond replied by telegram in September:

> We are grateful for your description of views held by President Wilson as to declaration of war by United States on Turkey and Bulgaria. Theory that presence of American missionaries in Turkish territory has up to now prevented massacres and atrocities is quite untenable. Armenian

massacres which were witnessed by Americans have probably surpassed for savagery anything in war. No doubt missionaries dislike idea of a war between Turkey and United States as this would imperil security of their important properties and institutions which they possess on Turkish soil. Morgenthau and Elkus influence and advice would also I believe be against declaration of hostilities. However this may be, it would seem we must abandon idea of declaration of war on Turkey by United States.[40]

In an unexpectedly Victorian twist, the presence of American Christian missionaries in the Ottoman empire (and the influence, perhaps, of two American Jewish ambassadors) was presumed to play a role in Wilson's hesitations about war with Turkey. During the nineteenth century, and especially after the Crimean War, it had been a basic pillar of the Eastern Question that foreign powers might exercise some role of protection on behalf of minority religious communities within the Ottoman empire. The British now feared that Wilson would be swayed by missionary considerations, and, would be hesitant, in spite of his own Turcophobia, to proceed to more open hostilities against the Ottomans.

In October 1918, a month before the armistice, Walter Lippmann and Frank Cobb, working with The Inquiry, prepared an extended, detailed memorandum for Wilson, interpreting for him his own Fourteen Points. This memorandum specified that "Anatolia should be reserved for the Turks," with a Greek mandate for the coastal areas with Greek population, with British mandates for Palestine, Mesopotamia, and Arabia, a French mandate for Syria, a British or French mandate for Armenia, and either a collective or unspecified single-power mandate for Constantinople and the Straits—all according to the principle of "autonomous development" for the peoples of the Ottoman empire. The memorandum, however, noted that "the same difficulty arises here as in the case of Austria Hungary concerning the word autonomous"—for in the case of the Habsburg monarchy, the authors had already noted that the promise of autonomy would actually imply a considerable degree of dismemberment, allowing for the creation of independent Czechoslovakia and Poland.[41] In the case of the Ottoman empire it was, analogously, becoming clearer that a system of mandates, while providing autonomy, would also bring about a restructuring that meant de facto dismemberment. Perhaps most interesting was the fact that the parallel between the Ottoman and Habsburg empires, suggested by the Fourteen Points speech, was now evolving into a more systematic attempt to deal with these two political entities in parallel fashion. The political logic of the Victorian Eastern Question concerning the Ottoman empire was finally acknowledged as the conceptual framework for addressing the restructuring—or dismantling—of the Habsburg monarchy, while the assumptions of Habsburg nationality and autonomy were being applied to Ottoman outcomes.

After the end of the war, the actual meetings of the peace conference consolidated, for Wilson, his sense of parallelism between the Habsburg and Ottoman empires. When he returned briefly to the United States for two weeks in the late winter, he gave a speech at the Metropolitan Opera House in New York in March 1919, attempting to rally the public behind the idea of the League of Nations. "The liberated peoples of the Austro-Hungarian Empire and of the Turkish Empire call out to us for this thing," declared Wilson. "The nations that have long been under the heel of the Austrian, that have long cowered before the German, that have long suffered the indescribable agonies of being governed by the Turk, have called out to the world, generation after generation, for justice, for liberation, and for succor."[42] Wilson almost ventriloquized the cries of the oppressed peoples of the enemy empires, allowing those cries to become intermingled in their parallel political appeals, while perhaps revealing his own most personal sympathies with the hyperbolic, indeed operatic, evocation of the "indescribable agonies" of the Ottoman subject peoples. His presidential oratory of 1919, when it touched upon the Ottoman empire, echoed the Christian political passion of Gladstone's outrage at the Bulgarian horrors in 1876.

■ ■ ■

"As though it were made of quicksilver"
The Lippmann-Cobb memorandum of October 1918 raised the question of mandates for the Ottoman provinces, and as the war concluded it remained to be seen whether Wilson himself would undertake one of these post-Ottoman mandates on behalf of America. The president arrived in

Paris on December 16, 1918, prior to the opening of the peace conference, and visited England in late December. Both Lloyd George and Balfour discussed with Wilson the possibility of American mandate responsibilities, following from the Gladstonian premise of "the Turks being cleared out of Europe," which Wilson endorsed:

> Mr. Lloyd George informed the Imperial War Cabinet that President Wilson expressed himself in favour of the Turks being cleared out of Europe altogether, but of their place at Constantinople being taken by some small Power, acting as a mandatory of the League of Nations. Mr. Balfour had told the President that the eastern Committee had been in favour of the United States acting as mandatory at Constantinople. With regard to this, President Wilson had pointed out that the United States were extremely proud of their disinterested position in this war, and did not wish to be deprived of that pride. It would be difficult to persuade them that such a mandate was not a profit but really a burden. Altogether he had shown himself very much opposed to any intervention on the part of the United States in these territorial questions.[43]

Wilson, speaking for the United States and presumably for the American public, claimed to prefer the moral high ground of not assuming territorial authority, while his British counterparts hoped to persuade him that imperial or mandatory responsibility constituted a righteous burden not a triumphant prize. Rudyard Kipling had called it "the White Man's Burden"—in the poem that he wrote in 1899 to mark the American assumption of an imperial role in the Philippines.

The historian Perin Gürel has studied the creation of the Turkish Wilsonian Principles League by Halide Edib, a leader of the Turkish movement for women's rights. The League endorsed the idea of an American mandate for postwar Turkey, and sent an appeal to Wilson in December 1918 requesting American assistance "for the solution of the problem of the heterogeneous religions and races in Turkey."[44] The appeal specified a period of fifteen to twenty-five years of American "guidance and instruction" for Turkey under the continuing sovereignty of the Ottoman sultan.

According to Robert Lansing, the whole notion of American mandates for Armenia and Constantinople—"both of which . . . would be a constant financial burden"—was intended by the Allies "to take advantage of the unselfishness of the American people and of the altruism and idealism of President Wilson." Lansing, writing later in a hostile spirit, after Wilson had dismissed him, regarded the president as a mere dupe in his post-Ottoman concerns: "The president apparently looked upon the appeals made to him as genuine expressions of humanitarianism and as manifestations of the opinion of mankind concerning the part that the United States ought to take in the reconstruction of the world. His high-mindedness and loftiness of thought blinded him to the sordidness of purpose which appears to have induced the general acquiescence in his desired system of mandates."[45] The other Powers, according to Lansing, might look for profitable mandates, but Wilson naively, blindly, believed in the moral stakes of the post-Ottoman settlement. Lansing, for all his retrospective antagonism toward Wilson, did not doubt that the president was sincerely interested in the Constantinople mandate.

In Paris the peace conference was dominated by the Big Four—Wilson, Lloyd George, the French prime minister, Georges Clemenceau, and the Italian prime minister, Vittorio Emanuele Orlando—and in March 1919, Wilson returned to the subject of Ottoman mandates in the Council of Four. He put forward a comparison between the Habsburg and Ottoman empires in their respective conditions of collapse. Drawing an unusual analogy from chemistry, he declared the Ottoman empire to be in a state of dissolution—"as though it were made of quicksilver"—while the Habsburg monarchy was simply in a condition of disintegration—"had been broken into pieces"—and therefore could be, and had been, dismembered into its component ethnographical parts. Because the Ottoman empire was so confusingly mixed in its populations, foreign powers would necessarily need to "take care of it" through purposeful political restructuring based on a mandatory system of responsibility. Wilson acknowledged that America should reluctantly assume some sort of mandatory role, though he rightly anticipated opposition at home:

> For his part, he was quite disinterested since the United States of America did not want anything in Turkey. They would be only too delighted if France and Great Britain would undertake the responsibility. Lately,

THE GREAT RENUNCIATION.

President Wilson. "NO! I DON'T THINK IT QUITE SUITS MY AUSTERE TYPE OF BEAUTY."

[It is reported that the United States of America have declined to accept a mandate for Constantinople.]

FIGURE 2. This cartoon of Wilson from *Punch* in May 1919 showed him in Ottoman costume with a hookah, and proclaimed "The Great Renunciation," explaining that "it is reported that the United States of America have declined to accept a mandate for Constantinople." Wilson's vanity is satirized as he looks into a mirror at himself in costume and comments, "No! I don't think it quite suits my austere type of beauty."

however, it had been put to him that he must approach his own people on this matter, and he intended to try, although it would mean some very good talking on his part. He admitted that the United States of America must take the responsibilities as well as the benefits of the League of Nations. Nevertheless, there was great antipathy in the United States of America to the assumption of these responsibilities. Even the Philippines were regarded as something hot in the hand that they would like to drop.[46]

The Ottoman empire was precisely the regional arena where Wilson anticipated that the United States might have to assume those morally complicated mandatory responsibilities that, at a superficial glance, appeared to resemble imperialist acquisitions.

When Wilson drafted a memorandum for the Council of Four, dated March 25, 1919, he explicitly emphasized the Armenian massacres as the crucial justification for establishing mandates in the provinces of the Ottoman empire.

> Particularly because of the historical mis-government by the Turks of subject peoples and the terrible massacres of Armenians and others in recent years, the Allied and Associate Powers are agreed that Armenia, Syria, Mesopotamia, Palestine, and Arabia must be completed severed from the Turkish Empire. . . . The Allied and Associated Powers are of the opinion that the character of the mandate must differ according to the stage of development of the people. . . . They [the Powers] consider that certain communities formerly belonging to the Turkish Empire have reached a stage of development where their existence as independent nations can be provisionally recognized, subject to the rendering of administrative advice and assistance by a mandatory power until such time as they are able to stand alone.[47]

The European peoples of the Habsburg monarchy were judged to be at a stage of development appropriate to political independence, whereas the Middle Eastern peoples of the Ottoman empire were deemed to be at some less advanced mandatory stage. The European portions of the Ottoman empire—Constantinople, the lands of southeastern Europe denominated as Thrace, and even Albania, which had been an Ottoman province up until 1912—would eventually be considered as possible places for mandates.

At a meeting of the Council of Four in Paris on May 5, 1919, Lloyd George "said he was very anxious to settle the question of the mandates" and Wilson, responding as if pressured, replied that "in regard to Turkey in particular, it was impossible for him to give a decision at present as to whether the United States could take a mandate." Wilson was already concerned that even the claiming of mandates would appear as old-fashioned imperialism, and if Lloyd George was "very anxious" to settle their assignment, Wilson himself was "very anxious to avoid the appearance of a division of the spoils."[48] Wilson's ambivalence about mandates followed from his anxiety that any appearance of "spoils" would be in arrant contradiction to the Wilsonian principles of the peace.

The next day, on May 6, in the Council of Four, Wilson addressed the possibility of America holding a mandate for the entire territory of Anatolian Turkey. He was interested in forestalling the Greek and Italian armies eager to occupy portions of Anatolia, but believed that an American mandate would be unacceptable to the American public:

WILSON: I am told that the Turks wish that the regions inhabited by their race not be divided, and also that there is a movement among them in favor of an American administration.

LLOYD GEORGE: That would not surprise me; of all Westerners, the Americans are those against whom they have the fewest grievances.

WILSON: I have no hope that American opinion will consent to it. Hatred of the Turk is unbelievable in America. What American opinion will approve is the protection of the Armenians or of some population which stands against the Turks. It will also approve the occupation of Constantinople, if it is conferred on us, because in that way Constantinople will be taken away from the Turks.[49]

The issue of mandates occupied a curious status in the Wilsonian world view, inasmuch as it depended, not upon the self-determination of individual nations, as in the Habsburg peace arrangements, but upon the intersection of Turkish readiness to tolerate the mandate and American readiness to undertake it, a balancing of reciprocal reluctances. The supposed American "hatred of the Turk" might have reflected, in part, a missionary-inflected Islamophobia, but also, in part, a Gladstonian abhorrence of political oppression and brutality. Such hatred, Wilson believed, would be an obstacle to international trusteeship, though he was optimistically hopeful that there might be public approval for an occupation of Constantinople. In this, as in so many other instances, he clearly misjudged the readiness of the U.S. Senate to take on any postwar international responsibilities.

Both Wilson and Lloyd George were anxious about how such mandates for Ottoman territory, especially over Constantinople, would be perceived in the Muslim world. Wilson had heard that "the Persians were much depressed at not being consulted in regard to the Peace Settlement," and Lloyd George replied that "he wished the Council to hear what the representatives of India had to say, particularly in regard to Constantinople and the future of Islam."[50] The Ottoman sultan was also the Sunni Muslim caliph, and depriving him of his secular domains might further offend his religious followers. A few days later, at the Council of Four, Wilson "produced an ethnographic map of Anatolia" (probably provided by The Inquiry) and indicated the mixed populations that would complicate the construction of mandates. Characteristically, Wilson was focused on issues of ethnicity, but Lloyd George reminded him that "it had to be borne in mind that the whole Mohammedan world would be aroused by this partition of Turkey."[51] The international dimensions of Constantinople were not only maritime, but also denominational, and the issue of Muslim public opinion was a delicate one for Wilson to assimilate, as the leader of a Christian nation instilled with "hatred of the Turk"—which he himself partly shared.

On May 17, 1919, Edwin Samuel Montagu, British Secretary of State for India, who partly represented British India at the peace conference, wrote to Wilson urging him to consider an American mandate for Constantinople. Montagu paid attention to Muslim interests at the conference, in deference to the concerns of Indian Muslims.

> Dear President Wilson, At the last moment as we were going out this afternoon you used the word "mandate" as applied to Turkey. My Mahomedan friends would hate a mandatory because they would be so suspicious that

it was disguised annexation. But their attitude of hostility would be largely modified if the mandatory were a country of undoubted integrity and disinterestedness . . .[52]

Certainly it could not be the Italians, wrote Montagu ("nothing will convince the Mahomedans that this is not annexation"), but it could plausibly be America, "whose disinterestedness is beyond dispute"—and the more so inasmuch as America had never declared war on Turkey. Wilson had his ethnographic map of Anatolia, and Montagu noted further that Constantinople had a Turkish plurality of population, but not an absolute majority—given the large communities of Greeks, Armenians, and Jews.[53] An American mandate would therefore affect and protect numerous non-Turkish Christians and Jews in Constantinople.

On May 21 in the Council of Four, Lloyd George was still pressing Wilson to consider a mandate for all of Anatolia, while seeming to take for granted that America would have mandates, at least, for Armenia and Constantinople. Wilson was more interested in sorting out ethnography than mandates, and again "brought out an ethnographical map of Turkey," noting that the issues of mixed (Greek and Turkish) population in Anatolia were analogous to those of Silesia (Polish and German) and the formerly Habsburg Adriatic (South Slavic and Italian). For Wilson, the map of Eastern Europe extended as far as the coast of Anatolia, and the peace settlement could not be discussed without reference to the populations themselves. He was willing to speak hypothetically about an American mandate for Constantinople ("if the United States were the Mandatory of the Straits"), but was prepared, still hypothetically, to allow the sultan "to inhabit a reserved area in Constantinople in the territory of the Mandatory." When Lloyd George pragmatically objected that the sultan would have a very large court and guard, which would be "a great inconvenience to the Mandatory Power," Wilson, pragmatic himself, replied that "the guards might be limited in number." Lloyd George thought that if the Americans did not accept a mandatory role, "it would be better for the Sultan to clear out of Constantinople." Wilson did not think that America would accept a mandate for all of Anatolia but claimed to be open to the possibility of a mandate for Armenia and for Constantinople with the Straits.[54]

Wilson's calculations reflected a counterfactual alternative American history that was never to be realized: control of Constantinople. This was a fantasy that went beyond Gladstonian Turcophobia, back to the Greek project of Catherine the Great when she aspired to conquer the Ottoman capital. "I ask your majesty for permission to come and place myself at her feet, and to pass some days at her court, as soon as it shall be established at Constantinople," Voltaire wrote to her in 1768.[55] In fact, Constantinople had been promised to Russia in 1915 by secret agreement with England and France as the reward of eventual victory in World War I, but the Russian claim was no longer recognized after the Bolshevik Revolution and the Treaty of Brest-Litovsk, Russia's separate peace with Germany. This was precisely the sort of secret agreement that Wilson denounced as the aggrandizing diplomacy of the nineteenth century, confidently practiced by imperial Russia. Yet now it was Woodrow Wilson himself, pleading perfect disinterestedness, who seemed to entertain the simultaneously moral and Orientalist fantasy of establishing his own American court at Constantinople.

On May 22, Wilson spoke with William Linn Westermann, the Columbia historian of the ancient world who advised the president on Greek and Turkish affairs in Paris: "The President said that the United States, if it held mandates over Armenia and Constantinople, would be in a strategic position to control that portion of the world." At the same time, he backed off from the idea of hosting the sultan within the American mandate, claiming that he had just seen "a document written by a Moslem Indian (whose name he had forgotten) . . . that the Eastern Moslems did not after all set so high a value on keeping the Sultan in his former position," and that "the Moslem world was not vitally interested even in maintaining the Caliphate."[56] In a letter of May 23, Wilson acknowledged the force of arguments against allowing the sultan to remain in Constantinople, observing that, "just such arguments are beginning to prevail in my mind, after further consideration of the matter." The hypothetical American mandate could be compromised by a rival authority in the person of the Ottoman sultan and Muslim caliph Mehmed VI. Yet, when asked generally about possible American mandates in Turkey on May 28, Wilson replied, "I've been giving it a good deal of thought . . . and have not yet made up my mind."[57]

On June 17, three Ottoman representatives, led by Grand Vizier Damat Ferid Pasha, the son-in-law of the sultan, addressed the victorious powers at the peace conference in Paris, and appealed for the territorial integrity of the empire. At this time Greek and Italian troops were already in Anatolia, and Mustafa Kemal Pasha, promising resistance, undiplomatically declared that "if we have no weapons to fight with, we shall fight with our teeth and nails."[58] On June 23, the Ottoman delegation in Paris submitted a memorandum, which Wilson read out to the Council of Four on June 25: "Memory glorifies the past of Turkey, recalling that she knew how to form and administer a great empire, that in it she respected the existence of all religious communities, and that she entered onto the path of reform as soon as she came into contact with the West. Turkey only desires to continue her advance toward progress."[59] The delegation insisted that the Ottoman empire, while willing to protect minorities and allow autonomies, refused to accept any foreign mandates that would compromise political independence or territorial integrity.

It was precisely this liberal interpretation of the Ottoman past and future which aroused the scorn of the peacemakers. "That delegation and its memorandum are good jokes," Lloyd George responded after Wilson finished reading aloud. "I have never seen anything more stupid," Wilson agreed. "It is the best proof of the complete political incapacity of the Turks," Lloyd George continued. "They have always placed men of other races at the head of their government."[60] It was true that Ottoman officials, including the sultan's grand viziers, were often drawn from the diverse peoples of the empire, and even Damat Ferid Pasha possibly had his family origins in Montenegro, but Lloyd George himself was the Welsh prime minister of Great Britain with its multiracial empire. What appeared most "ridiculous" and "stupid" to the Big Four was the Ottoman claim to a tradition of tolerant and progressive government, coming from a nation that was despised in defeat for its supposed barbarism.

Wilson wondered, "Is it necessary to reply to a document of this kind?" Lloyd George believed it would be enough "to acknowledge the receipt of this memorandum and to say to the Turkish delegation: 'You can go home.'" Wilson agreed that the delegation itself was entirely dispensable:

WILSON: The solution which we will reach has nothing to do with these three ridiculous people
LLOYD GEORGE: If we could only make peace summarily and finish with it.
CLEMENCEAU: I really fear that that is not possible.⁶¹

Wilson, with his principled belief in observing the will of the people, was prepared to deal with Turkey summarily, without regard for "these three ridiculous people" of the Ottoman delegation. Once again, as when he and House had joked about the likely execution of the American ambassador, he seemed to approach the subject of Turkey in the spirit of comic opera.

In that day's discussion in the Council of Four, Lloyd George pressed the question of whether the Turks should cease to rule over Constantinople, and Wilson replied decisively that "he had studied the question of the Turks in Europe for a long time, and every year confirmed his opinion that they ought to be cleared out." The words "cleared out" echoed Gladstone's emphatic phrasing from the "Bulgarian Horrors" pamphlet of 1876, which demanded that the Ottomans "clear out from the province they have desolated and profaned." Yet Wilson's inclination to displace the Ottomans from their capital also committed him still further to supporting an American mandate, which would certainly face public resistance back in the United States. Wilson was ready to send the Ottoman delegates "home" to Constantinople—but it was only to await being "cleared out" according to the terms of the prospective postwar settlement.

The next day, on June 26, Wilson was still indignant over the Ottoman memorandum and declared that the delegates exhibited a "complete absence of common sense and a total misunderstanding of the West"; that they "imagined that the Conference knew no history and was ready to swallow enormous falsehoods."⁶² Based on his own early Gladstonian initiation into the Eastern Question, and further armed with the research of The Inquiry, Wilson believed that he had nothing to learn from the Ottoman delegates and the "enormous falsehoods" of their memorandum. He came away from this encounter still fully committed to the concept of post-Ottoman mandates, though still unsure of what role America might play. The Turkish presumption of teaching the Council of Four a lesson in Ottoman history, a history of alleged religious toleration and political reform, outraged Wilson's own sense of the gulf between the civilization of the West and the barbarism of the Ottomans.

■ ■ ■

Amputations

In late June 1919 the question of whether America would accept a mandate for Ottoman territory—in Constantinople or in Armenia—was still unresolved. Nevzat Uyanik has noted that there was even significant support from U.S. diplomats and especially American missionaries for a mandate over all of Anatolian Turkey.[63] Wilson, however, believed that the mandate issue might be left provisionally unresolved, as long as Turkey was made to renounce in the treaty the specified territories whose future was still to be determined. This was to be done, according to Wilson, with the same procedure as the Austrian peace treaty: "He suggested that the portions which Turkey was to lose might be cut off and the Treaty might provide that she should accept the dispositions of the Allied and Associated Powers in regard to them, just as had been done in the case of Austria." Thus both peace treaties were to map the dismemberment of the two empires, Habsburg and Ottoman, without specifying the future rearrangement of sovereignties and authorities. Wilson noted that "the amputations would involve Mesopotamia, Syria, and Armenia," and that "the Allied troops would remain there to keep order until the final settlement." Constantinople and the Straits "should be left as a neutral strip." Wilson had finally decided that "he would make the Sultan and his Government move out of Constantinople."[64] In fact, the Eastern Question of "Turkey in Europe" was probably the aspect of the whole peace settlement that Wilson had contemplated longest, dating to the long-ago Eastern crisis of the 1870s when he was a student. The whole impetus to rearrange the map of Eastern Europe at the Paris Peace Conference may be traced back to its origin in Wilson's long-standing conviction that Turkey in Europe was a geopolitical and moral anomaly, and that such anomalies—all across Eastern Europe—were susceptible to political correction by the redrawing of the map and reassignment of sovereignty.

Wilson returned with ever greater emphasis to the formula of Ottoman renunciation of territory in the peace treaty, without specifying the political future of the territory renounced: "It might be possible to tell the Turks that they must abandon their possessions in Europe and in certain specified territories in Asia, or else they might be told 'Your territory will be bounded as follows—Turkey must renounce all rights over territories outside the boundary and accept in advance the disposal of these areas to be made by the Allied and Associated Powers.'"[65] The Turkish treaty (like the Austrian treaty) would involve drawing a map to define clearly what was not-Turkey, having Turkey renounce the territories beyond the specified boundary on the map, and surrendering all stake in the to-be-determined affiliation or sovereignty of those territories. Lloyd George returned to the question of Constantinople:

> MR. LLOYD GEORGE said that this proposal was practicable if it be decided at once to take Constantinople from the Turks.
> PRESIDENT WILSON observed that Constantinople was not a Turkish City, other races there were in the majority.
> MR. LLOYD GEORGE said this amounted to a final expulsion of the Turks from Europe.[66]

Lloyd George's posing of the Eastern Question in its classic form, the taking of Constantinople and the removal of the Ottoman empire from Europe, was met here by Wilson's offering of ethnographic justification, his analysis of the ethnic composition of the Ottoman capital. Here, as the two men seemed to complete each other's thoughts, the nineteenth-century politics of the Eastern Question met the new twentieth-century calculus of ethnographic mapping, the determination that Constantinople could not be politically Turkish because it was not ethnographically Turkish.

Clemenceau chimed in to agree that Constantinople should be taken from Turkey, that the Ottoman conquest of Constantinople all the way back in the fifteenth century had been a traumatic event for Europe—but "since then Europe had made every effort to maintain the Turks there." Wilson showed his familiarity with the history of the Eastern Question when he replied to Clemenceau: "doubtless because no successor could be found for them." This was the fundamental dilemma of the Eastern

Question: what power would replace the Turks at Constantinople? Disraeli had supported the sultan for fear of Russia controlling the Straits. Wilson, however, had replied too quickly, for the probable designated successor was none other than himself, the hypothetical American mandatory of Constantinople. Clemenceau now took some satisfaction in pointing this out: "Constantinople had been offered to President Wilson, but he did not seem anxious to accept it."[67] Wilson's ambivalence about the proposal for an American mandate was partly pragmatic, deriving from a well-founded doubt about whether the U.S. Congress or the American public would accept it, but also, as a matter of principle, out of antipathy to formulations like this one—"Constantinople had been offered to President Wilson"—which so powerfully suggested the old diplomacy that he absolutely rejected.

Wilson had to satisfy himself morally that an American mandate would not appear to the world as American aggrandizement. This was, in fact, precisely how Wilson judged the presence of Italian troops in Anatolia in 1919: as Italian aggrandizement, Italy seeking to obtain territories for its own advantage. For Wilson Ottoman issues were becoming increasingly entangled with Italian issues, especially given his strong opposition to observing the terms of the Treaty of London, the secret agreement of 1915 by which Britain, France, and Russia obtained Italy's entry into the war on the side of the Entente (in spite of prewar Italian participation in the Triple Alliance with Germany and Austria-Hungary). The crucial enticement was the promise of Trieste, Istria, and northern Dalmatia, to be taken from Austria-Hungary, in addition to Trentino and South Tyrol. Since America was not a participant in the secret treaty, Wilson was in no way bound by its promises, and was determined that Italy should not obtain Dalmatia, with its largely South Slavic population. There were, however, also clauses of the treaty that pertained to Ottoman lands, promising Italy the Dodecanese islands, which Italy had seized from the sultan in the Italian-Turkish War of 1911–12, and formerly Ottoman Albania, independent since 1912, but now promised to Italy as a protectorate. Furthermore, by the ninth article of the treaty, Italy was promised a share of the Anatolian Mediterranean, around Antalya, "in the event of total or partial partition of Turkey in Asia."[68] Concessions to Italy in Anatolia now became one possible strategy for persuading Italy to abandon her claim to Dalmatia, but Wilson, by June 1919, had become so frustrated by Italian self-aggrandizement that he suddenly found himself playing the role of protector of the Ottomans.

Orlando resigned as Italian prime minister on June 23 (partly because he was failing to obtain satisfaction of Italy's demands at the conference), and on June 26 the remaining Big Three were waiting in Paris for Rome to supply a new prime minister to join them as the Big Four. Under these circumstances, it was possible for the Big Three to be frankly disparaging about the Treaty of London and Italy's subsequent conduct in the war.

> WILSON: I hope that you will seize the favorable occasion to rid yourselves of a treaty which, speaking in all conscience, I have never considered continued to bind you.
> LLOYD GEORGE: We must take into account the critical moment when Italy joined us, and the 500,000 dead which the war cost her.
> CLEMENCEAU: Do not take that figure too literally.
> WILSON: The truth is that Italy went to the highest bidder.
> LLOYD GEORGE: That is a harsh word; but I fear that there is truth in it.
> WILSON: During this conference, Italy was uninterested in everything that did not directly affect her . . .
> LLOYD GEORGE: I went through the entire war, and, unfortunately, I always saw Italy try to do as little as possible.[69]

With Italy represented so unflatteringly, as lazy and cowardly in war, utterly selfish at the conference, and exaggerating the number of her war dead, Wilson proceeded to object strenuously to the presence of Italian troops in Ottoman lands. "I do not see what rights the Italians have in Asia," Wilson declared.[70]

Britain and France, of course, considered that they themselves held legitimate imperial rights in Asia, and, furthermore, considered themselves bound to Italy by the Treaty of London. The literal-minded Balfour took up the text of the Treaty of London and actually read the relevant clause aloud to Wilson.

WILSON: The case anticipated is that of a partition of the Ottoman empire.

CLEMENCEAU: This partition has not yet taken place.

WILSON: There will be no partition. The territories of the Ottoman Empire will not be distributed among us like properties; they will be administered, for the good of their peoples, according to the system of mandates. This is not a partition.[71]

In defending Turkey from Italian predation, Wilson made himself the spokesman for the Ottoman "peoples"—not only the Armenians, Greeks, and Jews, but also the Turkish population of Anatolia. Wilson's insistence on the difference between mandates and partitions was all the more emphatic out of the reasonable anxiety that some observers would not clearly recognize the distinction.

A few days later Wilson himself was reading aloud the memorandum that the Council proposed to present to the Italian government. The memorandum began by looking back to the Treaty of London in 1915 and arguing that the promises of the treaty had become irrelevant. Italy could no longer claim Dalmatia from the Habsburgs, since the Habsburg empire no longer existed. The Ottoman empire did still exist, and would be shorn of some of its provinces, but, in accordance with American principles, Turkey would not be simply dismembered in defeat to provide spoils for the victors.

> It [the Treaty of London] contemplated a victorious peace with the Austro-Hungarian Empire; but while victory of the completest kind has been achieved, the Austro-Hungarian Empire had ceased to exist. It [the Treaty] assumed that if Turkey was completely defeated, fragments of the Turkish Empire might be assigned to the victors; but while Turkey has indeed *been* completely defeated, and the alien peoples which she misgoverned are to be separated from her Empire, they are not to be handed over in possession to the conquerors.[72]

Contemplating the Habsburg and Ottoman empires analogously, Wilson stood ready to defend even the defeated Ottoman peoples and territories, like the Habsburg peoples and territories, from arbitrary claims and predations. "If for example Italy insists, after our earnest protests, on maintaining troops in Anatolia," the memorandum continued, "it can only be because she intends to obtain by force all she claims to be hers by right"—which would lead to Italy's complete "isolation" from the Allies in Paris.[73]

A separate memorandum on American-Italian relations called on Italy to withdraw its armies from Anatolia, and to desist from unilaterally occupying Turkish territory, lest it become "impossible for the other Powers to cooperate with it [Italy] or to assist it in any way." The United States could not consent to "the sacrifice of any of the principles upon which the present negotiations have been conducted," principles that were manifestly violated by Italy's unauthorized occupations in Anatolia.[74] Strangely, Wilson had made himself into a limited advocate for Turkish territorial integrity, even as the Ottoman empire was being dismembered by the mandate system.

On June 27, the day before the signing of the Versailles peace treaty with Germany, Wilson spoke with American press correspondents in Paris, and placed the Ottoman issues of the conference before the American public:

> Regarding the proposition that the United States accept a mandate for Armenia, the President said he considered that he had no right to make a personal decision without consulting the American people. He regarded Anatolia as an integral part of Turkey, not to be linked with Armenia. He was personally inclined to favor accepting a mandate for Armenia and stated that the question of Constantinople was like that of Armenia. He said that the moment you separate Constantinople from the Turkish Empire, it is of small consequence. The real job about Constantinople was like the Panama Canal job—one of keeping the Black Sea passage open. Asked if he was going to put this question before the people or Congress, he answered, "Both."[75]

Here Wilson frankly recognized the limits of what he could promise in Paris, acknowledged that the creation of an American mandate for Armenia or Constantinople lay beyond his personal prestige and political authority. He would have to present Armenia to Americans as the victim of "indescribable agonies," and Constantinople as a mere convenience for shipping. While Clemenceau was sufficiently aware of the weight of history to recall that the conquest of Constantinople in 1453 had been a shock for Renaissance Europe, Wilson would acknowledge no special historical mystique of the city on the Bosphorus, at the maritime frontier of Europe and Asia, but rather compared the legendary straits to the modern engineering project of the Panama Canal—where American commercial interests were self-evident.

When Wilson found himself speaking before the U.S. Senate a few weeks later, on July 10, he offered a Gladstonian moral indictment of the Ottoman empire, justifying its dismemberment by extolling the suffering of its peoples, but only cautiously making a general argument for mandates to facilitate the protection of peoples not quite ready for self-government in his opinion. He insisted now on a perfect parallel between the Ottoman and Habsburg empires, but the post-Habsburg scenario did not involve the assumption of mandates by the great powers of Western Europe, let alone by the United States. Crucially, Wilson argued that the Turkish empire had disintegrated spontaneously, and therefore was not being purposefully dismantled by the allied powers at the peace conference, the same powers who were claiming post-Ottoman mandates;

> The Turkish Empire, moreover, had fallen apart, as the Austro-Hungarian had. It had never had any real unity. It had been held together only by pitiless, inhuman force. Its people cried aloud for release, for succour from unspeakable distress, for all that the new day of hope seemed at last to bring within its dawn. Peoples hitherto in utter darkness were to be led out into the same light and given at last a helping hand. Undeveloped peoples and peoples ready for recognition but not yet ready to assume the full responsibilities of statehood were to be given adequate guarantees of friendly protection, guidance, and assistance.[76]

As he had ventriloquized the "indescribable agonies" of the Ottoman peoples at the Metropolitan Opera House in March, so now, in the Senate in Washington, Wilson gave voice to the "unspeakable distress" of those same peoples. The Ottoman empire was "inhuman," and its suffering peoples remained "undeveloped." They would require a "helping hand" to be led from darkness to light, and were therefore candidates for the "friendly protection" that Wilson did not here specify as the mandate system. The Covenant of the League of Nations, also under consideration by the Senate as part of the Versailles treaty, made this explicit: "Certain communities formerly belonging to the Turkish Empire have reached a stage of development where their existence as independent nations can be provisionally recognized subject to the rendering of administrative advice and assistance by a Mandatory until such time as they are able to stand alone."[77] Wilson's own long-standing hostility to the Ottoman empire nevertheless allowed him to entertain political sympathies for the Ottoman peoples, even while assigning them to an intermediary level of civilized development in the hierarchy of nations implicated in the peace settlement.

"I will withdraw the French treaty rather than consent to see the Turkish Empire divided as spoils!" Wilson wrote to Lansing in the summer of 1919, casting himself as a defender of Turkish integrity.[78] He approved the system of League mandates, but would permit nothing that would give the appearance of annexations by force. A memorandum by Lansing on "The President's Feelings as to the Present European Situation" noted Wilson's parallel disgust with forceful incursions in the lands of Austria-Hungary and Ottoman Turkey. Particularly outraged at "the rapacity of Roumania," which had seized Transylvania from Hungary, Wilson also spoke "with considerable heat" about Turkish territories: "When I find Italy and Greece arranging between themselves as to the division of western Asia Minor, and when I think of the greed and utter selfishness of it all, I am almost inclined to refuse to permit this country to be a member of the League of Nations when it is composed of such intriguers and robbers. I am disposed to throw up the whole business and get out."[79] Ultimately, it would be the Senate that would make this decision for him, though Wilson's refusal to make compromises and accept amendments helped bring about the failure of the treaty.

It was, however, precisely concerns about "rapacity" and "spoils" with reference to the Ottoman settlement that roused Wilson to the rhetorical intensity of wanting to renounce the entire peace settlement over which he himself had labored so purposefully. Lansing further elaborated: "This is the third time that the President has said to me that the present conduct of the nations makes him consider withdrawing from the League, though he never before spoke so emphatically. The other occasions were when the Greeks were demanding all of eastern Thrace, and when France was insisting on her claim to Syria."[80] Thus, all three occasions for threatening to renounce the League were provoked by Turkish territorial issues: Thrace in Ottoman Europe, Syria in the Ottoman Middle East, and finally Asia Minor or Anatolia. Lansing recognized that Wilson was concerned with having to give an American guarantee, through the League, to "unjust territorial arrangements," but the secretary of state also noted Wilson's underlying moral rigor, his detestation of "inordinate cupidity and disregard of right" in international affairs.[81] The issue of "right" in all these cases was, unexpectedly, a matter of rightness toward the Ottoman empire and the Ottoman peoples.

Frank Lyon Polk, who represented America in Paris after Wilson and Lansing returned home, wrote to Wilson in August 1919, concerned about whether it was legitimately possible to assume mandates over territories that remained nominally under Ottoman imperial sovereignty. The Covenant of the League, in article 22, specified that mandates were intended for "those colonies and territories which, as a consequence of the late war, have ceased to be under the sovereignty of the states which formerly governed them and which are inhabited by peoples not yet able to stand by themselves under the strenuous conditions of the modern world."[82] Colonel House had therefore come up with a fill-in-the-blank formula, for the purposes of the peace treaty, by which the Ottoman empire renounced sovereignty over particular territories, which might then be assigned to mandates. This applied to any and all territories: "The Turkish Empire having by article blank of the Treaty of [blank] signed at blank the blank [date] renounced all rights over blank . . . "[83] A similar formula was proposed for the Habsburg monarchy in the Austrian peace treaty, though not for the purpose of mandates, but rather for the reassignment of territory to new states. Indeed the formula constituted a sort of "blank check" for disassembling multinational empires. It is notable that after sponsoring the huge historical research project known as The Inquiry, House could only offer such a strikingly ahistorical modeling of those empires: constructed of seemingly interchangeable blanks, to be renounced, detached, entrusted, and reassigned in almost mechanical fashion.

In September 1919, Wilson was campaigning around the country on behalf of the Treaty of Versailles, which would have to be approved or rejected by the Senate, where it was opposed by the leading Republicans, who demanded modifications. The president was speaking in St. Louis on September 5, and Turkey did not figure large in his mobilization of public feeling for the treaty and, along with it, the League of Nations. He pointed out to his audience that Turkey would not be immediately included in the League (inasmuch as no peace treaty with Turkey had yet been signed), but he made it into a somewhat lame joke, which did, at least, entertain the crowd: "We can at any rate postpone Turkey until Thanksgiving."[84] The joke was greeted with laughter from the public. Wilson's engagement with the Turkish settlement seemed to be flagging during this final phase of his political activity on behalf of the peace. When Turkey could be dismissed with a joke about Thanksgiving, the American president had come a long way from Gladstone's fervent moral abomination of the Ottoman empire.

■ ■ ■

Constantinople: The Washington of the Balkans
With the war ending late in 1918 Henry Morgenthau published a memoir of his term in Turkey, *Ambassador Morgenthau's Story*, with a full account of the Armenian massacres during the war. He dedicated the book "To Woodrow Wilson, the exponent in America of the enlightened public opinion of the world, which has decreed that the rights of small nations shall be respected and that such crimes as are described in this book shall never again darken the pages of history." It was a salvo heralding the Wilsonian perspective on the Ottoman empire, even as Wilson prepared for the peace conference. One year later, on Sunday, November 9, 1919, ten days before the Senate voted on the Versailles treaty, Morgenthau published an article titled "Mandates or War?" in the *New York Times Magazine*, commencing with a very direct endorsement of mandates: "I am one of those who believe that the United States should accept a mandate for Constantinople and the several provinces in Asia Minor which constitute what is left of the Ottoman Empire. I am aware that this proposition is not popular with the

American people." He believed that the former Ottoman lands were at risk of lapsing into chaos, and that "unless the United States accepts a Turkish mandate the world will again lose the opportunity of solving the problem that has endangered civilization for 500 years." Morgenthau emphasized the importance of "the expulsion of the Turk from Europe," and the safeguarding of the formerly oppressed Ottoman peoples. The alternative, he believed, was "another Balkan war" with the risk of "another world conflagration." His orientation with regard to the nineteenth-century Eastern Question was evident from the article's celebration of Gladstone and his denunciation of the Ottoman empire in the 1870s, complete with citations from the "Bulgarian Horrors" pamphlet. "It might be necessary for us to remain in Constantinople longer than elsewhere," Morgenthau observed, because he envisioned the city as "the Washington of the Balkans and perhaps of Asia Minor." The city where Europe met Asia at the Bosphorus was the geographical point from which American guidance would instill American values to bring about the definitive transformation of the former Ottoman lands: "We can not hope sanely for peace unless America establishes at Constantinople a centre from which democratic principles shall radiate and illuminate that dark region of the world."[85] The article strongly suggests how ideologically essential—and diplomatically plausible—this project of an American mandate for Constantinople appeared within the broader Wilsonian vision of the postwar settlement.

On November 19, 1919, still before Thanksgiving, the American Senate rejected the Treaty and the League, and then rejected it definitively, for a second time, in March 1920. Even after that, in May 1920, Wilson proposed an American mandate in Armenia—from "an earnest desire to see Christian people everywhere succored in their time of suffering, and lifted from their abject subjection and distress"—and this too was rejected by the Senate, a final insult to the Wilsonian vision of the peace.[86] In the meantime the Turkish peace negotiations were taking place in Paris. In a letter to Wilson, Lansing noted that "I am instructing Mr. Wallace [the U.S. ambassador in Paris] to attend the meetings of the Heads of Governments should he be invited to do so, but to make it clear to those present at the meetings that he is participating in them unofficially and as an observer."[87] In 1920, Archibald Cary Coolidge, back at Harvard, published in the *New York Evening Post* an anonymous lament about Constantinople being left under Turkish sovereignty. Writing contemptuously of the Turks, he insisted that "as elements in the progress of mankind they have contributed nothing," and, given Constantinople's economic position as a great port, "there seems a strange irony of fate if such a position is to remain in the hands of a backward people notoriously little addicted to trade." The professor's academic Turcophobia was consistent with the president's political view, and now, in 1920, Coolidge could only regret that "an American mandate for Constantinople would have been an easy and simple way out of the difficulty . . . but America today appears in no mood for commitments of this kind."[88] The "difficulty" was at least in part inherent in the broader Wilsonian perspective: the incapacity to envision the Ottoman empire outside the framework of Victorian moral outrage, the failure to envision modern Turkey without benefit of Western tutelage. It was an oddly unscholarly perspective—combining knowledge and prejudice—for a professor who had hoped to write a book about Suleiman the Magnificent.

Constantinople was left to the Ottoman empire by the Treaty of Sèvres, with no mandate and no free state. Though signed by the Ottoman representatives including Damat Ferid Pasha, that treaty was rejected by Mustafa Kemal Pasha, who drove the Greek armies out of Anatolia and forced a massive exchange of populations between Greece and Turkey before agreeing to the much more favorable treaty of Lausanne in 1923. The sultan was removed from power and went into exile, ending the seven-century rule of the Ottoman sultanate and making way for the Turkish republic. The only "independent" Armenia was Soviet Armenia. Wilson's mandated Armenia—sometimes called "Wilsonian Armenia"—disappeared from the agenda of hypothetical history.[89]

Wilson joked about Turkey and Thanksgiving in 1919 at a moment when serious American involvement in the Turkish settlement already appeared increasingly unlikely. In fact, the president had already drawn from the Turkish circumstances the model that he required for the disassembling of empires. Wilson began with the moral, even religious, conviction that Turkey did not belong in Europe, that it should be relegated to Asia. His moral conviction of Turkish misgovernment evolved into a model of imperial dismemberment that ultimately informed his approach to the Habsburg monarchy too. Yet imperial dismemberment had to be uncoupled from any tainted association with the spoils of victory, and Wilson's commitment to maps and mapping introduced him to the ethnographic framework that finally justified his remaking of Eastern Europe. The moralism of "indescribable agonies," as developed in response to the Armenian massacres, was inscribed upon an ethnographic map in which suffering peoples were understood to have an international significance. The logic of the Victorian Eastern Question thus came to shape Wilson's morally and politically modern approach to the remapping of Eastern Europe.

2

"This War of Emancipation"
The Wilsonian Deliverance of the Habsburg Peoples

Condolences

On June 28, 1914, the heir to the Habsburg throne, Archduke Franz Ferdinand, and his wife Sophie were assassinated in Sarajevo by Gavrilo Princip, a student member of the Young Bosnia group, opposed to Austrian rule and favoring South Slavic unification with the kingdom of Serbia. It was not known at the time that the assassin was linked to Belgrade through the Black Hand, a secret conspiratorial society of Serbian army officers. On the day of the assassination U.S. Ambassador Frederic Penfield in Vienna notified Wilson in Washington, and the president promptly wired his condolences to Emperor Franz Joseph, the dead archduke's uncle:

> Deeply shocked at the atrocious murder of His Imperial and Royal Highness Archduke Francis Ferdinand and Consort at an assassin's hands, I extend to Your Majesty, to the Royal Family, and to the Government of Austria-Hungary, the sincere condolences of the Government and people of the United States and an expression of my own profound sympathy.[1]

These conventional condolences made no reference to the possible political implications of the assassination, information not included in Penfield's telegram. Possibly the news called to mind the attempted assassination of Theodore Roosevelt in Milwaukee in 1912, during the three-way presidential campaign pitting former President Roosevelt and sitting President Taft against Wilson himself, the eventual winner. The unbalanced assassin claimed to be acting on the instructions of the ghost of former President McKinley who was himself assassinated in Buffalo in 1901. Roosevelt in 1912 was not seriously injured and, with tremendous sangfroid, proceeded to give a ninety-minute campaign speech with a bullet in his chest. With this recent and relatively benign American scenario in mind, Wilson may not at first have recognized the huge political significance of the assassination at Sarajevo, which would lead to four years of European world war, ultimately involving the United States during Wilson's second term.

After the war, in September 1919, addressing U.S. voters in Helena, Montana, on behalf of the treaty of Versailles, Wilson presented a fully political—and largely sympathetic—account of the assassination. "Don't you remember?" he asked the Montanans:

> The Crown Prince of Austria was assassinated in Serbia. Not assassinated by anybody according to order from the government of Serbia or anybody over whom the government of Serbia had any control, but assassinated by some man who had at his heart the memory of something that was intolerable to him, something that had been done to the people he belonged to.[2]

By the time Wilson spoke in Helena in 1919, after the war was over and the peace concluded, he had a powerful political sense of what the assassination meant; he could frame it as an admirable enactment of the principle that small nations like Serbia had as much right to stand up for their rights as great empires like Austria-Hungary. He had perhaps forgotten that the assassination did not take place in Serbia, but in Habsburg-ruled Bosnia, and he could not have known that the killing was in fact supported by forces close to the government of Serbia in Belgrade.

Wilson was so sympathetic to the national aspirations of small nations that he claimed to be able to intuit the secrets of the heart of the assassin, to be able to feel his intolerable psychic pain at the oppression of his people. Gavrilo Princip had died as an Austrian prisoner at the fortress in Terezin, or Theresienstadt, in 1918, but his posthumous celebrity would survive in Yugoslavia and, more briefly, as an object of Wilsonian sympathy in Montana, where there were many Serbian immigrants working in the coal and copper mines.[3] Wilson almost seemed to suggest to his public in Helena that any of them, including himself, might have pulled the trigger under the intolerable sense of injustice experienced by the assassin.

These two perspectives on the assassination—condolences to Franz Joseph in 1914 and the conjuring up of Princip in 1919—bracketed a period in which Wilson himself shed every possible sympathy for Habsburg Austria-Hungary and led the peacemakers in Paris to embrace the demolition of the multinational Habsburg monarchy and its supplantation by supposedly national successor states, including Czechoslovakia and Yugoslavia. Wilson did not arrive at this conclusion all at once. In 1917, before the United States entered the war, and even in 1918, after it did so, Wilson still entertained the possibility of arranging a separate peace that would detach Austria from Germany and allow the Habsburgs to withdraw from the war with their empire largely intact. In January 1918, his Fourteen Points speech moderately urged, in Point Ten, that the peoples of Austria-Hungary should receive "the freest opportunity to autonomous development"—which was already plausibly politically possible within the constitutional system of the monarchy. Historian Victor Mamatey traced some of the diplomatic intricacies of Wilson's turning against the Habsburg monarchy, and Nicole Phelps, more recently, in her study of U.S.-Habsburg relations, analyzed America's "giving up" on Austria-Hungary.[4] This diplomatic reversal however, was also closely connected to Wilson's evolving political theory of national "emancipation" and his mental mapping of Eastern Europe.

■ ■ ■

"Like the voice of Lincoln"

In the Wilsonian peace proposals of January 1917, the German ambassador Johann Heinrich von Bernstorff, in correspondence with Lansing, observed that the Entente was determined "to destroy Austria-Hungary and to annihilate Turkey." The former objective was remote from Wilson's thoughts at that time, though the latter aim was of Gladstonian interest to him.[5] Eventually he would come around to equating the geopolitical elimination of the Ottoman and Habsburg empires, but in February 1917 Lansing explained Wilson's perspective as follows:

> The chief if not the only obstacle [to peace] is the threat apparently contained in the peace terms recently stated by the Entente Allies that in

case they succeeded they would insist upon a virtual dismemberment of the Austro-Hungarian Empire. Austria needs only to be reassured on that point, and that chiefly with regard to the older units of the Empire. It is the President's view that the large measure of autonomy already secured by those older units is a sufficient guarantee of peace and stability in that part of Europe. . . . The President still believes and has reason to believe that, were it possible for him to give the necessary assurances to the government of Austria, which fears radical dismemberment and which thinks that it is now fighting for its very existence, he could in a very short time force the acceptance of peace upon terms which would follow the general lines of his recent address to the Senate regarding the sort of peace the United States would be willing to join in guaranteeing.[6]

Although he distinguished the "older units" (implicitly, Hungary and Bohemia) from newer ones (certainly Bosnia, annexed in 1908, and probably Galicia, annexed in 1772), Wilson thus accepted the basic integrity of the Habsburg monarchy, and Ambassador Penfield was authorized to inform the Habsburg foreign minister, Ottokar Czernin, that the Allies had "no desire or purpose to disrupt the Austro-Hungarian Empire by the separation of Hungary and Bohemia from Austria."[7] At this point, certainly, the Habsburg monarchy was not condemned to Wilsonian annihilation.

This was confirmed in House's conversations with Balfour in Washington in April about a hypothetical postwar settlement: "It was agreed that Austria must return Bosnia and Herzegovina." Austria had annexed Bosnia from the Ottoman empire, but House and Balfour were determined to "return" it to Serbia. That notwithstanding: "We thought Austria should be composed of three states, such as Bohemia, Hungary and Austria proper." House believed that Trieste should be left to the Habsburgs as an outlet on the Adriatic, and Balfour informed House about the secret treaty of London by which Italy was promised Habsburg Dalmatia—but also "referred to Italy as being greedy." With a map spread out between them, Balfour supposedly told House that he regretted the treaties that "divided up the bearskin before the bear was killed."[8] The bear, though more usually the symbol of Russia, presumably represented here the Habsburg monarchy, and both men, with the map between them in preparation for Balfour's meeting with Wilson, considered the possibility that the Habsburg monarchy might substantially survive the war. According to Colonel House's biographer Charles Neu, it was House who attempted to persuade Balfour to accept the prospect of a negotiated settlement that would allow for such survival.[9]

American ambivalence about the Habsburg monarchy was partly apparent in the notable eight-month interval between the declaration of war on Germany in April and on Austria in December 1917. It was Germany's unrestricted submarine warfare and the German Foreign Office's Zimmerman Telegram, attempting to bring Mexico into the war on the side of the Central Powers, that provoked Wilson to go to war with Germany. His Flag Day speech of June 14, 1917, articulated a complex indictment of both Germany and Austria-Hungary, with the latter seen principally as the vassal and victim of the former.

> The war was begun by the military masters of Germany, who proved to be also the masters of Austria-Hungary. These men have never regarded nations as peoples, men, women, and children of like blood and frame as themselves, for whom governments existed and in whom governments had their life. They have regarded them merely as serviceable organizations which they could by force or intrigue bend or corrupt to their own purpose.[10]

The chief villains here were the Germans, but the indictment—regarding nations as objects of domination rather than peoples with political rights—would soon be applied to Austria-Hungary.

Wilson went on to elaborate a complex and confused mental mapping of Germany's relation to Eastern Europe, a vision of German domination achieved through asymmetrical alliances in which allies were actually pawns.

> Their plan was to throw a broad belt of German military power and political control across the very centre of Europe and beyond the Mediterranean into the heart of Asia; and Austria-Hungary was to be as much their tool and pawn as Servia [sic] or Bulgaria or Turkey or the ponderous

states of the East. Austria-Hungary, indeed, was to become part of the central German Empire, absorbed and dominated by the same forces and influences that had originally cemented the German states themselves. The dream had its heart at Berlin. It could have had a heart nowhere else! It rejected the idea of solidarity of race entirely. The choice of peoples played no part in it at all. It contemplated binding together racial and political units which could be kept together only by force—Czechs, Magyars, Croats, Serbs, Roumanians, Turks, Armenians—the proud states of Bohemia and Hungary, the stout little commonwealths of the Balkans, the indomitable Turks, the subtile peoples of the East.[11]

Wilson here conjured up a mental map in which German ambitions, directionally oriented by the *Drang nach Osten*, the drive to the East, were envisioned as devouring the far-flung territories of Eastern Europe—and reaching even into "the heart of Asia." The peoples of Eastern Europe were "proud" (in spirit) and "stout" (of heart), and the Turks were "indomitable," but the more eastern peoples of the Ottoman empire were suspiciously labeled as "subtile" (that is, crafty). In any case, Germany intended to subjugate and degrade them all. Wilson's June Flag Day speech thus enumerated the far-flung peoples of both the Habsburg and Ottoman empires who were supposedly objects of German domination.

Already in late May, however, Washington's *Official Bulletin* had announced that the Fourth of July would be celebrated in wartime by having citizens of foreign birth—America's immigrant communities—"demonstrate loyalty." The commitment to loyalty was signed by an alphabetical enumeration of communities, including "Czechoslavs" (represented by the Czecho-Slovak National Council), Hungarians (represented by the American Hungarian Loyalty League), Poles (represented by a Polish National Department), Romanians (represented by the Roumanian National League), and South Slavs (represented by the South Slavic National Council). The term "Czechoslavs" was new enough to require parenthetical explication as Bohemians, Moravians, Silesians, and Slovaks, while "South Slavs" were defined as Croats, Serbs, and Slovenes. Though Germans were included on the list of loyal citizen communities, Austrians were not: the Armenians and Assyrians were followed alphabetically by the Belgians, Chinese, and Czechoslavs.[12] In the plans for the 1917 Independence Day celebration, the Habsburg monarchy was thus already, in effect, dissolved into its component nationalities, and the list of immigrant communities intimated the possibility of a new Wilsonian national mapping of Eastern Europe.

On Flag Day, Wilson charged that Germany "rejected the idea of solidarity of race entirely." From his perspective "solidarity of race" within one political or economic domain was a desirable thing, which may not have been altogether unrelated to his own sense of racial solidarity as a white Virginian born in 1856 on the eve of the Civil War. German war aims would, however, produce enforced political heterogeneity. Wilson believed that "race" (by which he clearly also meant nationality) was the naturally integrating force of government, and that "binding together racial and political units" created an imperial domain that "could be kept together only by force"—and could not derive legitimacy from the consent of the governed. This indictment of German war aims would require only the most minor adaptation to be refashioned as a condemnation of the Habsburg monarchy with its numerous nationalities.

By August 1917, Wilson was certainly familiar with the basic ideas of Naumann's *Mitteleuropa* (translated and published that year in New York as *Central Europe*) which the president discussed in Washington with the visiting Belgian diplomat Baron Ludovic Moncheur. Wilson was now more critical of the Habsburg monarchy, but still favored its postwar survival, according to Moncheur: "We then talked of ways of combating the political system of *Mitteleuropa*. The President believed that, even as a democratic regime will be instituted in the German Empire after the war, the races forming the Austro-Hungarian agglomeration would wish to be emancipated. The Dual Monarchy would continue to exist, but each people of the confederation would have liberal autonomy."[13] The notion of a racially miscegenous polity was here represented under the somewhat pejorative term "agglomeration"—a sort of refusal to acknowledge the Habsburg monarchy as an authentic state.

To say that the monarchy would "continue to exist" was at least to suggest that its nonexistence could be contemplated as a possibility, and clearly the concession of autonomy to its peoples was the condition of that continuance. Most striking was the recognition here that the peoples of the monarchy "would wish to be emancipated"—a powerful word in Wilson's lexicon—and one that would come to play a radical role in reconsidering the future of the Habsburg monarchy. When the Polish nationalist ideologue Roman Dmowski urged specific war aims for America in November 1917, he proposed not only "the reconstitution of an independent Polish state" (predictably) but also "the emancipation of nationalities in Austria-Hungary."[14] The word "emancipation" was already being spoken in 1917 with reference to the Habsburg monarchy, and even foreign statesmen seemed to understand that it might carry some special valence in American political culture.

On December 4, in Wilson's State of the Union address, he finally asked Congress to declare war on Austria-Hungary, calling it an "embarrassing obstacle" to the war effort that America was not also at war with Germany's allies. He meant for war to be declared on the Habsburg monarchy but fought on behalf of the Habsburg subjects: to "deliver the peoples of Austria-Hungary, the peoples of the Balkans, and the peoples of Turkey" from Prussian domination. The Habsburg peoples were not yet, however, to be delivered from their own Habsburg rulers: "We do not wish in any way to impair or to rearrange the Austro-Hungarian Empire. It is no affair of ours what they do with their own life, either industrially or politically. We do not purpose or desire to dictate to them in any way. We only desire to see that their affairs are left in their own hands."[15] Even as the language of deliverance implied a commitment to transforming the political future of the Habsburg monarchy, the protestation of noninterference in Habsburg domestic political affairs remained explicit, even emphatic, at the very moment that Wilson was asking for a declaration of war.

On December 5, 1917, the very next day, a telegram was sent to Wilson from the self-styled Bohemian National Alliance of America, asking that Bohemians in America not be considered as Austrians and therefore as enemy aliens. Rather, they declared themselves eager, as Czechs and Slovaks, to enlist to fight against Austria-Hungary, and they flatteringly compared Wilson to Lincoln: "Like the voice of Lincoln . . . so your voice gives new strength to millions of oppressed." In Wilson's speech, oppression was attributed entirely to the evils of German military and economic ambition, but the Bohemian National Alliance now implicitly identified the oppressor as the Habsburg monarchy: "We welcome America's declaration against Austria-Hungary. It will encourage wonderfully our loyal allies in the very heart of Europe, the Czechoslovak people in their defiance of [the] oppressor."[16] The Bohemian National Alliance was created in Chicago after the outbreak of the war in 1914 for the purpose of agitating on behalf of the Czech and Slovak cause, and against Habsburg rule. The Alliance now gave Wilson's own commitment to deliverance precisely the anti-Habsburg direction that he himself still hesitated to affirm, while invoking Lincoln in such a fashion as to imply that deliverance from Habsburg oppression was a matter of Lincolnesque emancipation.

■ ■ ■

"The continued existence of the Austro-Hungarian Monarchy"

On January 4, when Wilson and House discussed the upcoming Fourteen Points speech of January 8, 1918, the two men reviewed a report from The Inquiry, prepared by Sidney Mezes, David Hunter Miller, and Walter Lippmann, outlining a strategy for "The Disestablishment of a Prussian Middle Europe." Responding thus to Naumann's *Mitteleuropa*, the memorandum did not, as in Wilson's previous formulations, see the problem as strictly one of Germany's domination of Austria-Hungary. In a more equitable assignment of responsibility, the authors argued for "the disestablishment of a system by which adventurous and imperialist groups in Berlin and Vienna and Budapest could use the resources of this area in the interest of a fiercely selfish foreign policy," while acknowledging that the strategic goal was to detach Austria-Hungary (that is, Vienna and Budapest) from Germany so that the Entente Allies might win the war.[17]

Considering how to bring about this detachment, the Inquiry memorandum proposed a strategic aggravation of Austria-Hungary's internal national tensions. The memorandum further noted "the nationalistic discontent of the Czechs and probably of the South Slavs," which was confronted with an imperial determination "to emerge from the war with the patrimony of Franz Joseph unimpaired." The Inquiry accordingly suggested a Machiavellian strategy of intimidation balanced by restraint.

> It follows that the more turbulent the subject nationalities become and the less the present Magyar-Austrian ascendancy sees itself threatened with absolute extinction, the more fervent will become the desire in Austria-Hungary to make itself a fit partner in a league of nations. *Our policy must therefore consist first in a stirring up of nationalist discontent, and then in refusing to accept the extreme logic of this discontent, which would be the dismemberment of Austria-Hungary.* By threatening the present German-Magyar combination with nationalist uprisings on the one side, and by showing it a mode of safety on the other, its resistance would be reduced to a minimum, and the motive to an independence from Berlin in foreign affairs would be enormously accelerated. Austria-Hungary is in the position where she must be good in order to survive.[18]

This cynical but risky strategy of provocative destabilization and ultimate restraint recognized nationality as an instrument of political warfare, to be encouraged and aggravated in order to terrorize the Habsburgs, but not to be followed to the "extreme logic" of forcing the monarchy's disintegration.

The authors of The Inquiry's memorandum well understood that the national forces that they hoped to manipulate were dangerously subversive of political order, and, following the Bolshevik Revolution of October 1917 in Russia, they certainly understood some of the risks of provoking political destabilization. The nationalities were to be encouraged, stroked, manipulated in their political longings—and then, at the last moment, prevented from finding any climactic political satisfaction. Austria-Hungary would have to "be good"—would have to break with Berlin—or the furiously nettled nationalities would be permitted to bring about her political annihilation. Such a strategy of destabilization was also being pursued by the Germans with respect to Russia: Germany had already created in 1916 a League of the Foreign Nationalities of Russia (Die Liga der Fremdvölker Russlands) in order to undermine political stability by lending support to the diverse nationalities of the Russian empire.[19] In November 1917, Lenin, too, encouraged national self-determination within the former tsarist empire in a "Declaration of the Rights of the Peoples of Russia," leading eventually to the postwar independence of Lithuania, Latvia, Estonia, and Finland. While members of The Inquiry endorsed the independence of the Baltic states in reports of 1917, Wilson himself did not contemplate a strategy of national destabilization in Russia, for fear that it would benefit Germany, as it indeed it did after the Peace of Brest-Litovsk. The Fourteen Points would propose "autonomous development" for the peoples of Austria-Hungary in Point Ten, while still preserving the empire, but Point Six concerning Russia was more restrained, urging Russia's "independent determination of her own political and national policy"—as if Russia were simply a unitary nation-state.[20]

Although the American Inquiry memorandum ultimately rejected the idea of Austria-Hungary's political extinction, an earlier British report of May 1917, written by R. W. Seton-Watson, who had made himself an expert on Austria-Hungary before the war, argued against a separate peace with the Habsburgs on the grounds that the empire had to be abolished after the war. Seton-Watson's report to the British Intelligence Bureau insisted that, because of the Allies' declaration of "respect for nationalities," and because of treaty commitments assigning Habsburg provinces to allied states like Italy and Romania: "the break-up of Austria-Hungary follows logically and inevitably." Furthermore, the promise of liberation and independence to the Czechs and Slovaks "would ipso facto . . . render impossible the continued existence of the Austro-Hungarian Monarchy." He argued that the Habsburgs would never be able to reform the monarchy to satisfy the Slavic nationalities—since "such a reconstruction would involve the overthrow of the overlordship of the German and Magyar elements" and "consequently these two races will never agree to any such plan."[21] Seton-Watson was already personally close to the Czech and South Slavic leaders who, with his supportive advocacy, would successfully create Czechoslovakia and Yugoslavia after the abolition of the monarchy at the end of the war.

The Inquiry was less closely involved with those national leaders and movements, but had already studied them well enough to understand that they threatened the stability of the Habsburg state, though without necessarily dooming that state, ipso facto, to political extinction. In contrast to Seton-Watson's report of May 1917, The Inquiry's memorandum of December 1917 offered an explicit, almost scientific, model of national destabilization, of the stirring up and curbing of national passions, in order to keep a whole empire in a suspended state of politically libidinous excitement on the verge of explosion. That model was based on the American academic experts' understanding of the Habsburg monarchy as a tensely fraught but still potentially viable state.

The Inquiry memorandum went on to summarize "a program for a diplomatic offensive" that reiterated the strategy of Habsburg provocation: "Towards Austria-Hungary the approach should consist of references to the subjection of the various nationalities, in order to keep that agitation alive, but coupled with it should go repeated assurance that no dismemberment of the Empire is intended, together with allusions to the humiliating vassalage of the proudest court in Europe [i.e., of the Hapsburgs to the Hohenzollerns]."[22] One might perhaps recognize Lippmann's affinity for Machiavellian realism in this phrasing, and certainly it was remote from the affirmation of principles that are usually associated with Wilsonian idealism. The Fourteen Points, often seen as Wilson's attempt to turn moral principles of statesmanship into practical propositions, should perhaps be considered with reference to the memorandum of The Inquiry that Wilson read and discussed with House four days before delivering the famous speech.

The Inquiry memorandum, furthermore, offered a "suggested statement of peace terms," and Wilson actually noted down his drafts for the Fourteen Points on the margin of his copy of the Inquiry text. The proposed Inquiry peace terms—written out in capital letters—were accompanied by an explanation of the underlying strategy:

> WE SEE PROMISE IN THE DISCUSSIONS NOW GOING ON BETWEEN THE AUSTRO-HUNGARIAN GOVERNMENTS AND THE PEOPLES OF THE MONARCHY, BUT THE VASSALAGE OF AUSTRIA-HUNGARY TO THE MASTERS OF GERMANY, RIVETED UPON THEM BY DEBTS FOR MONEY EXPENDED IN THE

INTERESTS OF GERMAN AMBITION, MUST BE DONE AWAY WITH IN ORDER THAT AUSTRIA-HUNGARY MAY BE FREE TO TAKE HER RIGHTFUL PLACE AMONG THE NATIONS.

The object of this is to encourage the present movement towards federalism in Austria, a movement which, if it is successful, will break the German-Magyar ascendancy. By injecting the idea of a possible cancellation of the war debts to Germany, it is hoped to encourage all the separatist tendencies as between Austria-Hungary and Germany, as well as the social revolutionary sentiment which poverty has stimulated.[23]

There was an almost taunting spirit in the citing of Austria's "vassalage" to Germany—"the humiliating vassalage of the proudest court in Europe"—and an almost smug satisfaction in Austria's indebtedness and consequent impoverishment. Yet one also has the sense that The Inquiry was perhaps too enamored of its own Machiavellianism, and while hoping to stir up "social revolutionary sentiment," did not dare openly to play upon national sentiment against Vienna and Budapest, offering only an implicit endorsement of Habsburg federalism. The final commitment to Austria-Hungary's "rightful place among the nations" was very remote from even hinting at the possibility of dismemberment or extinction.

Wilson was not interested in actually incorporating into his speech the proposed text in capital letters, and his shorthand comment in the margin of the memorandum was, concisely, "The peoples of Austria-Hungary, whose place among the nations of the world we wish to see safeguarded and assured, must be accorded the freest opportunity of autonomous development."[24] With very small adjustments—and with "must be accorded" altered and weakened to "should be accorded"—this marginal comment found its way into the speech and into history as Point Ten of the Fourteen Points: "The peoples of Austria-Hungary, whose place among the nations we wish to see safeguarded and assured, should be accorded the freest opportunity to autonomous development." Having read The Inquiry's suggestion, Wilson was able to craft a more concise and more meaningful phrasing that reflected the proposed strategy for confronting the future of the Habsburg monarchy and its peoples.

Point Ten was equivocal in its political significance, advocating both the autonomy of the nationalities and the safeguarding of Austria-Hungary. Furthermore, the ambiguous relative pronoun "whose" might affirm the "place among the nations" of Austria-Hungary as a whole or might affirm "the place among the nations" of "the peoples of Austria-Hungary." On January 22, two weeks after the speech, the French ambassador in Washington, Jean Jules Jusserand, asked for a clarification of this grammatical ambiguity in a note to Frank Lyon Polk at the State Department, which was then referred to Wilson:

> The French Ambassador tells the Department that he has received reports that item number 10 in the peace program outlined in your address to Congress on January 8th is not clearly understood abroad, especially in Italy, the impression being that we desired to see the place of Austria-Hungary among the nations "safeguarded and assured." The Ambassador interprets your statement to mean that we wish the place of the peoples of Austria-Hungary "safeguarded and assured," but desires our confirmation.[25]

Wilson immediately replied to Polk that "the French Ambassador has correctly interpreted my peace terms with regard to Austria-Hungary."[26] The president had seemed to affirm simultaneously the sovereign place of Austria-Hungary within Europe and the autonomous place of the Habsburg nationalities within Austria-Hungary. These were not inconsistent affirmations, but the more forceful, and ultimately decisive, interpretation—now confirmed in Wilson's reply to Polk—was that those nationalities could also be considered to have some political standing within Europe apart from their embedded status within Austria-Hungary.

Czernin himself, responding for the Habsburg government to Wilson's speech on January 24, interpreted the Fourteen Points as sympathetic and acceptable to Austria-Hungary. "I think there is no harm in stating that I regard the recent proposals of President Wilson as an appreciable approach to the Austro-Hungarian point of view and that to some of them Austria-Hungary could joyfully give her approval," declared Czernin. He did not, however, accept the force of Point Ten on the autonomous development of the Austrian nationalities:

I have to observe that we courteously but resolutely reject the advice as to how we are to govern ourselves. We have in Austria a parliament elected by universal, equal, direct and secret franchise. There is no more democratic parliament in the world and this parliament together with the other constitutionally authorized factors alone has the right to decide upon the internal affairs of Austria. I speak only of Austria because I should regard it as unconstitutional to speak in the Austrian delegation of the internal affairs of the Hungarian State. We do not interfere in American affairs and we do not want any foreign guardianship by any State.[27]

He did not refuse to concede the autonomous development of the nationalities in Austria; he simply refused to acknowledge any American entitlement to discuss the matter, while affirming that Austria was no less democratic than America itself.

In fact, the basic Austrian constitutional law of 1867 allowed collective national rights to language, education, justice, and administration for the different nationalities, going far beyond anything that ethnic minorities in America might have claimed. While he rejected American interference, Czernin did acknowledge that, of all the warring states, "Austria Hungary on the one side and the United States on the other are composed of States whose interests are least at variance with one another"—and their exchange of views might therefore become the basis for discussing terms of peace. Victor Mamatey has observed that the Habsburg nationalities, especially the Czechs, were deeply disappointed in Point Ten. Edvard Beneš noted that the Czechs were surprised to learn that "Wilson was not a partisan of the destruction of the Monarchy, and his plan for the liberation of the peoples of Austria-Hungary did not call for the creation of independent national states but only for the organization of self-government or some sort of federation."[28]

Wilson's Fourteen Points did not call for the Habsburg monarchy to be abolished in favor of independent national states, but the ambiguities and contradictions of Point Ten were entirely consistent with the strategic policy of The Inquiry's memorandum: encourage the nationalities by affirming autonomous development, thus menacing the monarchy with the possibility of disintegration, while holding back from actually endorsing that outcome.

The purpose of Point Ten—as initially sketched by Wilson on the margin of the memorandum—was not to dissolve the Habsburg monarchy, but to hint at destabilizing developments that might have the effect of detaching it from the wartime alliance with Germany. The idea of Wilson as the great emancipator of the Habsburg peoples was still evolving.

■ ■ ■

"The golden bridge between Vienna and Washington"
On November 21, 1916, Habsburg Emperor Franz Joseph died in Vienna at the age of eighty-six after a reign of sixty-eight years. The *New York Times* reported in a series of sub-headlines the succession of his grand nephew Karl, the condolences of President Wilson, the expected arrival in Vienna of Kaiser Wilhelm for the funeral, and, in strong capital letters: "DEATH NOT TO AFFECT WAR." The text of the article reported from Vienna a public sense of "regret that the Emperor had not been spared long enough to see the end of the war, which, according to the accepted view here, nobody regretted more than he." At the same time it was noted: "During the progress of the war he took the keenest interest in the fortunes of his own and the allied armies with never-tiring zeal. He declared that it was a bitter disappointment that he was not allowed by reason of his age and the solicitation of his entourage to lead his troops himself."[29] Franz Joseph thus appeared to the American public at the moment of his death in the contradictory aspects of fierce military zealot and regretful partisan of peace. If this accurately reflected some degree of ambivalence in the aged emperor, it also certainly suggested the ambivalence of the American public and Wilsonian government with regard to Austria's wartime intentions.

Wilson's sending of condolences at this juncture was complicated by a peculiar miscarriage in Austrian-American diplomatic relations, which occurred already in 1915, well before America went to war. At that time it was discovered that Franz Joseph's ambassador Konstantin Dumba was conspiring to encourage labor unrest in American munitions factories (which could have been supplying England), and Washington insisted that he be recalled. However, the next Habsburg ambassador, Adam Tarnowski—appointed by Franz Joseph shortly before his death—arrived in

Washington just as America declared war on Germany in 1917. Though America was not yet at war with Austria-Hungary, Wilson declined to receive Tarnowski who thus never managed to present his credentials and eventually returned to Europe. Moreover, U.S. Ambassador Penfield was recalled from Vienna. The historian Nicole Phelps, in her account of this affair, points out that Wilson was implicitly declining to acknowledge Habsburg sovereignty by refusing to receive Tarnowski.[30] This question of sovereignty would become significant later, as Wilson hesitated over whether to commit himself to the postwar persistence of the monarchy, but the absence of accredited ambassadors would also compromise diplomatic relations when Wilson attempted to explore the possibility of a separate peace with Franz Joseph's successor, Emperor Karl.

In the fall of 1917—before the American declaration of war on Austria-Hungary—an American journalist in Stockholm, George Talbot Odell of the *New York Evening Mail*, met with another journalist Geza "Sil-Vara" Silberer, associated with the leading Viennese newspaper, the *Neue Freie Presse*. Silberer, the son of a Jewish Hungarian dentist and the journalistic protégé of Theodor Herzl, was an Anglophile, the author of a book on English gardens in 1914 and another on English statesmen in 1916. Meeting Odell in Stockholm, Silberer was authorized by Foreign Minister Czernin to deliver an oral message—in his presumably fluent English—concerning Emperor Karl in Vienna, to be passed on in some fashion to President Wilson in Washington, for "under present circumstances it was practically impossible to communicate these things through diplomatic channels." Odell was persuaded that the message did come directly from Emperor Karl, and that, furthermore, Silberer "has long been a close personal friend of the Emperor"—which, given their respective social stations, would have seemed not altogether likely.[31]

Upon his return from Europe to America, Odell wrote to Lansing on November 10, 1917, to relay Silberer's message ("I quote his words as accurately as possible") which was then sent by Lansing to Wilson, for whom it was clearly intended:

> Kaiser Karl is a thorough democrat. He desires to give his people a thoroughly democratic form of government. He has abolished all forms

of monarchical oppression; he has done away with all the court forms which pertained to the old court regime. Great stress must be laid upon the fact that he is parading before the people of Austria-Hungary as a democratic sovereign, because he believes that he can thereby show his people what democracy means, educating them by showing them the difference between monarchy and democracy in terms they can understand. . . . The Emperor goes about a great deal in civilian clothes. He has done away with the formalities which the old Emperor always required, such as requiring his barber always to attend him in evening clothes. . . . Emperor Karl mingles much with the crowds on the streets and rides on tramcars in order to hear what the people are saying.[32]

The literary style of the paraphrase suggested the spirit of Silberer's own literary generation, the fin-de-siècle aesthetic culture of fantasy and fairy tale, conjuring up Karl as a sort of Caliph Harun al-Rashid, going among his people in the Baghdad of the *Thousand and One Nights*. Hugo von Hofmannsthal might have envisioned such a fairy tale, and was, in fact, just then in 1917, creating a mythological emperor in the libretto for *Die Frau ohne Schatten*, to be set to music by Richard Strauss, and finally performed in 1919 after the war's end. The fantasy of a refashioned emperor was powerful in Austrian culture at this moment of succession, after the conclusion of Franz Joseph's sixty-eight-year reign, and the son of a Hungarian Jewish dentist would certainly have relished the idea of a democratic emperor who could even have been his own "close personal friend." What Silberer offered Wilson, however, was the image of the emperor refashioned in Wilson's own American image, a true democrat, bringing democracy to unenlightened peoples ("in terms they can understand")—which was precisely how Wilson would come to understand his own role when he came to Europe in 1918 and 1919.

Presenting Wilson as the mirror image of Kaiser Karl constituted a last-minute Austrian effort to ward off the coming American declaration of war on the Habsburg monarchy, while also laying the ideological groundwork for possible future peace negotiations. Just when The Inquiry was emphasizing the importance of detaching Austria from Germany, Vienna was offering Washington a politically appealing scenario of mutual democratic recognition: an emperor in civilian clothes, an emperor on the tram, an emperor on terms of informality with his own barber. *Frank Leslie's Popular Monthly* published a tale in New York in 1891 about the teenage Beethoven encountering the Habsburg emperor Joseph II in Vienna in the 1780s, with the emperor incognito and pretending democratically to be his own barber. Beethoven made some deprecating comments about the emperor's musical knowledge, which "seemed to amuse the barber mightily; he simply roared with laughter." Later, when Beethoven was presented to Joseph, "intense was the young musician's horror to learn that the supposed barber and the Emperor were one!" The emperor responded with such good humor and magnanimity, however, that Beethoven was put at his ease, and learned that the emperor further enjoyed the companionship of Mozart in a spirit of democratic congeniality.[33] It was in a similar spirit that Silberer, transcribed by Odell, represented to Wilson the supposedly democratic spirit of Emperor Karl.

In January 1918, the Austrian legal scholar Heinrich Lammasch arrived in Switzerland for an unofficial meeting with an American expatriate, George Herron, formerly a Congregationalist minister and theology professor. According to Hugh Wilson, the American diplomatic representative in Switzerland, Herron resembled an Old Testament prophet with "the fervor of a fanatic"—and idolized Wilson for "leading the world into new relationships between men and men and States and States." Lammasch suggested to Herron that Emperor Karl might be willing to break with Germany and accept a separate peace for Austria on Wilsonian terms, even perhaps to countenance the federal reform of the monarchy based on the principle of nationality.[34]

Herron wrote up his own conversation with Lammasch which was forwarded to Washington as a highly confidential memorandum, dated February 3. Lammasch told Herron that "the Emperor, urged on by the Empress, was getting more and more anxious for a change, and they wanted to find some way of getting a confidential message through to President Wilson that would not be known by Germany." Not only Karl, but his wife Empress Zita, formerly a princess of Bourbon-Parma, of Italian origin and Italian sympathies, was implicated in this eagerness to reach out to Wilson and try to make peace for Austria. Herron rather grandly wrote of meeting Lammasch "with the fate of the world hanging on building some kind of a bridge between Vienna and Washington." Lammasch declared that "the whole heart of the Emperor is in effecting a great change in the constitution of the Monarchy, in getting extricated from Prussian hegemony, and in getting a reorientation, especially with America." Supposedly, Empress Zita—"extraordinarily clever and forcible"—also supported this change. Lammasch wanted Wilson to make a public address, acknowledging "some sort of preparedness on the part of Austria toward peace." Czernin, according to Lammasch, was not to be trusted, but Emperor Karl was entirely sympathetic to Wilson's perspective.[35]

More important, Herron was told that the emperor was sympathetic to Lammasch's own political program for Austria:

> Then follows Professor Lammasch's scheme for the new Austria which is to integrate, to put together, all the different peoples of Austria, each in separate states. He would group all the Yugo-Slavs that are in the hands of the Austrian Empire into a new state. That includes Croatia, Slavonia, Bosnia, Herzegovina, Dalmatia into one single state. . . . And he would group all the Poles into another state; the Austrians into another state; Transylvania into another; the Magyars or Hungarians strictly speaking into another state; the Italians left within the bounds of the Empire into a province . . . making Trieste an international port.[36]

Here was a commitment not only to democracy under Emperor Karl but to precisely the empire of autonomous national units that Wilson claimed to seek. This supposedly indigenous program of Habsburg constitutional federalism also corresponded to Wilson's Point Ten.

Lammasch went one step further, however, utterly rejecting Czernin's insistence on noninterference, and—according to Herron—actually calling upon America to bring about the desired transformation of the Habsburg monarchy.

> America must help us to do this. . . . I [Herron] naturally said—but this is quite in contradiction to Czernin. Do you mean to say that you would

permit us to dictate as to the internal construction of your Empire? His [Lammasch's] reply was extraordinary: We will not only permit you, we beg you. The Emperor will embrace you. I [Herron] could hardly believe my own ears.[37]

What was envisioned here was a conspiratorial collaboration in which the president and the emperor would together bring about the peace of Europe and the political reform of the Habsburg monarchy based on Point Ten.

Herron, however, was skeptical about Karl already from the beginning of 1918. The American expatriate, with his theological background and his messianic devotion to Woodrow Wilson, passed strict judgment upon the messianic fantasies of others. Karl's fantasies, as suggested by Lammasch, could be summed up as "a dream of the young Emperor encouraged in every way by the Pope to restore again in a modernized form the Holy Roman Empire." Pope Benedict XV had appealed for peace from the beginning of the war, and in August 1917 again offered a proposal for peace without annexations or compensations, which, in some ways, corresponded with Wilson's agenda. Protestant that he was, Herron could not, however, accept the sincerity of the papal vision. He wondered if Austria was "playing the Pope's game" and suggested that Lammasch was perhaps misrepresenting Karl, given that "he has a very paternal feeling toward his pupil, toward the young Emperor personally." Beyond this protective impulse toward the emperor, Lammasch had only one sincere goal—"to save Austria"—and, to that end, "he sees that the old order passeth, and that whatever the future is it must be by some sort of seizure of the new order."[38] Herron believed that he was living through biblical times, expressed in biblical verb forms—"the old order passeth"—and that the purity of the new order had to be preserved from false pretenders.

Though Lammasch insisted on Karl's readiness to embrace Wilsonian perspectives, Herron believed that Austria was not actually committed to Wilson's vision of a future peace:

> My whole attitude was of one wanting to see a door through which a possibility of building a bridge could be seen. But the whole attitude of the Emperor and even of Professor Lammasch . . . is that of wanting to capture and use the new order, and not to serve the new order. There is

as much difference between the two as between heaven and hell, or black and white. It is the old method by which Constantine adopted Christianity and destroyed it; by which the Roman Catholic Church adopted St. Francis. . . . And then this idea of handing out in a paternal way as of a benevolent autocrat liberties of a kind to peoples, thereby binding them by better chains, chains with more gold even, to the throne, seemed to me simply reactionism masquerading. . . . It was an attempt to really establish a benevolent autocracy in place of the old Habsburg autocracy. In other words across the golden bridge between Vienna and Washington it seemed to me that Austria wouldn't be walking into the future, but America would be walking into the past . . . [39]

In Herron's grandiose and millenarian vision Karl waited at one end of the golden bridge in the Habsburg archaic and autocratic past (which rested upon the even more remote past of the Roman emperor Constantine the Great and the medieval popes in Rome), while Wilson waited at the other end in the American democratic future, as different as heaven from hell. Europe lay between them, and Herron and Lammasch, meeting in Switzerland in neutral territory, sought to determine the construction, sturdiness, and direction of the bridge as it seemed almost to materialize in the Alpine skies above them. In the absence of normal diplomatic relations—dating back to the recall of Dumba and the refusal to receive Tarnowski in Washington—the metaphorical bridge served as the structural basis for envisioning the Habsburg-American encounter. Herron's imaginary engineering project offered an intimation of the millenarian spirit that would envelope Wilson's eventual remaking of Europe.

Herron's memorandum proposed not only an argument for rejecting the Austrian peace overture but, even more important, the rationale for rejecting the continued existence of the Habsburg monarchy. Wilson's favorable reading of Herron's recommendation was encouraged by its flattering, indeed worshipful, framing of the Wilsonian project:

Good man that he [Lammasch] is, I couldn't see that he understood . . . the programme which President Wilson had presented to the world of wanting, of literally making the world a world of democratic peoples, of free, self-governing peoples. I couldn't see that either he or the Emperor, as he presented it, had grasped that with mentality, that after all it was only a somewhat glorified and yet no less masquerading and sordid self-preservation that they were seeking for.[40]

In Herron's understanding of self-determination, the normal, even self-evident, politics of self-preservation was rejected as "sordid"; the Habsburg monarchy was indicted merely for seeking to continue its existence. The egoistic drive for self-preservation—all the more deplorable when disguised in a masquerade of pretended democratic principles—was in itself a moral reason for rejecting that preservation. "We could take advantage of the situation and make separate peace with Austria," Herron wrote, but warned that this would be a betrayal of "the hopes of all these peoples of the world that are looking to us"—including, and perhaps principally, the peoples of Austria-Hungary.

> The world has never looked to a man as it now looks to President Wilson and has never trusted a man as it trusts President Wilson. And I came away feeling what I didn't want to feel. I wanted to find an open door, you see. I came away feeling that . . . we must let Austria wait, we must keep on . . . if it costs all these millions of our lives and actually breaks up and smashes the old world, and makes a new one, it is worth it. I came away with the feeling that this is a case of Satan appearing as an angel.[41]

It was Professor Lammasch, or perhaps Emperor Karl, who was being revealed as Satan, in Herron's relentlessly eschatological imagery, and the masquerade involved dressing up in the principles of Woodrow Wilson. The old world was satanic, the new world was angelic, and it was impossible to read Herron's indictment without concluding that Austria-Hungary was a fundamental part of the old world to be smashed. It would, no doubt, only have confirmed Herron in his deep suspicion of Catholicism were it possible for him to know that the satanic Karl would one day, in 2004, be beatified by the Vatican, in part for his efforts to negotiate peace in wartime.

■ ■ ■

"The subject races of Austria whom the President desires to help"
Herron's account of his meeting with Lammasch would have reached Wilson just as the president was preparing his next major address to Congress, the so-called Four Principles speech, on February 11, 1918, his elaboration on the principles underlying the original Fourteen Points of January 8. On January 8 the Habsburg monarchy was only discussed in Point Ten, but the principles formulated on February 11, while framed in general terms, all seemed pointedly directed toward Austria-Hungary. In fact, Wilson began by citing the Austrian friendliness of Czernin in his sympathetic response to the Fourteen Points, which compared favorably to the less forthcoming response of Germany. Czernin was particularly commended by Wilson for recognizing that "national aspirations must be satisfied even within his own Empire, in the common interest of Europe and mankind."[42] The word "within" was important here, and suggested, on the one hand, American respect for Habsburg territorial integrity, while, on the other hand, assuming some American entitlement to infringe upon Habsburg sovereignty by setting the parameters of internal political life.

Wilsonian principles received their most explicit formulation in the February 11 speech, beginning with a rejection of the old diplomacy of the Congress of Vienna, following the Napoleonic wars, and the whole nineteenth-century international order based on the balance of power. Rather, Wilson now called for "a new international order based upon broad and universal principles of right and justice—no mere peace of shreds and patches." He insisted that "national aspirations"—the aspirations of peoples, not governments—would shape the postwar order.

> Peoples are not to be handed about from one sovereignty to another by an international conference or an understanding between rivals and antagonists. National aspirations must be respected; peoples may now be dominated and governed only by their own consent. "Self-determination" is not a mere phrase. It is an imperative principle of action, which statesmen will henceforth ignore at their peril. . . . This war had its roots in the disregard of the rights of small nations and of

nationalities which lacked the union and the force to make good their claim to determine their own allegiances and their own forms of political life. Covenants must now be entered into which will render such things impossible for the future.[43]

The Fourteen Points had proposed that sovereign nationality should be the basis of a future peace with reference to Italy, to the Balkan states, and to Poland, but Points Ten and Twelve, concerning the Habsburg and Ottoman empires, had stressed the importance of "autonomous development" for nationalities under imperial rule. Now Wilson connected the right of "autonomous development" within an imperial context to the more comprehensive right of political self-determination that might shape post-imperial sovereignties on the map. Wilson's new emphasis on "national aspirations" allowed for the conceptual amplification of "autonomous development," so as to envision for the Habsburg and Ottoman nationalities "their own forms of political life."

The term "self-determination," emphasized in the Four Principles speech, had not even been used in the Fourteen Points speech a month earlier. It had previously figured in a 1914 article by Lenin on "The Right of Nations to Self-Determination [*Samoopredeleniye*]," and was now presented cautiously by Wilson within quotation marks. In 1915 Tomáš Masaryk delivered a lecture in London on "The Problem of Small Nations in the European Crisis." He was thinking of the small nations of the Habsburg monarchy, the Czechs among them, and Wilson now borrowed Masaryk's emphasis on "small nations" to stress the broad applicability of the right to national self-determination.

Each of Wilson's four principles was relevant to Austria-Hungary. According to the first principle, every aspect of the peace settlement was to be based on "the essential justice of that particular case"—suggesting a peace by components, separately addressing the component parts of an imperial state. This was confirmed by the second principle, which specified that the likely components were "people and provinces," for, according to Wilson, "peoples and provinces are not to be bartered about from sovereignty to sovereignty as if they were mere chattels and pawns in a game, even the great game, now forever discredited, of the balance of power." Considerations of justice, rather than considerations of power, were to be applied to each province and to each national community. In his third principle Wilson proposed that peace be created "in the interest and for the benefit of the populations concerned"—rather than to suit the interests of rival states. And, finally, he specified, "fourth, that all well defined national aspirations shall be accorded the utmost satisfaction that can be accorded them without introducing new or perpetuating old elements of discord and antagonism that would be likely in time to break the peace of Europe."[44] Promising that national aspirations would receive "the utmost satisfaction" seemed to offer a great deal more than "the freest opportunity to autonomous development," as proposed in the original Fourteen Points. While "autonomous development" clearly lay still "within" Austria-Hungary, "the utmost satisfaction" might well lie beyond Habsburg sovereignty. Wilson acknowledged that aspiration to the utmost satisfaction had to be limited by the need to avoid provoking new discords and new risks of war. The peace conference would later demonstrate that competing national aspirations could not necessarily be satisfied simultaneously, and the arbitration of satisfaction led inevitably to fierce discord.

Having enunciated his four principles, in the speech of February 11, Wilson then affirmed his commitment to "this war of emancipation—emancipation from the threat and attempted mastery of selfish groups of autocratic rulers."[45] The word "emancipation" now emerged as fundamental to Wilsonian principles. The year 1918 marked the fiftieth anniversary of the Fourteenth Amendment, ratified in 1868 and constitutionally confirming the citizenship rights of emancipated slaves in America. Wilson himself was a child of the Confederacy, born in Virginia in 1856; his earliest memories dated from 1860, when his family was living in Georgia: "When I was four years old and hearing someone pass and say that Mr. Lincoln was elected and there was to be war . . . I remember running in to ask my father what it meant."[46] Wilson had just turned six at the time of Lincoln's Emancipation Proclamation of January 1, 1863—and had the boy run for an explanation to his minister father, a Confederate army chaplain, Wilson would probably not have heard a sympathetic perspective. The Reconstruction Laws of 1867 and 1868 and the confirmation of the Fourteenth Amendment in 1868 belonged to Wilson's childhood, and it was of course his own party, the Democratic Party, that undermined both Reconstruction and Emancipation during his adulthood in the later nineteenth century, allowing for the establishment of Jim Crow laws in the southern states.

The Lincoln Memorial was under construction in Washington while Wilson served his two terms as president from 1912 to 1920, and its architectural structure was already almost complete in 1918, though the colossal statue by Daniel Chester French was not yet in place. Wilson's call for a "war of emancipation" in 1918 could hardly have been made without some significant awareness of the precedent of the Civil War and Lincoln's emancipatory purpose fifty years earlier. Yet Lincoln's message of emancipation was implicitly displaced by the newly designated war of emancipation—which promised to emancipate not the African Americans of the United States, but the oppressed peoples of Europe, notably those of the Habsburg and Ottoman empires. The Habsburg emperor and the Ottoman sultan were implicitly indicted for the "autocratic" mastery of multiple peoples and provinces. George Herron had just suggested to Wilson that the Habsburg peace proposals should be rejected as merely "an attempt to really establish a benevolent autocracy in place of the old Habsburg autocracy." In November the Polish national leader Roman Dmowski had urged the "emancipation" of the nationalities of Austria-Hungary, and in December, the Bohemian National Alliance had invoked Lincoln in addressing Wilson: "'Like the voice of Lincoln . . . so your voice gives new strength to millions of oppressed." Now, in the speech of February 11, Wilson put together these pieces and formulated the war as a "war of emancipation"—with the Habsburg nationalities implicitly indicated as the targets of emancipation.

Wilson's speech may have been partly shaped by Herron's evaluation of Heinrich Lammasch's proposal, but that proposal was still being discussed at the end of February when British Foreign Secretary Arthur Balfour, having been shown Herron's memorandum in confidence at Wilson's request, expressed a critical perspective in writing to Colonel House.

> Professor Lammasch lays down with great emphasis and in quite clear language the right of peoples to choose their own form of Government, and the Emperor is reported as expressly desiring to see this principle applied to his own Dominion. As far as it goes this scheme is in harmony with the principles laid down by the President and might therefore form a starting point for discussions. But there are two very serious objections. In the first place it ignores Italy and in the second place, unless it is very carefully handled, it may alienate the subject races of Austria whom the President desires to help. Various Slav peoples have so often been fooled by the phrase "self government" that they will be disposed to regard all schemes which are so described as giving them the old slavery under a new name.[47]

Italy had, in fact, been promised territory from Austria-Hungary by the secret treaty of London in 1915, territory including large Slavic populations, and it was therefore perhaps disingenuous of Balfour to be worrying, in the very same sentence, about alienating the Slavs of Austria through promises of mere self-government instead of full independence.

The hyperbolic notion that "subject races" languished in "slavery" in constitutional Austria-Hungary was in itself disingenuous in its rhetorical recoloring of Habsburg politics. In fact, parliamentary representation in the Vienna Reichsrat was based on universal male suffrage, and constitutional law guaranteed the collective rights of the nationalities. There were perhaps nationalist political agitators who themselves believed that they lived as slaves under the Habsburg monarchy, and there were certainly British advocates like R. W. Seton Watson and Henry Wickham Steed who embraced those national causes and that formulation of national oppression. By 1918 Balfour himself was clearly susceptible to that perspective, and now that Wilson was inclined to see the war as one of "emancipation," it was an opportune moment for Balfour to present national life in Austria-Hungary as "the old slavery."

Balfour's remark on the "slavery" of the Habsburg Slavs was not intended to promote moral righteousness, however, for his objections to Lammasch turned out to be entirely strategic. Above all, the Allies had to win the war:

> The future of the war largely depends on supporting Italian enthusiasm and on maintaining [the] anti-German zeal of [the] Slav population in Austria. Both Italians and Slavs are very easily discouraged and are quick to find evidence in foreign speeches that their interests are forgotten or betrayed. I fear that Austrian statesmanship will not be above using any indication that the President has a tenderness for the Austrian Empire as a means of convincing the Slavs that they have nothing to hope for from the Allies and had best make terms with the Central Powers.[48]

Seton-Watson, in his report of May 1917, had suggested that Austria-Hungary could never satisfy its Slavic populations—inasmuch as such satisfaction "would involve the overthrow of the overlordship of the German and Magyar elements." Balfour, however, now obviously feared that Vienna might well find terms to satisfy the Slavs if the Allies were not promising even better terms. He took a somewhat slighting view of Italian and Slavic touchiness ("very easily discouraged") and a somewhat suspicious view of Wilson as a man of "tenderness," of emotions and inclinations, rather than political principles. Just as The Inquiry encouraged Wilson to try to hold the Habsburgs in a condition of finely tuned suspense, so Balfour had come to feel—probably with encouragement from Seton-Watson—that the Habsburg nationalities had to be stoked to a proper pitch of political anticipation. In February 1918 Seton-Watson reported again to the British Intelligence Bureau, noting "the absence of any serious evidence (beyond mere hearsay) that the leading statesmen of Austria and Hungary really contemplate adequate constitutional reform," and denouncing "the gross misgovernment of the Slav and Latin elements by Budapest and, to a lesser degree, Vienna."[49] That "lesser degree" suggested that there might be reason for concern that the Slavs were not absolutely alienated from the Viennese government.

On February 25, the Spanish embassy in Washington delivered to Wilson a message from King Alfonso XIII (a neutral leader) containing within it a quoted personal response from Emperor Karl to the February 11 speech. Karl declared himself in agreement with Wilson's points and therefore ready for a "direct exchange of views" that would bring about a negotiated peace. The emperor approved of Wilson's principle that populations should not be transferred like chattels or pawns, but interpreted this nontransference to imply a multilateral renunciation of conquests and indemnities, such that "no State should gain or lose, admitting as a standard the territorial situation of all the States before the war." His interpretation would preserve the complete territorial integrity of Austria-Hungary within the borders of the status quo ante. In the case of Wilson's fourth point, mandating "the utmost satisfaction" of national aspirations, the chain of translations and retranslations now emerged from the Spanish embassy rephrased as "the most ample satisfaction"—and here too Karl offered a reservation. He promised that his government would "produce evidence that there exist national aspirations the satisfaction of which would not bring the good and lasting solution"—and he cited as an example "the national aspirations of Italy to Austrian territory."[50] The national aspirations of any designated population, Karl implied, could be conveniently, even cynically, invoked by one power in order to make claims upon another power, in precisely the predatory spirit of aggrandizement that Wilson claimed to deplore.

Karl insisted that he and Wilson were thinking along the same lines: "that between the fundamental bases mentioned by the President on one side and my aspirations on the other, there exists the requisite degree of coincidence," so that they might be able to negotiate peace. The letter was signed simply "Charles" and forwarded with a note from the king of Spain, offering his own royal cooperation.[51] Wilson's reply was drafted on February 28, and on March 5 was already being forwarded from Madrid to Vienna, with an assurance from Wilson "that in order to maintain secrecy he had himself typed on the typewriter the message."[52] At this point Wilson would have already read Balfour's message of hesitation, and the president's reply was polite but not overly enthusiastic.

While "gratified that my recent declaration of the principles to be observed in formulating the conditions of peace are so largely agreed to by His Majesty the Emperor of Austria," Wilson nevertheless asked Karl to be more concrete, emphasizing that the possibility of peace negotiations would depend upon Karl's "explicit programme." Wilson himself, after having formulated his own points very generally, wanted Karl to be very specific and questioned him accordingly: "I should like to know how His Majesty proposes to end the dispute in the Balkans and to satisfy the national aspirations of the Slav peoples who are so closely related to masses of his own subjects, and what solution he would suggest for the Adriatic coast?"⁵³ Wilson, perhaps influenced by Herron's and Balfour's reserve, would not immediately engage in the proposed peace discussions, and demanded explicit explanations as a precondition for entering into negotiations. At the same time the questions that he posed would have satisfied the strategy of The Inquiry's memorandum, pointedly reminding the emperor of the fragility of his own empire.

Wilson, perhaps with the assistance of the Inquiry memorandum, was able to come up with a mapping of Eastern Europe—of Slavic peoples in the Balkans and on the Adriatic coast—for presentation to the Habsburg emperor, with the issue of "national aspirations" as the key to a series of related political vulnerabilities. He challenged Karl to solve these problems on the basis of the Wilsonian principles that the emperor supposedly embraced. Yet, before Karl even received Wilson's message, he faced a different challenge in the Reichsrat in Vienna, when Lammasch attempted to make the case for a negotiated peace without annexations and was shouted down by the parliamentary representatives, crying, "We want war and victory." Victor Mamatey concludes that Karl had no support for his peace policy, so that "even if he had wished to, he was in no position to make a separate peace."⁵⁴ The emperor's exchange of views with the president did, however, contribute significantly to the evolution of Wilson's own perspective on the Habsburg monarchy: the dissipation of the mirage of "the golden bridge between Vienna and Washington" made the disintegration of the monarchy seem more thinkable.

Wilson's reply to the emperor was delivered to Vienna on March 5, two days after Germany and Austria-Hungary made peace with the Bolshevik government by the treaty of Brest-Litovsk, taking Russia out of the war, and freeing the Central Powers for a renewed effort on the Western front. Karl's next reply to Wilson was dated March 23, a few days after the opening of that spring offensive, and the emperor's message was held up in Madrid and not delivered to Washington. The possibility of a negotiated peace was now rendered unlikely by the escalation of the war, and Vienna's peace initiative was definitively destroyed when Clemenceau, in

Paris, disclosed a message from Karl to his brother-in-law Prince Sixtus of Bourbon-Parma, who was acting as a secret intermediary between Vienna and Paris. The publication of the message revealed to Berlin that Vienna was pursuing a separate peace negotiation and was even willing to consider the return of Alsace-Lorraine from Germany to France. This was extremely embarrassing for Karl, even as his undelivered letter to Washington affirmed a commitment to Wilsonian principles. In that letter the emperor observed that "we are not pursuing any policy with reference to the Adriatic coast which conflicts with any of M. Wilson's principles," while noting that "Italy is striving for the possession of territory inhabited by a larger number of Slavs and Germans than Italians."[55] Karl actually understood Wilson's principles very well, and already foresaw some of the contradictions—concerning Italian claims, for instance—that those principles would create at the future peace conference.

■ ■ ■

"The artificial Austrian Empire"

It was Lansing, in a message of May 10, 1918, who pushed Wilson to declare himself for or against the Habsburg monarchy. The publication of the Sixtus message by Clemenceau meant that Austria had been compelled to cleave closer to Germany and could no longer pursue a separate peace. "My dear Mr. President," wrote Lansing. "I feel that the time has arrived when it is wise to assume a definite policy in relation to the various nations which make up the Austro-Hungarian Empire." In a series of four numbered questions—"considered always from the standpoint of winning the war"—Lansing matched the enumerative style of Wilson's four principles.

1. Is there anything to be gained by giving support to the conception of an Austria-Hungary with substantially the same boundaries as those now existing?

2. Is there any peculiar advantage in encouraging the independence of the several nationalities such as the Czech, the Jugo-Slav, the Roumanian, &c, and if so, ought we not to sanction the national movements of these various elements?

3. Should we or should we not openly proclaim that the various nationalities subject to the Emperor of Austria and King of Hungary ought to have the privilege of self-determination as to their political affiliation?

4. In brief, should we or should we not favor the disintegration of the Austro-Hungarian Empire into its component parts?[56]

The creation of such an agenda was entirely consistent with, even clearly inspired by, Wilson's emphasis on self-determination in the Four Principles speech and his affirmation "that all well defined national aspirations shall be accorded the utmost satisfaction."

Although Wilson's statement of political principles never explicitly countenanced the disintegration of Austria-Hungary, Lansing treated it as a strategic agenda for winning the war. Lansing, a supporter of the Entente cause, had been appointed secretary of state in 1915; his predecessor William Jennings Bryan had been too strictly in favor of neutrality to satisfy Wilson. Now in 1918, with America at war, Lansing was committed to victory, and his pragmatic perspective went so far as to cite the example of Germany undermining Russia, "by appealing to the national jealousies and aspirations" of the peoples of the Russian empire: "The resulting impotency of Russia presents a strong argument in favor of employing the same methods in relation to Austria's alien provinces. I do not think that it would be wise to ignore the lesson to be learned from Germany's policy toward the Russian people." That America should learn Machiavellian lessons of political intrigue from Germany was not a suggestion that Wilson, so much a man of righteous principles, was likely to receive with satisfaction, and Lansing's tone, as he reached his conclusion, actually took on an air of impatience, as if he really felt that Wilson was hopelessly beset by vacillation and indecision: "I would be gratified, Mr. President, to have your judgment as to whether we should continue to favor the integrity of Austria or should declare that we will give support to the self-determination of the nationalities concerned. I think that the time has come to decide definitely what policy we should pursue."[57] Lansing presented it as a choice between alternatives, just as he presented his four questions as nominally open and undetermined, but there was little doubt that he himself believed that the time had come to embrace the destruction of the Habsburg monarchy.

Seemingly in alignment with Lansing's sense of urgency was the passionate, almost mystical, letter addressed to Wilson on May 31 by George Herron in Geneva. Herron appealed to Wilson's "shepherdship of the nationalities"—and declared that "the peoples are trusting you to speak the word that shall gather them all into one fold." The nationalities were Wilson's sheep, and he their pastoral oracle. "Not in the whole history of mankind, dear Mr. President, has the world turned to one man as it now turns to you," wrote Herron with the pious fervor of a former minister.

> No hand but yours can open the door of this unprecedented and predestinative opportunity. Will you open it? If you will, I believe the whole race of man will pass through the door, no matter what the travail and the tragedy of the passing, and that therethrough the race will enter upon a world of such fellowship and felicity, such new and nobler progress, as now seems incredible and Utopian.[58]

The sheep, once herded into a single fold, would pass through a single portal that would open only at Wilson's command.

It was a boldly biblical appeal to the president, but Herron finally moved beyond biblical phrasing to aim his appeal at Wilson's mental mapping of Eastern Europe. Now the sheep took the form of specific peoples, designated nationalities: "The Serbians, the Czechs, the Poles, the Lettonians, and all the weaker peoples Germany has practically annexed—all the uprising nationalities of the doomed and dissolving Hapsburg Empire—would take your summons as their pledge of deliverance."[59] If the Habsburg monarchy was already "doomed and dissolving," it would be Wilson who pronounced the word that would consummate that doom and dissolution by calling forth a new world, a new society of nations to displace the empire of nationalities. The nationalities would pass through the portal to the utopian future, but Austria-Hungary would be left behind in the rubble of the old world. Wilson himself would bring about the millenarian "deliverance" of the Habsburg nationalities.

On June 24, Lansing was still urging Wilson to declare himself. The message of May 10 was now formalized as a "Memorandum on the Policy of the United States in Relation to the Nationalities Included within the Austro-Hungarian Empire." Lansing noted that "the principle of 'self-determination' was hostile to the idea of holding in subjection to the imperial rule of Austria-Hungary the Poles, Czechs, Ruthenians, Rumanians, Italians, and Jugo-Slavs." The United States had already endorsed an independent Poland—this was one of Wilson's Fourteen Points. Lansing further proposed "an independent Bohemia and an independent Southern Slav State," and suggested that the Habsburg Romanian and Italian subjects should be allowed "their natural allegiance"—namely, Romania and Italy. "This would mean in effect the dismemberment of the present Austro-Hungarian Empire into its original elements," Lansing wrote, adding, in the spirit of justification, that "the Austro-Hungarian Monarchy was organized on the principle of conquest and not on the principle of 'self-determination.' "[60] Lansing repeatedly placed "self-determination" in quotation marks, highlighting its significance as a new principle of international politics—and perhaps also to emphasize that he was quoting Wilson to Wilson, that this was the president's own principle.

Following the logic of The Inquiry, Lansing pursued the maximal provocation of chaos in the monarchy, but no longer felt that it was necessary to hold back from the ultimate declaration of doom. The Habsburg monarchy had to be abolished: "If this is the wise policy to adopt, it should be done *now* when the political, military, and social conditions of Austria-Hungary are in the greatest confusion and when the spirit of revolution is rife. It should be done unconditionally and without ambiguity. The entire surrender of the Dual Monarchy to the German Empire should remove all sympathy and compassion for the Habsburg rulers."[61] Just as Balfour worried over Wilsonian "tenderness" toward the Habsburgs, Lansing, too, seemed to suspect Wilson of being excessively sympathetic and compassionate in his hesitation to make a full commitment to the destruction of the monarchy.

Considerable ambiguity had hovered over Wilsonian policy concerning the Habsburgs dating back to the Fourteen Points and the commitment to "autonomous development." Lansing now formulated the necessary clarity in the draft of a message to be sent to the Serbian minister in Washington, Ljubomir Mihailović, clarifying the already articulated American sympathy with "the nationalistic aspirations for freedom of the Czecho-Slovaks and Jugo-Slavs." Lansing proposed to explain, very explicitly, "that the position of the United States Government is that all branches of the Slav race should be completely freed from German and Austrian rule."[62] Whereas Wilson had earlier supported national aspirations in general (within but not necessarily against the Habsburg monarchy), Lansing now specifically advocated the liberation of the nationalities from imperial rule.

Lansing handed his memorandum to Wilson on June 25, and on June 26, the president replied with a note of formal agreement: "I agree with you that we can no longer respect or regard the integrity of the artificial Austrian Empire. I doubt if even Hungary is any more an integral part of it than Bohemia." Wilson thus introduced into the discussion the notion of imperial artificiality—in contrast to authentic and natural national polities. He also indicated a readiness to go beyond the freeing of the Slavs to contemplate the condition of the Magyars, who had been themselves long denounced (by Seton-Watson, for instance) as oppressors of the Slavs. Lansing's draft letter to the Serbian minister had originally called for freeing the Slavs from German, Austrian, and Magyar rule, which Wilson now amended by asking Lansing to "leave out Magyar in the closing sentence." The president had recently met with a group of Hungarian-Americans and his easily awakened sympathy had been extended to the Hungarian people, even as America waged war on the dualist state of Austria-Hungary.[63] Ten years before, in an academic essay of 1908 on "Constitutional Government in the United States," Wilson had observed that medieval Hungary, unlike medieval England, had failed to achieve constitutional government, that the Hungarian Golden Bull of 1222 had established the privileges of a noble class, whereas the English Magna Carta of 1215 had created the rights of a nation.[64] Hungary had thus, even before the war, occupied a place on Wilson's mental map of Europe as a site of thwarted freedoms, and in 1918, as he decisively turned against the Habsburg state, he allowed for the exemption of Hungary from the official indictment of Austria-Hungary, and the mental reinscription of the Hungarians on the map of authentic nationalities in Eastern Europe.

Encouraged by Wilson's agreement, Lansing now presumed to push the president even further, writing to him on June 27 to solicit an immediate declaration against the existence of Austria-Hungary: "An opportunity should be taken or made, it seems to me, to announce this policy to the world.... Would not such an opportunity be the occasion of your address to oppressed races on the 4th of July?" Wilson, however, declined to make his announcement in accordance with Lansing's sense of urgency. "I had assumed that we should make no formal public declaration," he replied to the secretary of state. "I do not know of any nearby public occasion on which I could embody it naturally in what I might have to say."[65] There was a certain chilliness in this refusal, as the fitting public occasion was precisely the one that Lansing had named, the imminent Fourth of July, when Wilson would address the diplomatic corps at George Washington's estate of Mount Vernon.

The anniversary of the Declaration of Independence would indeed have been the most apt moment for endorsing the independence of the subject nationalities of the Habsburg monarchy—which Wilson resolutely declined to do. In his speech he spoke of the era of Washington and the founding fathers as directly relevant: "We here in America believe our participation in the present war to be only the fruitage of what they planted," inasmuch as the aim was to "make not only the liberties of America secure but the liberties of every other people as well." He advocated the cause of peoples "who suffer under mastery but cannot act; peoples of many races and in every part of the world"; he called for a settlement that would bring about "the destruction of every arbitrary power" or "at the least its reduction to virtual impotence"; he called for the spirit of American independence, as celebrated on the Fourth of July, to serve as the inspiration for "the spread of this revolt, this liberation, to the great stage of the world itself!" In the final peroration he denounced "the blinded rulers of Prussia," but did not explicitly condemn the Habsburg emperor in Vienna.[66] Implicitly, perhaps, the monarchy may have been seen as a target for "reduction to virtual impotence."

On August 19, Lansing took up again the question of Austria-Hungary's ongoing existence, informing Wilson of the British, French, and Italian recognition of the Czecho-Slovak National Council, as the representative of a "sovereign nation," presumably independent of Austria-Hungary. Lansing hesitated for the moment about full formal recognition of "the Czecho-Slovaks as a sovereign nation," lest the

Yugoslavs "clamor for similar recognition and feel offended," but he was unequivocal in his view of Austria-Hungary: "I feel strongly that Austria-Hungary as an Empire should disappear since it is the keystone of Mittel-Europa." He therefore proposed, first, a partial recognition of the belligerency of the Czechs and, second, a general denunciation of the Habsburg government and general endorsement of the Habsburg nationalities: "a frank declaration that the utter subservience of Austria-Hungary to Germany, whether the result of coercion, fear, or inclination, forfeits whatever right the Dual Monarchy had to be treated as an independent state; that the nationalities aspiring to be free from Austro-Hungarian rule are still more entitled to be saved from German domination." The rhetorical argument suggested that because Austria-Hungary did not act independently in wartime, it therefore could not be legitimately considered as sovereign and independent, either in wartime or thereafter. In effect, the weakness of the monarchy became the argument for its illegitimacy, even as Lansing paradoxically determined to notify the world "that this Government intends to support and give substantial aid to all little nations which have been held in subjection against their will by the exercise of superior force."[67] Austria-Hungary was the coercive superior force with respect to its own nationalities but the subservient tool of the superior power of Germany in the wartime alliance. This conjunction of passive subservience and active oppression was articulated as the argument for the monarchy's illegitimacy and the justification for its proposed disappearance.

Wilson replied on August 22 somewhat tentatively, agreeing that "it is time we took definitive action in this important matter" but still hesitating to undertake a full public denunciation of the Habsburg monarchy. He admitted with some mystification that "my inclination would be to take the second course you outline [affirming the illegitimacy of the monarchy]; but I am restrained by considerations . . . too complex for a brief memorandum." Instead, he agreed to Lansing's first proposal, the partial recognition of the role of the Czecho-Slovak National Council, acknowledging that this "to a certain extent carries with it by implication the principle of the second." Wilson's caution in formulating his Habsburg policy was fully on display in this cryptic note which never mentioned the names "Habsburg" or "Austria-Hungary" and could scarcely be decoded by any reader not in possession of Lansing's original message.[68] The abolition of the Habsburg monarchy was endorsed only by implication, and Wilson's reticence appeared not so much as a matter of diplomatic discretion but rather as a more compelling reluctance to articulate what amounted to a dramatic alteration in his own international perspective.

On August 31, Masaryk wrote a memorandum for Lansing and Wilson, urging the recognition of the Czecho-Slovak National Council (of which he was the leading figure)—though Victor Mamatey concludes that it arrived too late for Lansing and Wilson to read it in advance of their imminent declaration of recognition. Masaryk argued that the Bohemian crown was elective, that it could not be simply inherited by the Habsburgs, and that therefore the Czechs could legitimately withdraw from the monarchy. "We invoke the principles of the Declaration of Independence," he wrote, appealing to American history—"and we are convinced that there is and cannot be a more just case before the political forum of the world than our case against the Habsburgs"—whom he further disparaged as "the degraded medieval Habsburg dynasty, covering its crimes with the sacrilegious pretension of being a chosen instrument of God."[69] Legitimacy based on allegedly divine election was not only sacrilegious but also completely opposite in political principle from that which claimed to rest upon national self-determination.

Without having time to consult Masaryk's memorandum, Lansing now drafted, and Wilson then approved, a statement of recognition of the Czecho-Slovak Council as a "de facto belligerent Government" fighting against "the common enemy, the Empires of Germany and Austria-Hungary" —and this statement was made public on September 3.[70] Wilson's long hesitation thus produced, only two months before the armistice, a formulation in which some of the peoples of Austria-Hungary (in this case, the Czechs and Slovaks, amalgamated as "the Czecho-Slovaks") were finally understood to be at war with Austria-Hungary itself. At the same time the recognition of a new de facto government not only envisioned the displacement of the existing Habsburg government of Austria-Hungary but also the remaking of the map in accordance with a new logic of belligerency and nationality.

Masaryk was present in Washington for the issuing of the recognition, but frequently visited Pennsylvania with its large Czech and Slovak immigrant communities. The crucial Czech and Slovak agreement to create an amalgamated state as Czechoslovakia was achieved in Pittsburgh in late May 1918. In early September, following the American recognition, Masaryk recalled making a visit to the battlefield of Gettysburg, and he wrote to Wilson to salute him as Lincoln's natural successor in advocating democratic principles, now as the basis for a new international order.

> At an historical moment of great significance Lincoln formulated these principles which were to rule the internal policies of the United States—at a historical moment of world-wide significance you, Mr. President, shaped these principles for the foreign policies of this great Republic as well as those of the other nations: that the whole mankind may be liberated, that between nations, great and small, actual equality exists—that all just power of governments is derived from the consent of the governed.[71]

In 1913 Wilson himself had spoken at Gettysburg on the occasion of the fiftieth anniversary of the terrible battle, but he had avoided addressing racial issues and "delivered a peculiarly hollow speech," according to historian A. Scott Berg. Now in 1918, with Masaryk's encouragement, Lincoln's war of emancipation became Wilson's war of liberation. The Czechs and the Slovaks, however, could only be liberated at the expense of Habsburg sovereignty. Wilson replied to Masaryk that "your letter of September 7 has given me a great deal of gratification"—indeed, with its comparison to Lincoln, it could hardly have been more gratifying—and affirmed "my earnest endeavor to be of as much service as possible to the Czecho-Slovak peoples."[72] The recognition of the Czecho-Slovak Council on September 3 certainly offered such service, and finally pointed toward an American policy dedicated to the disappearance of the Habsburg monarchy.

Masaryk, having invoked the American Declaration of Independence in August and the Gettysburg Address in September, now actually wrote and issued a Czecho-Slovak declaration of independence on October 18—carefully rendered into English with the help of an Oberlin College sociology professor, Herbert Miller, so that the declaration would resonate with Americans. On October 19, Wilson drafted and Lansing submitted to the Austrian government a note in which the American government formally revised its commitment to "autonomous development" for the peoples of Austria-Hungary as specified in the Fourteen Points. According to the note, Wilson saw himself as "no longer at liberty to accept the mere 'autonomy' of these peoples as a basis of peace," but rather as "obliged to insist that they, and not he, shall be the judges of what action on the part of the Austro-Hungarian Government will satisfy their aspirations and their own conception of their rights and destiny as members of the family of nations."[73] Welcoming the peoples of Austria-Hungary into the family of nations meant, by implication, condemning Austria-Hungary itself to dissolution and disappearance.

■ ■ ■

"Liberation from the yoke of the Austro-Hungarian Empire"
On October 18, the same day that Masaryk declared independence, Pope Benedict XV communicated with Wilson through James Gibbons, the archbishop of Baltimore, asking for the president's "benevolent consideration" of the Austrian request for an armistice based on the Fourteen Points. Even the pope felt the need to declare, through Gibbons, that he felt "that Divine Providence has reserved for you and for our great Republic the merciful mission of restoring peace to the world."[74] Wilson replied the very same day, saying, "I have every inclination of the heart to respond to the suggestion of His Holiness," but that the "whole matter of dealing with Austria-Hungary" had changed since the Fourteen Points address (with its reference to autonomous development). America had now "created obligations of honor" to the Slavic peoples of Austria-Hungary and would therefore have to recognize more fully their national aspirations.[75] Wilson thus put the pope on notice in Rome, at the same time that he communicated his message to the Habsburg government in Vienna, that autonomy would no longer constitute the necessary concession for achieving peace.

Wilson's message to Vienna of October 19, renouncing the standard of autonomy, was transmitted through neutral Sweden's ambassador in

Washington, August Ekengren, who then delivered a reply from Vienna to Lansing ten days later on October 29. In this communication the Habsburg government desperately conceded its agreement to "the previous declarations of the President and his opinion of the rights of the peoples of Austro-Hungary" and begged him to arrange an armistice.[76] During the intervening days, however, beginning on October 24, the battle of Vittorio Veneto in northeastern Italy, north of Venice and Treviso, had already begun, and the Austrian army was on the point of being definitively defeated by the Italians and their allies (including an American regiment held in reserve). On November 3, the collapsing Habsburg army suffered the loss of 30,000 dead and 300,000 prisoners and agreed to a humiliating armistice that gave over vast territories to Italian occupation; this also meant that the government in Vienna was in no condition to resist the claims to independence coming from the Slavic provinces of the monarchy. Wilson's long-delayed refusal to guarantee the integrity of the Habsburg monarchy, his renunciation of the standard of autonomy for its subject peoples, was now rendered altogether unnecessary, and even self-evident, on the battlefield.

On the day of the last desperate Viennese appeal to Wilson for an armistice, October 29, The Inquiry submitted a memorandum written by Walter Lippmann and Frank Cobb reviewing the Fourteen Points, including the issue of autonomous development for the peoples of Austria-Hungary, and stating: "This proposition no longer holds." Wilson himself had informed Vienna that "autonomy" was now insufficient, suggesting that it had now given way to the possibility of independence. Lippmann and Cobb, however, believed that the proposition did not hold for a different reason, indeed an opposite reason, inasmuch as they now pointed out to the president—too late to make a difference—that the achievement of national autonomy (let alone national independence) would not be unproblematic: "This proposition no longer holds: instead we have to veto [today] the following elements: one, Czechoslovakia. Its territories include at least a million Germans for whom some provision must be made."[77]

Another veto would concern Galicia as part of Poland: "Eastern Galicia is in large measure Ukrainian (or Ruthenian) and does not of right belong to Poland." Additional vetoes were related to German Austria, Yugoslavia,

Transylvania, and Hungary, all of which were too nationally complex to be settled according to a straightforward principle of nationality. Furthermore, Lippmann and Cobb discerned similar problems in regulating any sort of national dissolution of the Russian empire and especially the Ottoman empire: "the same difficulty arises here as in the case of Austria-Hungary concerning the word autonomous."[78] Wilson now envisioned the expansion of autonomy into independence—even as the Austrian defeat at Vittorio Veneto made that vision inevitable—while Lippmann and Cobb, too late, reminded the president that even "autonomy" was a problematic ideal. The memorandum suggested, implicitly, that the existence of the Habsburg monarchy (however degraded, sacrilegious, and medieval in Masaryk's eyes) resolved some of the problems of multinational complexity and coexistence that would be radically exacerbated by dissolution according to the principle of national self-determination.

The final appeal from the Habsburg government arrived in Washington on October 29, and Secretary of the Interior Franklin Knight Lane reported on November 1: "At last week's Cabinet we talked of Austria.... The President said that he did not know to whom to reply, as things were breaking up so completely. There was no Austria-Hungary."[79] The framework of American-Habsburg relations, even as mediated by the Swedish ambassador in wartime, disintegrated along with the Habsburg state, and American policy did not need to condemn the monarchy, inasmuch as it suddenly seemed no longer to exist. Wilson, in the cabinet meeting, puzzled over what would happen to the pieces of the monarchy: "Theoretically, the President said, German-Austria should go to Germany, as all were of one language and one race, but this would mean the establishment of a great central Roman-Catholic nation which would be under control of the Papacy."[80] This particular anxiety about German-Austrian union, or *Anschluss*, as an instrument of Roman Catholic aggrandizement and papal domination, suggests some of the eccentricities of Wilson's perspective on the European map: the president's ongoing ambivalence about the Habsburg monarchy was imbued with Protestant anxieties about Roman Catholicism. It was true that the pope in Rome had on several occasions encouraged the arrangement of an armistice with Austria, most recently through the archbishop of Baltimore, but Wilson did not seem to regard such papal interventions as merely the services of a convenient intermediary. A few months later, in January 1919, Wilson would come face to face with Pope Benedict in the Vatican and would respond awkwardly, declining to kneel for the papal blessing.[81] In October 1918, as Austria-Hungary collapsed, leaving a political vacuum to be filled according to the principles of Wilsonian self-determination, Wilson himself was clearly worried about what other forces might attempt to occupy the contested spaces on the new map of Europe.

Thomas Nelson Page, the U.S. ambassador to Italy, seemed less preoccupied with the papacy when he wrote to Wilson on November 5 that "the break-up of Austria to any extent, such as appears likely at present, introduces a whole new system of problems in Europe." The disputed succession of sovereignty over the mixed Italian and Slavic populations of the Habsburg Adriatic would become one of the thorniest of those problems, but Page, for the moment, remained optimistic simply because of Wilson himself, because "we have in you a leader who has shown a vision which, if not prophetic, has been broad enough to take within its scope all the problems which have hitherto arisen and solve them in a way to give promise that those which arise hereafter will also be solved with courage and wisdom."[82] Wilson had been far from prophetic in his contemplation of the future of the Habsburg monarchy, and the recent memorandum by Lippmann and Cobb underlined the inadequacy of the formulation of "autonomous development" in the Fourteen Points—even as Wilson himself was engaged in somewhat fantastical preoccupations with papal dominion.

On November 5, Wilson issued a general statement, to be distributed from Switzerland, addressed to "the peoples of the constituent nations of Austria-Hungary that have achieved liberation from the yoke of the Austro-Hungarian Empire." It was to be given the "widest possible distribution" in multiple translations. For the first time, Wilson spoke directly as liberator to the peoples of the Habsburg monarchy:

> May I not say, as speaking for multitudes of your most sincere friends, that it is the earnest hope and expectation of all friends of freedom everywhere and particularly of those whose present and immediate task it

is to assist the liberated peoples of the world to establish themselves in genuine freedom, that both the leaders and the peoples of the countries recently set free shall see to it that the momentous changes now being brought about are carried through with order, with moderation, with mercy as well as firmness, and that violence and cruelty of every kind are checked and prevented, so that nothing inhumane may stain the annals of the new age of achievement.[83]

The warning against violence suggested the anxieties of the moment when the Habsburg emperor had not yet stepped down (as he would on November 11) but the political vacuum was ominously looming. Civil war between Poles and Ukrainians in eastern Galicia had already begun, while the Hungarians and Romanians were poised for the imminent struggle over Transylvania, and Czech armies imposed themselves in the name of Czechoslovakia on recalcitrant Sudeten German populations. While never mentioning the Habsburg monarchy that was about to be displaced, Wilson offered a mental map of the "liberated" post-Habsburg lands that was fraught with potential disorder, violence, and inhumanity, the chaos of the political vacuum.

■ ■ ■

"Broken into pieces"
In mid-November 1918, The Inquiry's Archibald Cary Coolidge received "instructions to proceed to Eastern Europe to investigate and report upon conditions there." Here "Eastern Europe" was specified as a destination, increasingly used as the general term for the territories where the Habsburg monarchy was collapsing. Lansing informed the American diplomatic representatives in Europe that the State Department "has just appointed Professor A. C. Coolidge of Harvard University a Special Assistant in the Department, with instructions to proceed to the Balkans and possibly later to the Ukraine for the purpose of making a careful study of conditions in those countries"—the disparate lands now connected by the concept of "Eastern Europe." Coolidge himself wrote in a letter to his mother that his assignment was to gain information about "goings-on in

Austria and Poland, making Vienna, if it seemed wise, my headquarters, and establishing people in Prague, Pesth, etc., when possible, to report to me."[84] Coolidge's reports would help provide the president in Paris with information about Eastern Europe. On December 26, 1918, Lansing informed Coolidge, "You are hereby assigned to the American Commission to Negotiate Peace for the purpose of proceeding to Austria for that Commission to observe political conditions in Austria-Hungary and neighboring countries."[85] When The Inquiry was formed in 1917, the Habsburg monarchy was naturally one of its principal objects of study, but now, in December 1918, Coolidge's assignment "to observe political conditions in Austria-Hungary" was more equivocal, even paradoxical; it was to be carried out at the transitional moment when Austria-Hungary no longer existed, following the removal of the last Habsburg emperor of Austria and king of Hungary.

Coolidge's team of American informants, including military officers and academics, were based in Warsaw, Prague, Budapest, and Zagreb, and traveled across the lands of the just-dissolved Habsburg monarchy, reporting on and sometimes intervening in regional border controversies, as between Poland and Czechoslovakia over Teschen-Silesia and between Austria and Yugoslavia over Carinthia. When there was fighting between Austrian Germans and Yugoslav Slovenes in Carinthia in January 1919, Coolidge's representatives Colonel Sherman Miles and Lieutenant Leroy King actually drew the border in order to end the hostilities, though, as Coolidge conceded, "it would be hard to exceed instructions further." Writing to Paris, Coolidge acknowledged "the dangers and disadvantages from the point of view of the United States in having its agents act as unauthorized arbiters in such delicate international matters."[86] Coolidge's team, in some cases, thus actually defined the borders and terms of post-Habsburg sovereignty.

Coolidge sometimes also played a more personal role, unofficially representing Wilson in meetings with heads of state in post-Habsburg capitals. He twice met with Masaryk in Prague, and he spent five days in Budapest in January 1919 at a time of outrage over the encroachments of Czechoslovakia and Romania on formerly Hungarian territory and anxiety over the possibility of a communist revolution in Hungary—which indeed occurred in March. Coolidge described a "topsy-turvy world" in which he himself occupied the Budapest opera box of a Habsburg archduke (probably Archduke Joseph August, briefly postwar head of state in Hungary) and took bows from the box before the cheering audience. He reported to Paris on the Hungarian preoccupation with the territorial integrity of formerly Habsburg Hungary, now facing foreign incursions, and, judging from the appeals made to him personally, he had no doubt that the Hungarians "look primarily to America for their salvation." Hungarian faith in America—"and particularly in President Wilson"—was "touching," Coolidge thought. Reporting on a conversation with President Mihály Károlyi, he wrote:

> Count Karolyi told me that in a speech of January 1st he had declared his foreign policy could be summed up in three words: "Wilson. Wilson. Wilson." There are many placards in the streets with President Wilson's picture and the statement, "We are for a Wilson peace only." Today one of the ministers said to me, "Our only hope is in God and in President Wilson."[87]

Hungary would be the country in postwar Eastern Europe where Wilson would eventually be least loved, indeed most execrated, following the Treaty of Trianon in June 1920, which ratified huge territorial losses for Hungary. The name of "Trianon" has remained traumatic for Hungarians during the whole following century. Coolidge actually believed that Hungary should not lose territory to Romania in Transylvania unless determined by Wilsonian plebiscites, and he later thought the Hungarians badly treated at Trianon: "I don't blame them for being very bitter. I did what I could for them."[88] Yet, in January 1919, the Hungarians, like most other nationalities of the former Habsburg monarchy, still looked to Wilson for the "salvation" that would permit Hungary to emerge as a post-Habsburg national state. The Harvard professor Coolidge in Budapest borrowed some measure of archducal mystique as he channeled the post-imperial charisma of Wilson himself.

In the draft of the Covenant of the League of Nations, composed by a committee under Wilson's chairmanship in January 1919, it was specified that "in respect of the peoples and territories which formerly belonged to Russia, to Austria-Hungary, and to Turkey, and in respect of the colonies formerly under the dominion of the German Empire, the League of Nations shall be regarded as the residuary trustee with sovereign right of ultimate disposal or of continued administration in accordance with certain fundamental principles."[89] The principles were specified as self-determination, the consent of the governed, and the interests of the people. The postwar political vacuum would be filled under the ultimate sovereign authority of the League of Nations, as originally conceived, which seemed to diminish the independent sovereignty of the national successor states. The purpose of the proposed trusteeship was to forestall external annexations after the lifting of Habsburg sovereignty. Italy especially had extensive claims in the Alpine and Adriatic regions of the Habsburg monarchy, some of them guaranteed by the secret clauses of the Treaty of London that had brought Italy into the war.

When Wilson drafted the covenant in January 1919, the cases of the Habsburg and Ottoman empires still appeared to be intimately related and seemed to offer parallel domains for League trusteeship. Ultimately, former Ottoman provinces would become League mandates, while former Habsburg lands would be assigned to independent states in Eastern Europe. League authority in the former Habsburg lands would be invoked largely with reference to the disputed rights of minority populations within those states.

When Wilson was back in the United States in March 1919, campaigning for the League of Nations, the League guarantee of the post-Habsburg and post-Ottoman national outcomes was one of the main themes of his speeches. "The liberated peoples of the Austro-Hungarian Empire and of the Turkish Empire call out to us for this thing," Wilson declared in his speech at the Metropolitan Opera House in New York on March 4. By "this thing," he meant the League of Nations. The convergence between the Habsburg and Ottoman empires, in Wilson's geopolitical conception, reflected the parallel dissolutions that occurred at the end of the war, and now made it possible for him to explain the need for the League with reference to both political successions:

> The Austro-Hungarian Empire has gone to pieces and the Turkish empire has disappeared, and the nations that effected that great result—for it was a result of liberation—are now responsible as the trustees of the assets of those great nations. You not only would have weak nations lying in this path, but you would have nations in which that old poisonous seed of intrigue could be planted with the certainty that the crop would be abundant, and one of the things that the League of Nations is intended to watch is the course of intrigue.[90]

Wilson's political vision reflected a striking conception of agency and passivity in which the "great nations" acted as liberators for the "weak nations" that were liberated—according little credit to the former Habsburg or Ottoman subject peoples for achieving their own emancipation. Rather, those peoples merely "called out to the world," until, eventually, the world responded. Indeed, those peoples, even in their passivity, were seen as highly susceptible to "intrigue" which might, in ways not clearly specified, poisonously undermine the results of liberation.[91] The disintegration of Austria-Hungary thus appeared to Wilson in 1919 as something ominously fraught with the dangers of disorder, chaos, violence, and intrigue—which became part of the justification of the League of Nations.

Wilson returned to Europe on March 5, immediately after his speech at the Metropolitan Opera House: "Leaving the Opera House the President was escorted to the Lackawanna Ferry, at the foot of 23rd Street, rushed across the North River, and speeded directly to the Hoboken Wharves, where the [USS] *George Washington* was in waiting."[92] Speaking at the Council of Four in Paris, two weeks later, Wilson elaborated upon the comparison between the Ottoman and Habsburg empires. The former was fully dissolved "as though it were made of quicksilver," but the latter was merely fragmented: "Austria, at any rate, had been broken into pieces, and the pieces remained."[93] The post-imperial condition of the former Habsburg monarchy—a set of solid fragments, nationally cohesive territories—would have to form the basis of its political reconfiguration.

Archibald Cary Coolidge analyzed those pieces in a March memorandum entitled "The New Frontiers in Former Austria-Hungary." He accepted that national self-determination had to be the "guiding principle" for determining future frontiers, but also noted the existence of "historic frontiers" that had defined the provinces of the former Habsburg monarchy. Coolidge warned against simply reinscribing those historic provinces of the old empire in the new context of post-Habsburg national states, for fear of simply preserving the same national tensions that had riven the former empire. In particular, he argued "that a large part of German Bohemia should not be incorporated into the Czechoslovak state even if the historical and geographical unity of Bohemia (including Moravia and Austrian Silesia) will suffer amputation, while Slovakia should be taken away from Hungary even though Hungary will thereby suffer still more." For Coolidge, "Bohemia" and "Hungary" were well-defined historic pieces of "former Austria-Hungary," but he believed that the conference had to intervene surgically to reconstruct those pieces through further amputation. It was not enough to break up the Habsburg monarchy into pieces, unless the pieces themselves could be further broken down and reshaped in such a way as to diminish national conflicts. He warned that the inclusion in Czechoslovakia of "millions of [German] people unwilling to come under Czech rule" would be "dangerous and perhaps fatal to the future of the new state"—which proved to be the case in the 1930s, when Hitler capitalized on the national resentments of Sudeten Germans in Czechoslovakia.[94]

In April 1919, Wilson presented a memorandum to the Italian government in which he reviewed the evolution of his own policy toward the Habsburg monarchy and the determining of post-Habsburg national frontiers:

> It will be remembered that in reply to a communication from the Austrian Government offering to enter into negotiations for an armistice and peace on the basis of the Fourteen Points to which I have alluded, I said that there was one matter to which those points no longer applied. They had demanded autonomy for the several states which had constituted parts of the Austro-Hungarian empire, and I pointed out that it must now be left to the choice of the people of those several countries what their destiny and political relations should be. They have chosen, with the sympathy of the whole world, to be set up as independent

FIGURE 3. This map shows the new postwar national states of Eastern Europe against the shaded background of the former Habsburg monarchy.

states. Their complete separation from Austria and the consequent complete dissolution of the Austro-Hungarian empire has given a new aspect and significance to the settlements which must be effected with regard at any rate to the Eastern boundaries of Italy.[95]

By the Treaty of London of 1915, Italy had been promised generous swaths of Habsburg territory, but the treaty had been signed with England, France, and Russia, before America entered the war, so Wilson was not a party to it and not bound by its commitments.

Those commitments were nonetheless awkward for Wilson, inasmuch as they were inconsistent with his principle of national self-determination, bringing German communities of Tyrol and South Slavic populations of Dalmatia into Italy. For that reason, the abolition of Austria-Hungary now became a crucial point in Wilson's memorandum to the Italian government: "The line drawn in the Pact of London was conceived for the purpose of establishing an absolutely adequate frontier of safety for Italy against any possible hostility or aggression on the part of Austro-Hungary. But Austro-Hungary no longer exists." Therefore, Italy should no longer require the territorial aggrandizements promised at London in 1915, and, according to Wilson, the provisions of the treaty were rendered null and void (could "no longer apply"). Wilson expressed the opinion that the "historical wrongs inflicted upon her [Italy] by Austro-Hungary" were now "completely redressed"—and that those wrongs would soon "sink out of the memory of men," along with the Habsburg monarchy itself.[96] The president remained anxious about the aggrandizing national claims that would be made upon the former Habsburg territories by powers like Italy, keen to benefit from the unprecedented political vacuum created by the empire's demise.

Karl, the last Habsburg emperor, was now living in exile in Switzerland, having left Vienna without formally abdicating, and, in April 1919, the new republic of Austria legally banished him forever. Yet, the nonexistence of Habsburg Austria-Hungary haunted the peace conference in the spring of 1919, inasmuch as it was not possible to conclude a proper peace treaty with the defeated but now nonexistent enemy. Discussing the separate treaties with Austria and with Hungary in the Council of Four on May 26, the British scholar and adviser to the British delegation James Wycliffe Headlam-Morley posed the question of "whether [the republic of] Austria was regarded as a New State or as an Old State, the inheritor of the Austro-Hungarian Empire," inasmuch as "some parts of the treaty appeared to have been drafted on the former hypothesis, some on the latter," and "it was dangerous to treat Austria as possessing the rights formerly belonging to the Austro-Hungarian Empire."[97] Consistent with Wilson's view that the monarchy left behind fragmented pieces without being fully dissolved, Headlam-Morley declared that "the present Austria is only a part of the former empire; she is not the former empire diminished." Wilson then wondered: "In this case, why are we treating her as an enemy state?" For if the new Austrian republic was not the inheritor of the Habsburg empire, "Austria would not have to cede any territories." Headlam-Morley agreed that Austria would merely have to "renounce her union with other nationalities, whose frontiers we would indicate"—but she should not be asked to make specific renunciations, because, paradoxically, "in asking Austria to renounce her rights over this or that territory, you implicitly recognize those very rights."[98] Only the Habsburg monarchy itself could have legitimately made those renunciations.

Lloyd George proposed a formula to the effect that "the Austro-Hungarian Monarchy has ceased to exist by the will of the populations," and that "the different parts of the Austro-Hungarian Empire are becoming states or are joining pre-existing states, Austria being nothing other than one of them."[99] For Wilson, who had ultimately declined to negotiate a separate peace with the Habsburg monarchy during the war, it was now a challenge to figure out how to make peace without the summonable presence of the defeated enemy state. The nonexistence of the Habsburg realm offered an unprecedented opportunity for creating a new political structuring of Europe, but also uncertain terrain upon which to build those new structures.

The Italian prime minister Vittorio Orlando was skeptical about the empire's nonexistence: "As for the disappearance of the former state of Austria, it is a debatable fact," he argued.[100] Furthermore, when the preamble to the treaty with Austria was drafted according to Lloyd George's formula—"whereas, by the free action of the peoples of the former

Austro-Hungarian Monarchy, this Monarchy has now ceased to exist"—Orlando demanded that the words "by the free action of the peoples" be removed from the draft, since "it would be taken as underrating the Italian military effort."[101] For the Italians, Austria-Hungary had to exist as a defeated enemy at least long enough for territorial claims to be made upon it. He was not the only one to embrace such contradictory premises. New states like Poland, Czechoslovakia, and the Yugoslav kingdom were eager to dissociate themselves completely from the Habsburg matrix out of which they had just emerged; they refused to acknowledge themselves as successor states, denied any responsibility for the war as component parts of the Habsburg monarchy, and even hoped to press reparations claims for wartime damage against the now nonexistent state to which they had belonged right up until the end of the war.

On May 27, Wilson argued that if the new states were not to pay reparations as provinces of the Habsburg monarchy, then they had to contribute to the cost of the war to the Entente: "The principle accepted is that they participate in the costs of the war to which they owe their independence." By this principle they owed their independence to the world war—and not to "the free action of the peoples." According to Lloyd George, "Mr. Beneš said to me: 'We cannot be held responsible for a war which we condemn.'" Beneš, however, was willing to commit Czechoslovakia to paying a part of the war costs—"provided that the word 'reparations' be not mentioned."[102] In June, the Council of Four agreed "that Poland, Czecho-Slovakia, Serbia and Roumania should be called upon to accept liability for the payment of contributions in respect of the expenses of the liberation of formerly Austrian territory to be acquired by them"—and if they declined to pay these "contributions," they were to be billed for "reparations" as parts of the former monarchy.[103] The Habsburg monarchy had ceased to exist, and successor states had come into being, but, while none were willing to acknowledge their connection to the former monarchy, that filiation was intimately and implicitly related to their newly established sovereignty. The interchangeable relation of "contributions" and "reparations" was one way of signifying that relation.

Archibald Cary Coolidge, having moved from Vienna to Paris to participate in the conference, noted on May 28, "I suppose I shall hang round as long as there is anything Austrian in the offing." Yet there would always be something Austrian in the offing, inasmuch as the settlement of post-Habsburg sovereignties remained contested. Coolidge was present when the Austrian representatives were confronted with the Entente's peace terms:

> The most interesting thing I have been to since my arrival in Paris was the presentation of the peace terms to the Austrians. It was an occasion that appealed to the imagination, this handing over of the formal death doom to a state that for so many centuries has been one of the great powers of the world and has made, for good or for bad, so much history. . . . To me personally the occasion was the climax of my visit to Vienna, although it did not actually take place there.[104]

As a historian, Coolidge naturally appreciated the historic significance of the moment, and neatly noted the irony of the fact that such a momentous Viennese occasion did not take place in Vienna. While the existence of the Habsburg monarchy was always focused upon its capital, its nonexistence was a more abstract affair, not confined to any precise geographical location. The ghost of the dual monarchy hovered over the Wilsonian reimagining of Eastern Europe at the Paris Peace Conference.

For the reading of the Austrian treaty, Lloyd George thought it was not necessary to assemble the full conference:

> LLOYD GEORGE: Why should Nicaragua and many others hear the summary of the Austrian treaty?
> LLOYD GEORGE: The nations directly involved must be summoned.
> LLOYD GEORGE: Assuredly: the Czechs, the Yugoslavs, the Rumanians, the Poles must be present.
> HOUSE: It appears natural to summon all the nations which declared war on Austria-Hungary, as well as the ones which are formed out of the fragments of the Austro-Hungarian Empire.[105]

The victorious powers attempted to conceive of the huge political absence in the center of Europe as the blank slate upon which a new European state system could be constructed. For the purpose of settling the peace, Austria-Hungary needed to be conjured up one last time, by summoning her victorious enemies and her surviving fragments.

"Enslaved peoples"

The Hungarian communist government which came to power in Budapest in the spring of 1919—acknowledging no filiation with the Habsburg monarchy—urged that the fragmentary new states be summoned to discuss the succession among themselves, not just to listen to the reading of a treaty drafted by the victorious powers. On June 16, Béla Kun, the Hungarian Soviet Republic's leader and commissar for foreign affairs, sent a telegram to Clemenceau, the presiding host of the Paris Peace Conference, asking him "to summon together the Governments of the Peoples of the former Monarchy to a Conference where they will be able to discuss the liquidation of the former Monarchy as parties equally interested."[106] The new Hungary, even more than the new Austria, was treated as an enemy state, and eventually through the treaty of Trianon lost two-thirds of its prewar territory, including very large Hungarian populations. Indeed, the communist seizure of power in March was partly facilitated by the general Hungarian feeling that Hungary was being treated "in opposition to the principles laid down by President Wilson."[107] The zero-sum game of post-Habsburg national sovereignties made it even harder to adjudicate national rights than within the political framework of the former monarchy.

For Wilson, however, the indictment of the Habsburg monarchy had to remain rhetorically central to his American campaign on behalf of the treaty and the League of Nations. Traveling across the United States in September 1919 he offered his audiences political lessons on the failed civic structure of the defunct Habsburg monarchy. He celebrated the treaty as "the redemption of weak nations" and underlined their victim status within Austria-Hungary. "The Austro-Hungarian Empire," he declared on September 4 in Columbus, Ohio, "was held together by military force and consisted of peoples who did not want to live together, who did not have the spirit of nationality as towards each other, who were constantly chafing at the bands that held them."[108] In Wilson's rhetorical characterization the Habsburg peoples had been chafing at bands or bonds suggestive of slavery. Indeed, Czech Bohemia was allegorized as a sort of sexual slave of Vienna: "Bohemia, an unhappy partner—a partner by duress, flowing in all her veins the strongest national impulse that was to be found anywhere in Europe." The partitions of Poland—between Russia, Germany, and Austria—were rendered in the spirit of *Uncle Tom's Cabin*, as a sort of heartbreaking slavery that separated families: "great bodies of Polish people never permitted to have the normal intercourse with their kinsmen for fear that that fine instinct of the heart should assert itself which binds families together."[109] The postwar creation of new national states was thus given some of the sentimental character of family reunification.

The League of Nations was declared necessary to oversee and guarantee the new order. "There are regions," Wilson explained, in Columbus, "where you can't draw a national line and say there are Slavs on this side and Italians on that. There is this people there and that people there. It can't be done. You have to approximate the line."[110] This need for approximation was inherent in the multinational character of the Habsburg monarchy, and therefore the approximate boundaries of the Habsburg successor states would particularly need to be guaranteed by the League.

In San Diego two weeks later, Wilson evoked Habsburg responsibility for the war, looking back to the assassination of Franz Ferdinand in 1914:

> In the treaty with Austria, the Austrian power is taken off of every people over whom they have no right to reign. You know that great portions of Bosnia and Herzegovina which lay between Austria and the Balkan Peninsula, were unjustly under the power of the Austro-Hungarian Empire, and it was in a city of Bosnia that the Crown Prince of Austria was assassinated—Bosnia, which was under the power of Austria. Though it was part of Austrian territory, Austria had the audacity to hold Serbia, an outside neighbor, responsible for the act of the assassin. And this war was started because an Austrian prince was assassinated in Austrian territory, and the Austrian government chose to believe that certain societies with which it connected the assassin, societies active in Serbia, had planned the assassination. And so the world was deluged in blood . . . because of an insurgent feeling in a great population which was ruled over by rulers not of their own choice. And the peace conference at Paris

knew that it would not go to the root of this business unless it destroyed power of that kind. This treaty sets those great people free. (applause)[111]

Of course the Austrian government had reason to believe that the Serbian government in Belgrade was implicated in the assassination in Sarajevo—through the secret society of the Black Hand. For Wilson, however, the assassination seemed to be implicitly justified as the act of an "insurgent" population who lay "unjustly" under Habsburg power.

In San Diego, Wilson indicted not just the Habsburg government of Franz Joseph, but the very nature of Habsburg rule over a multinational empire. From the remote perspective of San Diego, the city of Sarajevo was perhaps too strangely foreign even to be named, an unnecessary complication in Wilson's geography lesson about Bosnia and Herzegovina. When Wilson declared that the peace conference was to be applauded (as it was in San Diego) for having "destroyed power of that kind"—he meant that the conference had destroyed the Habsburg monarchy, or more accurately, had ratified its collapse.

In Omaha, on September 8, Wilson tried to sum up the evils of empire for a public of farmers, urging his audience to imagine what would happen if someone tampered with the land records so that landholding rights were contested in Nebraska: "All the farmers would be sitting on their fences with shotguns." And this, in essence, according to Wilson, was true for nationally contested parts of Europe. "There are peoples in Europe who never before could say that the land they lived on was their own," Wilson explained, specifically mentioning the Poles.[112] He spoke as if those peoples were serfs who worked the lands of others, though in fact he meant something quite different, meant that they did not possess, as a nation, the lands that they collectively farmed. With his rhetorical appeal to farmers with shotguns, he seemed to suggest that this absence of national ownership was what had brought about the war.

In San Diego, on September 19, in Balboa Park Stadium, with a seating capacity of 15,000, he translated this farmer's perspective into a Lincolnesque political denunciation of slavery. "And the heart and center of this treaty is that it sets at liberty people all over Europe and in Asia who have hitherto been enslaved by powers which were not their rightful sovereigns and masters," Wilson orated. "So long as wrongs of that sort exist, you ought not to bring permanent peace to the world, because those wrongs ought to be righted, and enslaved peoples ought to be freed to right them."[113] The struggle against slavery, for Wilson, was an ongoing campaign, reaching back to Lincoln's Emancipation Proclamation and culminating now in the Treaty of Versailles.

"Pitiable Poland, divided up as spoils among half a dozen nations, is by this document united and set free," Wilson proclaimed. The crucial case, however, was that of the Habsburg monarchy: "In the treaty with Austria, the Austrian power is taken off of every people over whom they have no right to reign."[114] Austrian power was "taken off" like shackles from the enslaved nations of the Habsburg empire. Between the American entry into the war in 1917 and the oratorical campaign for the peace treaty that Wilson brought back to the American public in 1919, he had come to understand the war and the peace as an emancipatory project. It was the Habsburg monarchy, in its political relation to its diverse peoples, that had brought vividly to life in Wilson's imagination, and on his mental map of Eastern Europe, the dynamics of national slavery and emancipation.

3

Wilsonian Friendship
Personal Sympathy and Geopolitical Transformation

"The cultivation of friendships"

"Austro-Hungary no longer exists," Wilson observed in April 1919 in his memorandum for Prime Minister Vittorio Orlando and the Italian public,[1] almost as if the Habsburg monarchy had ceased to exist by his own declaration. He had not fully embraced its demise, however, until the war was almost over and the monarchy collapsed in military defeat. He emphasized its nonexistence in his Italian memorandum, and repeatedly in his dealings with the Adriatic question, in order to insist that the Treaty of London could now be discarded, since it had been intended to protect Italy from a Habsburg threat now absent. This highlighted a profound postwar conundrum, fraught with anxieties for the peacemakers, including Wilson: the utterly unanticipated political vacuum created by the simultaneous abolition of the Ottoman and Habsburg empires.

Citing the German Lutheran theologian Ernst Troeltsch (1865–1923), who commented on "the dreamland of the armistice period," the historian Jörn Leonhard characterizes the immediate postwar moment as a sort of dreamscape of international fantasy and unpredictable possibilities. Leonard Smith sees this same moment, above all, as one of lapsed sovereignty in the lands of the defeated empires, permitting the peacemakers, with Wilson the leading figure among them, to consolidate their own control in assigning postwar sovereignties, defining new borders, and recognizing new governments.[2] Mental mapping was crucial for Wilson's sense of the hypothetical permutations of postwar sovereignty and the reimagined borders of post-imperial Eastern Europe.

Wilson, in his memorandum for the Italians, was especially concerned about the new state system that would replace the Habsburg monarchy, a system that would emerge from a unique moment of political creation and international genesis: "organized for the purpose of satisfying legitimate national aspirations . . . created states not hostile to the new European order but arising out of it, interested in its maintenance, dependent upon the cultivation of friendships, and bound to a common policy of peace and accommodation by the covenants of the League of Nations."[3] The "cultivation of friendships" was part of Wilson's strategic and sentimental approach to the creation of a new international order, and his own sense of personal friendship—for national leaders, and even for whole nations—shaped his vision for the remapping of Eastern Europe.

The "newness" of the newly created states in Eastern Europe, and the new international system that framed them, was both a virtue and a source of vulnerability. When Wilson spoke in Washington on behalf of the settlement in February 1919, he worried over a possible future German upset of the system:

> We are setting up right in the path that German ambition expected to tread a number of new states that, chiefly because of their newness, will for a long time be weak states. We are carving a piece of Poland out of Germany's side; we are creating an independent Bohemia below that, an independent Hungary below that, and enlarging Rumania, and we are rearranging the territorial divisions of the Balkan states. We are practically dissolving the empire of Turkey . . .[4]

The notion that the peoples of Europe were deciding their own future was undercut by Wilson's rhetoric—we are carving, we are rearranging, we are dissolving—but it conveyed his own sense of the rapidity with which the whole of Eastern Europe, from Poland to Turkey, was being decisively reimagined and reconstructed. The Habsburg and Ottoman aftermaths, in the context of the German defeat and the Russian revolution, led into and then out of a moment of exceptional political formlessness. "Unless you expect this structure built at Paris to be a house of cards," Wilson noted, "you have to put into it the structural iron which will be afforded by the League of Nations." He was aware that he was building rapidly in Paris, and that brand new structures were inevitably fragile.[5]

Wilson was outlining a new and interlocking political geography—what is above and what is below, what is carved and what is enlarged—which he himself had come to learn from studying the maps that were presented to him throughout the peace process. The Inquiry sent more than a thousand maps to Paris with Wilson, and historian Steven Seegel has demonstrated the importance of an international cohort of "map men"—academic geographers—for whom the Paris Peace Conference represented the ultimate challenge of cartography applied to the goals of national self-determination. Seegel argues that the apparent scientific rationality of their map-making masked intensely political loyalties and personal emotions. Isaiah Bowman, director of the American Geographical Society and a leading figure in The Inquiry, was Wilson's "Chief Territorial Specialist" in Paris, and Bowman's network of international colleagues—for instance, his friendship with the Polish geographer Eugeniusz Romer—helped to shape Wilson's understanding of the map of Eastern Europe.[6]

The young historian Robert Howard Lord was quickly identified by Romer as The Inquiry's Polish expert, "whose influence on Wilson in Polish matters was already then pronounced," and who therefore had to be carefully courted. Romer went to Lord's room bearing a geographer's gift—"I brought with me a map"—to assist in their discussion of Poles and Ruthenians in Eastern Galicia. He was hopeful of persuading Lord to appreciate the Polish perspective, and in what was perhaps intended as a religious pun, called him *nasz Lord*, "our Lord."[7] Having published his Harvard doctoral dissertation on the partitions of Poland, Lord now had the opportunity to participate in the undoing of the eighteenth-century partitions and restoring Poland as an independent country.[8]

Robert Kerner, another recent Harvard doctoral student who served on The Inquiry, was similarly engaged, and perhaps more strongly opinionated. Of Czech descent and certainly interested in the creation of independent Czechoslovakia, Kerner, who had studied South Slavic languages, also had a research interest in the movement for South Slavic unity, which was about to produce a new Yugoslav state. Speaking with academic conviction, Kerner opined that "any solution which does not treat the Jugoslavs as one nation is based on unscientific foundations." More ominously, he contended that "International Jews . . . wish to save

Austria in order to save their securities and to exploit especially the Jugoslav territories."[9] Academic expertise, personal prejudice, and political sympathy all commingled among the members of The Inquiry. The young sociologist Max Handman, born in Romania, participated as an expert on Romania, and the journalist Albert Sonnichsen, who had reported from the Balkans, now served as The Inquiry's expert on Macedonia. Albert Lybyer, who had published his classic study of *The Government of the Ottoman Empire in the Time of Suleiman the Magnificent* just before the war, was considered to be overly partisan in his reports on Bulgaria. Of the circle of Eastern Europe experts, it was the two young historians Lord and Kerner who were included among the twenty-three Inquiry members (out of a total of 113 passengers) to travel across the Atlantic with Wilson on the USS *George Washington* in December 1918 for the peace conference.[10]

The presence of members of The Inquiry in Paris produced an almost comical impression on the journalist William Allen White who witnessed intensely mutual engagement between the scholars and the president himself:

> Down the gangplank walked this Yankee knight errant followed by a desperate crew of college professors in horn-rimmed glasses carrying textbooks, encyclopedias, maps, charts, graphs, statistics and all sorts of literary crowbars with which to pry up the boundaries of Europe and move them around in the interests of justice as seen through the Fourteen Points.[11]

The maps were crucial, studied through horn-rimmed glasses, and the Fourteen Points could only become meaningful if applied with a studious sense of geography to the prying up of boundaries, most notably in Eastern Europe. Lawrence Gelfand writes that "Inquiry scientists and engineers were ready to fashion a new world order," and "the peace conference was to take on the appearance of a huge laboratory whose director would be the American president."[12] The geopolitical engineering of the Inquiry experts was particularly focused on the map of Eastern Europe, which became, at the peace conference, the principal experimental domain for Wilson's transformative visions.

In September 1919, when Wilson campaigned fiercely for the treaty and the League of Nations, he offered geography lessons on the new Europe to crowds all over America. He sketched out a map when he spoke in Des Moines:

> Upon Poland center some of the dangers of the future. And south of Poland is Bohemia, which we cut away from the Austrian combination. And below Bohemia is Hungary, which can no longer rely upon the assistant strength of Austria, and below her is an enlarged Rumania. Alongside of Rumania is the new Slavic kingdom that never could have won its own independence, which chafed under the chains of Austria-Hungary, but never could throw them off. We have said: "The fundamental wrongs of history center in these regions. These people have the right to govern their own country and control their own fortunes."[13]

Wilson thus delineated "these regions" as one unified and interlocking domain whose fundamental past political condition was chafing at imperial subjection and "the wrongs of history." The new condition, which righted those wrongs, was characterized by a new map of adjacent spaces whose rightness was rendered tenuous by their newness. Lansing believed that Wilson worked too slowly as he operated upon the map in Paris, postponing the peace settlement by fussing over the details of the League Covenant. The menace of Bolshevism, according to Lansing, made such a settlement all the more urgent: "Eastern Europe seemed to be a volcano on the very point of eruption. Unless something was speedily done to check the peril, it threatened to spread to other countries and even to engulf the very foundations of modern civilization."[14] Lansing's idea of Eastern Europe as a volcano emphasized the region's extreme volatility in the post-imperial moment.

Wilson was someone who was quite ready to invoke gradualism, even as a convenient excuse, as in his response to the African American delegation who came to see him in October 1918 to protest against discrimination and segregation in the offices of the federal government. Wilson promised that "everything in my power to accomplish justice will be accomplished," but also pleaded that "we have to be patient with one another," since "human nature doesn't make giant strides in a single generation."[15] His sense of the future of Eastern Europe, at exactly that same time, with the war about to conclude and the Habsburg and Ottoman empires falling apart, was that "justice" would have to be achieved on the map of Europe in one single stride and in one studiously prepared moment of geopolitical genesis.

■ ■ ■

"The foster-father of a chiefless land"
When Wilson noted that the new states of the new Europe were "dependent upon the cultivation of friendships," he pointed to one of the crucially underlying aspects of his relation to Eastern Europe, whose new names and spaces had been envisioned, outlined, and imbued with color and character through his own personal elective affinities. "Dear and great Friend," Crown Prince Alexander of Serbia wrote, addressing Wilson in October 1917, six months after America's entry into the war. He was writing from Thessaloniki (Belgrade was occupied by the Germans and Austrians) to express "the deep gratitude myself and my people feel for the Chief of the great American Republic," based on "the principle which You have proclaimed in declaring war on Germany: that the small Nations have the same rights to existence and the same rights to dispose of their destinies as the Great World Powers." Alexander further remarked that Serbia was fighting "for the deliverance of its brothers who are expecting with impatience the day when they will be able to proclaim their decision to unite themselves all together in free Serbia."[16] The ultimate epistolary purpose was the remaking of Wilson's mental map with the feature of a dramatically expanded Serbia—the future Yugoslavia—envisioned as following upon the "deliverance" of all the South Slavs from Habsburg rule.

For Alexander the crucial point to emphasize in contemplating a new mapping of southeastern Europe was his friendship with the American president: "I avail myself with the greatest pleasure of this opportunity, very dear and great Friend, to send You, with the wishes I am forming for the greatness and the welfare of America, the renewed expression of my highest esteem and my sincerest friendship."[17] Such friendship for Wilson was both rhetorical and sentimental, conditioning the allegiances and alliances in wartime anticipation of the peace settlement. Signed with "sincerest friendship," Alexander's letter was an epistolary model of attempting to connect with the American president as an individual friend and simultaneously cultivating Wilson's future friendship for the whole Serbian nation. This message was reinforced by a South Slavic National Council, which wrote to Wilson around the same time, in September 1917, to inform the president that "the Slavs have been the most steady admirers of the policies of the President, and look upon him as the great champion of liberty of the small oppressed races of Europe."[18] Royal friendship for Wilson was thus amplified by the collective admiration of all the Slavs—and especially the South Slavs or Yugoslavs—locating themselves on the European map as small and oppressed peoples.

Colonel House's Inquiry was supposed to provide academic expertise to illuminate the map of Europe and understand the ethnographies that might form the basis of a future peace settlement, but the experts were always in competition with representatives of the communities of Eastern Europe, who themselves sought to cultivate and rearrange Wilson's mental map. When George (or Jerzy) Jan Sosnowski, a Polish political activist, was in America making contact with Polish American communities, he sought to address Wilson on the subject of Poland and the Poles, with particular attention to the president's mental map of the Slavic world. Sosnowski regretted "the Allies' ignorance of the Slavic question"—thus affirming the existence of a Slavic question—but he assured Wilson that "the Slavs have unbounded confidence in the United States and in your leadership." The Poles were "the purest Slavic race," according to Sosnowski, who, sketching a map for Wilson, explained that "today the Poles in Europe are the actual leaders of all the Slavic peoples of Austro-Hungary and partly so of the Lithuanians and Ruthenians"—and were therefore the key to Allied victory in the war.[19] The ethnographic lesson presented to Wilson was in itself somewhat casually inaccurate, inasmuch as the Lithuanians, speaking a Baltic language, were certainly not Slavs. Sosnowski's intention was in part to consolidate Wilson's support for Polish independence (which Wilson would explicitly endorse in the Fourteen Points in January 1918), but also to suggest the possibility of Polish political hegemony over the Lithuanians and Ruthenians.

Sosnowski enclosed a further letter to Wilson from the Polish National Defense Committee—formed by Polish Americans in Pittsburgh in 1912 to work toward Polish independence—writing now "to inform the President of the United States that all Poles expect a betterment of their lot from the action of the United States and that they wish to express their deep gratitude and their sincere friendship for the United States of America."[20] The dynamics of friendship were even more complex when invoked by Polish Americans, whose votes were relevant in American elections—speaking on behalf of "all Poles," whose friendship for Wilson and America was envisioned as a principle of international relations.

The person who would take up the particular role of Wilson's Polish friend was the famous Polish pianist Ignacy Jan Paderewski, who during the war became a spokesman for the Polish national cause. In 1916, Paderewski played Chopin at the White House and made a patriotic Polish impression on Wilson. The president himself had some musical training on the violin, and his daughter Margaret, who was a presence in the Wilson White House, played the piano and the harp and sang as a soprano. The connection to Paderewski was perhaps relevant to Wilson's reelection campaign in 1916, and the pianist actually paid a visit to the president on election day November 7. Paderewski was notified in advance that Wilson's "Peace without Victory" speech in the Senate on January 22, 1917, would be favorable to Poland. "No right anywhere exists to hand peoples about from sovereignty to sovereignty as if they were property," Wilson orated. "I take it for granted, for instance, if I may venture upon a single example, that statesmen everywhere are agreed that there should be a united, independent, and autonomous Poland."[21] At this point Wilson's abstract principle of national self-determination was illustrated by the "single example" that Paderewski had presented to him so persuasively.

Paderewski meanwhile pursued a friendship with Colonel House, taking House and his wife to dinner at Delmonico's in New York in April 1917. At the dinner, "no one was allowed to talk politics," but the friendship was of course implicitly political. House reported to Wilson that "Paderewski declares the world has never seen your equal," and Paderewski would later acknowledge "the powerful support of President Wilson whose heart has been won to our cause by our best friend,

Colonel House."²² Paderewski himself eventually funded a statue to honor Colonel ("Pułkownik") House as a friend of Poland ("Przyjaciel Polski") in Skaryszewski Park in Warsaw; the statue was removed in 1951, during the Stalinist period, but restored at the end of the Cold War in 1991.

Paderewski wrote to Wilson from Chicago in October 1917 on behalf of Polish organizations in the United States and all Polish Americans, saying: "They are hard-working people. Out of over four millions of them not one is a millionaire. But every one is willing to take his humble share in the glorious work of Poland's reestablishment so magnanimously proclaimed by you, Mr. President."²³ Polish Americans were also voters, of course, as Wilson was certainly aware. There was a history of solidarity between America and Poland that was as old as the American Revolution, when Tadeusz Kościuszko and Kazimierz Pułaski had fought under George Washington. Now, in the month that marked the centennial of Kościuszko's death (he died on October 15, 1817) Paderewski appealed to Wilson to support the creation of a Polish national army and to consider official recognition of a political authority for the future independent Poland.

In a 1917 memorandum for Wilson, Paderewski had offered a geographically generous conception of the future independent Poland, envisioned as a revival of the Polish-Lithuanian Commonwealth, which had been partitioned and abolished at the end of the eighteenth century. Paderewski's Poland not only included Lithuania, Galicia (with its significant Ukrainian population), and Polesia (including Belarusian territory), but he also assigned royal titles to those lands: "The President of the United States of Poland, in order to satisfy the provincial ambitions of the people, to strengthen his authority, should bear the title of King of Poland, King of Lithuania, King of Polesia, and King of Halicia."²⁴ Paderewski's fanciful vision of a sweepingly expansive presidency over a federally American-style "United States of Poland," adorned with multiple antique crowns, offered Wilson a geography lesson in the territorial building blocks of Eastern Europe.

In January 1917, before America entered the war, Wilson had suggested in the "Peace without Victory" speech that "statesmen everywhere are agreed that there should be a united, independent, and autonomous

Poland." In January 1918, in the Fourteen Points speech, with America now a combatant nation, he affirmed with more meaningful impact that "an independent Polish state should be erected." In fact, The Inquiry at the beginning of 1918 was not firmly focused on Polish independence and actually proposed that "in our opinion the best solution of the Polish question, both economically and politically, would consist in the inclusion of Poland as a federal state in democratic Russia"—and, "second best," be made an autonomous land within the Habsburg monarchy.[25] Paderewski's sensitive touch had helped to steer Wilson toward the more geopolitically extreme solution of independence.

Paderewski particularly sought to cultivate a sense of personal connection between Wilson and the people of Poland:

> You are the foster-father of a chiefless land. You are Poland's inspired protector. For many a month the spelling of your name has been the only comfort and joy of a starving nation. For many a month among the ruins of a devastated country millions of people have been feeding on you.[26]

Such hyperbole was supposed to have a flattering effect, but it was also meant to cultivate a very personal sense of Wilson's relation to Poland on the map of Europe—on an imminent map, that is, rather than an actual map—where Wilson himself played an almost paternal role. Poland was chiefless because it was stateless, which made it all the more possible to propose to Wilson a set of vivid geopolitical fantasies. Poland was the the place where Wilson was being personally, perhaps eucharistically, consumed by a starving nation. After the war, Poles would receive food assistance from Herbert Hoover's American Relief Administration, but during the war they already received the spiritual nourishment of Wilsonian politics. Poles were reverently spelling Wilson's name, while every American regarded names like Ignacy Paderewski and Tadeusz Kościuszko as hopelessly unspellable. Paderewski's letter was already preparing Wilson's Polish apotheosis, even as he prepared himself to assume the role of Wilson's special Polish friend.

Wilson's most important wartime friend from Eastern Europe was, however, Tomáš Garrigue Masaryk, the future founder and president of

Czechoslovakia. His importance was noted for Wilson in January 1917 in a letter from the American journalist Norman Hapgood, reporting from London that Masaryk was the leader of the movement for independence in the Czech lands. Hapgood noted that he himself did not favor such independence, and that other authorities on Austria and the Balkans "favor merely local autonomy for Bohemia, without breaking up the Empire"—"but I think Professor Masaryk deserves a hearing." Hapgood also reported that the Polish political leader in London, Roman Dmowski, "wants to unite Bohemia with Poland"—but the British expert R. W. Seton-Watson disagreed, thinking that "the only relation between Bohemia and Poland should be merely an arrangement that will give Bohemia access to open water."[27] Hapgood enclosed a map with his letter, allowing Wilson to visualize Masaryk's imagined homeland, Bohemia's

FIGURE 4. This poster from wartime, probably 1918, represented the friendship between Poland and America. Washington and Wilson preside above the Polish and American flags, flanked by American Revolutionary War heroes Kościuszko and Pułaski, with Paderewski down below. The slogan reads "Let Us Fight United for Freedom and Right." Photographer unknown. WS Collection / Alamy Stock Photo.

relation to Poland, and the place of Bohemia within the Habsburg empire.

Masaryk's connection to Wilson was furthered by the Chicago businessman and diplomat Charles Crane, who had known Masaryk when he lectured at the University of Chicago in 1902. Crane wrote to Wilson on May 8, 1918, to recommend Masaryk: "I hope you can set aside a little time for a talk with Professor Masaryk. He is the wisest and most influential Slav of our day, and probably only a Slav of such dimensions could fully understand and sympathize with what you are trying to do." Wilson wrote on the same day to Senator John Sharp Williams of Tennessee, "I have the same sympathy with the Bohemians that you have, and you may be sure I will speak sympathetically to them if I have the opportunity." Yet Wilson seemed to prefer to evade that opportunity, even in the context of reciprocal sympathies, and sent a message to Crane declining to set up a meeting with Masaryk.[28]

On the next day May 9, Wilson wrote to Paderewski's wife—"My dear Madame Paderewska"—regretfully declining her suggestion for the proclamation of a national "Polish Day" in America:

> I am sorry to say that I have been forced to the conclusion, after consulting many persons whom I regard as wiser than myself, that it would not be wise to proclaim an official Polish Day. In view of the many national elements of which our population is composed . . . you will probably have observed that there is a very strong movement among Americans of Bohemian origin in this country to take some active part against the Central Powers, and questions are arising with regard to their wishes very similar to those which have arisen with regard to the very admirable and commendable purposes of the Polish people.[29]

Wilson's friendship for the Poles and the Czechs was, from the beginning, complicated by the awkwardness of his fear that favoring one nation would inspire resentful rivalry in the other.

The Czechs and Poles were not the only national communities who might—if there were a precedent—demand a national day. Just the previous week Wilson had met with representatives of the Lithuanian National Council at the White House and received a petition that claimed to represent a million Lithuanian Americans pledging "loyal support and lasting affection" to Wilson and beseeching his support for Lithuanian independence. This affection was also explicitly rivalrous: "To Poland has been vouchsafed, in the Thirteenth Condition of your program for the world's peace, such assurances and guarantees as Lithuania would fain apply to herself." In February 1918, Lithuania declared independence from Bolshevik Russia, but in March Russia withdrew from the war and implicitly ceded the Baltic lands to Germany. The Lithuanian petition in May offered Wilson a very vague mapping of Lithuania, "this ancient of nations and infant of republics, bounded on the east by chaos and on the west by despotism."[30] With such a roiling map of despotism that merited demolition, of chaos that cried out for form, Wilson could begin to envision a transformational moment for generating a new postwar map, marked by the creative genesis of infant republics in Eastern Europe. Before the end of the war The Inquiry would generate reports endorsing the independence of Lithuania, Latvia, and Estonia—with a fiercely partisan tribute to the "racial virility, ambition, intelligence, and character" of the Lithuanians.[31]

At the end of May, writing to Wilson about the president's "shepherdship of the nationalities," George Herron designated "the Serbians, the Czechs, the Poles, the Lettonians" as among the peoples who looked to Wilson for their "deliverance." Herron mapped Eastern Europe ethnographically for Wilson from the South Slavic Serbians to the northern Baltic Lettonians or Latvians. The future belonged to new nations about to be born: "The Czechs and the Yougo-Slavs are already each a nearly-born nation, with their potential government already formed and drilling. These wait only for your word."[32] Herron thus offered Wilson a mental map of fetal nations, on the point of coming into geopolitical life at his summons. Wilson's sympathy was here characterized as pastoral shepherdship, a specifically Christian relation of sympathy and care for the flocks of Eastern Europe.

Charles Crane wrote to Wilson in July 1918 to comment on Slavic rivalries and antagonisms that, according to Crane, might be attributed to manipulative German engineering. Wilson was presumed to be able to communicate directly with all the Slavs, to encourage them to overcome their divisions and bring them together as a unified ethnographic body. Crane advised the president:

> Sometime you might call the attention to the Slavic people of the damage Germany has done to them and their wonderful mission in the world by keeping them divided—Russian against Pole, Serb against Bulgar, and Bohemian kept away from all the rest—and urge them from now on to adjust their differences and bring out the best there is in the whole race. To do this of course it will be the duty of the rest of us after this war to see that the various Slavic states are so well established that it will be possible for this to come about.[33]

Laying out a map for Wilson of the Slavic world divided by rivalries, Crane also hinted at a redemptive mission that belonged as much to the Slavs themselves as to Wilson their champion. They were to redeem the map of Europe against the autocratic ambitions of Germany and Austria-Hungary, bringing about this geopolitical redemption both as a single Slavic people and as various Slavic states.

Wilson, who was unsympathetic to both tsarism and Bolshevism alike, was also interested in the possibility of establishing democracy in Slavic Russia, and in July 1918 he agreed to American participation in the Allied intervention in the Russian Civil War on the side of the Whites against the Bolsheviks. In the "Polar Bear Expedition," American troops would land at Arkhangelsk, in the far north of Russia on the White Sea. "The whole heart of the people of the United States is with the people of Russia in the attempt to free themselves forever from autocratic government," Wilson declared.[34] The American intervention, however, was particularly aimed at extricating the Czechoslovak Legion, which had formerly been fighting against Germany and the Habsburg monarchy alongside the tsarist army and was now seeking to leave Bolshevik Russia by way of Siberia, so that the soldiers could return to Europe and fight on the Western front. Wilson's intervention in the Russian Civil War was thus partly motivated by a sense of the interconnectedness of the Slavic peoples, and his anxiety about Bolshevism would later be particularly driven by concerns—not only about the presence of Bolsheviks in the United States—but by the possibility that Russia might introduce Bolshevism to the wider Slavic world, based on the linguistic and ethnographic affinity of Slavic peoples.

U.S. troops arrived in Arkhangelsk in early September, but Archibald Cary Coolidge, the scholar who contributed more than anyone to the establishment of "Slavic" studies in the United States, was already there in late August. Coolidge had introduced relevant Slavic history courses at Harvard, while also advancing the study of Slavic literatures and building the Slavic collection of the university library. In 1891, he had spent some time in St. Petersburg and had even been presented to Tsar Alexander III. Now in 1918 Coolidge found Arkhangelsk to be "typically Russian," and he described it according to the established conventions for writing more generally about Eastern Europe: "broad streets deep in mud . . . plank side-walks in various stages of disrepair, long bearded coachmen in blue gowns driving their dirty, diminutive carriages . . . the sights, sounds, and smells so characteristic of Russia whatever the form of government."[35] Coolidge's role in The Inquiry guaranteed that a sense of common Slavic history, language, character, and civilization would inform the reports that consolidated an American perspective on Eastern Europe.

In 1918, Crane imagined a past world in which the Slavs were divided against one another, but a future map on which the various Slavic states would exist in cooperative unity. The notion of Slavic ethnographic kinship dated back to the German philosopher Johann Gottfried Herder's writings in the late eighteenth century. Herder saw the Slavs as peaceful, freedom-loving peoples, oppressed by foreign rulers, and, he prophesied: "so also will you too, so deeply sunken, once industrious and happy peoples, finally one day be awakened from your long, sluggish sleep, be freed from your chains of slavery."[36] In the nineteenth century, as the linguistic relation of the Slavic languages was more carefully explored, pan-Slavism became a political movement that alternately expressed solidarity among Habsburg Slavic subjects and served as a slogan to advance Russian influence in Eastern Europe. Appeals to Wilson in the twentieth century borrowed from the intellectual legacy of Herder's enlightened anthropology, envisioning the creation of newly liberated Slavic nation states, linked to one another within the systematic remapping of post-Habsburg and post-Ottoman Eastern Europe. It was also inevitable, however, that jealous rivalries would attend the passage from the old system to the new one. Wilson himself, with his privileged American relation of shepherdship, was the person most likely to excite such rivalries, even as he sought to resolve them.

In the summer of 1918, Democratic Senator Gilbert Hitchcock of Nebraska was corresponding with Wilson about a possible Senate bill endorsing Polish independence. Though Wilson had already declared for independence in the Fourteen Points, he consulted Lansing, and then cautioned Hitchcock that such a bill might cause "very serious embarrassment." The problem, again, was rivalry for American and Wilsonian sympathy:

> The Czecho-Slovaks and the Jugo-Slavs have recently effected, as you know, an organization very similar to and quite as influential as the organization which the Poles have effected, and we are dealing with both. The Poles may be said to represent a definable territory, but the Czecho-Slovaks and the Jugo-Slavs do not. It is not likely that if they followed their own preferences, they would unite in a single state. I should not like in the present circumstances of unrest in the Austrian Empire to throw the least cold water upon the Bohemians and the Slavs to the south of them, and I fear separate action with regard to Poland would have that effect.[37]

Wilson, in the summer of 1918, was aware that American sympathies were the subject of jealousy and rivalry among the peoples of Eastern Europe, whom he himself could not yet sort out on the map or even definitively name. He thought for the moment that Poland constituted a definable territorial and ethnographic entity (though he would learn better), but that neither Czechoslovakia nor Yugoslavia could be so defined (though he would be the one to help define them on the map). He also thoughtfully doubted the readiness of diverse peoples to join together as Czecho-Slovaks or Jugo-Slavs, and, though he later suppressed those doubts, history would show that he was right to be dubious. As he sought to construct a mental map of the lands and peoples of Eastern Europe, he was very much aware that their ambitions were curiously competitive with regard to himself and the American sympathies that he both guided and represented.

"You gave a definite form to the desire of all civilized peoples"

Wilson met with Masaryk on June 19, 1918, in the White House, and they discussed the Czechoslovak Legion in Siberia. "By the way, I saw Professor Masaryk today," Wilson informed Lansing.[38] The casualness of "by the way" underlined a certain lack of excitement surrounding an encounter that would soon be caught up in a mythology of friendship between Wilson and Masaryk. Certainly Masaryk was aware of the political value of Wilson's sympathy, aware that the meeting was an enviable mark of favor, even if the encounter was not yet awash in the rhetoric of championship and shepherdship.

By September Masaryk was writing to thank Wilson—"in the name of our whole nation" and with references to Lincoln, Gettysburg, and the liberation of mankind—for recognizing the Czechoslovak National Council. Wilson thanked Masaryk in turn for a letter that "has given me a great deal of gratification" and the reassurance "that I have followed the right course in my earnest endeavor to be of as much service as possible to the Czecho-Slovak peoples."[39] When Masaryk issued his Czechoslovak declaration of independence on October 18, Wilson responded effusively: "I need not tell you with what emotions I read the Declaration of Independence put out by the National Council."[40] Indeed, the declaration must have been gratifying in its affirmation, on behalf of the Czechs and Slovaks, that "we accept the American principles as laid down by President Wilson"—as if the Czechoslovak pronouncement were a public continuation of Wilson's ongoing private dialogue with Masaryk.[41] Thus, Wilson's very personal set of contacts, inclinations, sympathies, and friendships conditioned the transformation of his mental map of Eastern Europe.

These personal contacts framed a highly personal diplomacy at the Paris peace conference, and Wilson refused to consider as part of the American delegation such eminent Republican figures as former presidents Theodore Roosevelt and William Howard Taft. Instead, he brought his confidant, Colonel House, and his secretary of state, Lansing—whose views tended to be disregarded. "The president and I are doing everything" House commented self-importantly, in preparation for the conference. His eagerness to play the leading role in Paris would eventually cost him some of Wilson's confidence.[42]

Archibald Cary Coolidge studiously collected information and made reports to Paris from Vienna: "Everywhere the people just tumble over themselves in their readiness to see us and to talk. It is pretty pathetic when one is in the midst of it. They feel that their fate is being settled for them in Paris." He noted that "many people seem to believe that I am a mighty person on intimate terms with the President, and that I have only to express an opinion for it to be listened to," and that "at times one has reason to feel that what one has said may really have some influence and affect the destinies of a good many people." Coolidge had no doubt that whatever confidence and influence he himself held in the post-imperial capital derived from the intimacy with Wilson attributed to him. Part of what Coolidge found "pathetic" was the strange delusion of people who, in talking to him, believed that they were speaking directly and personally to Wilson himself. When Coolidge met with émigrés in Switzerland he showed himself to be a master of the ethnography of Eastern Europe, as reported in a letter to his mother, dated January 2, 1919: "Poles, Bulgarians, Roumanians, Hungarians, Lithuanians, Austrians, some of them triumphant, some of them pathetic, all convinced of the justice of their claims, and all hoping or fearing great things from the Peace Commission in Paris and from President Wilson."[43] In the political void created by the absence of imperial authorities over disparate peoples, a sort of imperial charisma had been temporarily assumed by Woodrow Wilson himself, presiding over the hopes and fears of the nationalities of Eastern Europe.

On January 2, 1919, Tomáš Masaryk greeted Wilson in Paris with a telegram from Prague, now the capital of Czechoslovakia, with the assurance that "our nation shall never forget that it was you Mr. President who by his kind sense of freedom and justice has brought about the disruption of the immoral state combination called Austria-Hungary, and it was you by his knowledge of our right in the most critical moment has made possible the revolution which brought us our national independence."[44] Wilson replied on January 10: "It is deeply gratifying to me that the Czecho-Slovak peoples should recognize in me their friend and the champion of their rights." The independence of Czechoslovakia gave Wilson "the profoundest pleasure," and he would be "always happy to serve the Nation," indeed hoped that Masaryk would "let me know from time to time what service of counsel or action you think I could render it."[45] In January 1919, Wilson allowed himself hopefully to imagine that the moment of geopolitical transformation was past, that the dynamics of friendship had shifted, needing now only auxiliary attentions "from time to time."

In fact, the peace conference was only just beginning to bring to Wilson's attention the complications of the post-Habsburg vacuum that would have to be sorted out as the peace treaties were negotiated. In March 1919, Coolidge, in his memorandum on "The New Frontiers in Former Austria-Hungary," warned against including in Czechoslovakia all the Germans of historic Bohemia. He was only nervously supportive of including Slovakia itself in Czechoslovakia at the expense of Hungary, questioning whether "Slovakia, in accordance with the principle of nationalities but doing great violence to those of history and geography, should be given to the Czechs and taken away from the Magyars," and

FIGURE 5. This postcard, probably from 1918 or 1919, shows Masaryk and Wilson as "Liberators of the Czechoslovak Nation," with the Bohemian lion between them.

adding "I should be surer of the fact if President Masaryk had not for lame reasons refused to hold a plebiscite there."[46] The definitive moment of geopolitical transformation—as Czechoslovakia emerged from "former Austria-Hungary"—would not be entirely a matter of self-congratulation, as Wilson and Masaryk might have momentarily imagined.

Masaryk was elected the first president of Czechoslovakia in November 1918 and began to govern from the Prague royal castle in December. His friendship with Wilson, in spite of the royal castle residence, was a friendship between two modern presidents, representing the supposed friendship between the peoples they represented and governed. Wilson also managed more difficult relations with crowned heads who spoke on behalf of their nations during and after the war. Although the principal imperial figures with whom the American president might have had to negotiate were removed from the scene—the Habsburg emperor, the German emperor, the Russian tsar—there were still lesser crowns in play at the time of the peace conference. While Masaryk was writing from Prague at the very beginning of 1919, King Nicholas of Montenegro was writing from Paris. Wilson was also in Paris, at the center of the deliberation of the Big Four, while the almost octogenarian Nicholas protested from the margins of the conference, having been deposed in November so that Montenegro might be merged with Serbia under the Karadjordjević dynasty of Crown Prince Alexander, and thus incorporated into the new Kingdom of Serbs, Croats, and Slovenes, which would eventually become Yugoslavia. "Very dear and great Friend," Nicholas wrote to Wilson. "You gave a definite form to the desire of all civilized peoples and to the principles on which perfectible humanity ought to build up its true happiness. In your person we are compelled to see the great conscience of our epoch."[47] Montenegro, one of the smallest states in Europe, thus made its claim on the American president who had staked out his position as the defender of small nations.

The merger of Montenegro and Serbia was carried out in the name of the popular will, but Nicholas depicted graphically for Wilson the dynamics by which the will of the people could be manufactured:

> Soon around us began to be heard the whisper of mischief-making, then the murmur of slander. Little by little rumours, at first of the vaguest

kind, took shape and grew in volume; subterranean slander broke out into definite accusation. What had so far only been said soon began to appear in print; clandestine libel was replaced by widely distributed printed pamphlets . . . [48]

The king was writing about Serbian efforts to manufacture sentiment against him, both among the people of Montenegro and among the diplomats in Paris. Curiously, he seemed to echo the famous speech on calumny written by Beaumarchais in *The Barber of Seville* for Paris in the 1770s:

> First the merest whisper . . . *pianissimo*—a murmur. . . . Someone picks it up and—*piano piano*—insinuates it into your ear. The damage is done. It spawns, creeps, and crawls and spreads and multiplies and then—*rinforzando*—from mouth to mouth it goes like the very Devil. Suddenly, no one knows how, you see Calumny raising its head. . . . and [it] breaks forth at last like a thunder clap to become . . . the general cry, a public *crescendo*, a chorus universal of hate, rage, and condemnation.[49]

In January 1919, Wilson, who believed that the peace settlement had to reflect the will of the populations involved, was just beginning to realize how difficult it might be to determine what those populations really wanted and how they viewed their political alternatives.

Not only had the people of Montenegro been purposefully manipulated by a campaign of calumny against him, Nicholas protested, but the peacemakers were being similarly manipulated:

> It was necessary to cause a people to become disgusted with its dynasty, with its Government and even its independence. It was necessary to wear down the sympathy that the Allies were disposed to show towards the misfortunes of the smallest of their number. It was necessary to bring the minds of all thinking people to accept the absorption of one people by another.[50]

Disgust with dynasties was something that Wilson tended to think entirely natural as he contemplated a new world without Habsburgs, Ottomans, Hohenzollerns, and Romanovs, but King Nicholas insisted that this sort of political disgust could be artfully produced—as in the Beaumarchais model, from *pianissimo* through *crescendo* to a full chorus of hatred and proscription. For Montenegro to be absorbed by Serbia was thus, the king explained to Wilson, "a violation of those very principles to which it has rightly become a habit to give your name."[51] Wilson himself believed devoutly in his Wilsonian principles, and, in January 1919, he was just beginning to perceive the ways in which the implications could be ambivalent and contradictory.

In a note to Lansing concerning the king's letter, Wilson seemed ready to reconsider the mapping of Yugoslavia with respect to Montenegro:

> This is a very moving letter, and I would highly value your advice concerning it. I am inclined to advise and request that you have a very frank talk with the representative of Serbia and say how much distress and what serious questions are arising in our minds because of the dealings of Serbia with Montenegro. Undoubtedly the sympathies of the people of the United States are as much with Montenegro as with Serbia. Our people have always admired the sturdy independence of the little kingdom, and I feel that the whole cause of Jugoslavia is being embarrassed and prejudiced . . .[52]

The sympathies of Wilson and Lansing were thus projected onto the American people, who would supposedly be offended—or even experience "distress"—at the mistreatment of sturdy little Montenegro. If the cause of Yugoslavia was "being embarrassed," it was also true that Wilson himself was being embarrassed by the political manipulation and undermining of his own much-vaunted principles.

Wilson could not easily find a way to reconcile his sympathies and principles when it came to Montenegro, however, and he wrote back to Nicholas as "my good friend," without committing himself to any course of action:

> I have received your letter . . . and read it with considerable interest. I must at present content myself with a brief acknowledgement of it, but I beg that you will believe that the days will not be too crowded or too hurried for me to drive the interests of sturdy Montenegro out of my mind . . .[53]

Montenegro was by no means sturdy enough to sustain its own dynasty against the claims of the new Yugoslav state, and it was small consolation to know that, while Montenegro was being politically absorbed, it nevertheless preserved its place—a very small place for a very small nation—on Wilson's mental map. He promised "sympathetic consideration"—even as his mental map was becoming confused with overlapping sympathies that could not be translated into a clearly interlocking political settlement.[54]

A few days later on January 12, at the peace conference, there was discussion of whether Montenegro was entitled to be represented at the conference, and Wilson was generally favorable: "President Wilson said that the action of Serbia in regard to Montenegro had gone somewhat towards prejudicing him against the Government of Serbia," for "to act with force like this was contrary to the principle of self-determination." His personal "prejudice" was thus closely related to his sense of "principle." Wilson declared that "the events of the last few months had almost made him a partisan of Montenegro." He now doubted whether the Podgorica Assembly of November 1918—which had deposed King Nicholas and proclaimed union with Serbia—had been "properly constituted," and he thought Montenegro entitled to representation at the peace conference in spite of Serbian objections. Wilson admitted that he was "anti-Serbian in this case," the case of Montenegro—though in general he was a great partisan of the new Yugoslav state, indeed perhaps its crucial foreign advocate.[55] The conference was beginning to impress upon him the awkward possibility of ambivalent partisanship, particularly awkward because his emotional sympathies were so closely tuned to his geopolitical advocacy.

The other member of the Council of Ten who most strongly agreed with Wilson was Sidney Sonnino, the Italian minister of foreign affairs, who in the interest of Italy's claims on South Slavic territories eagerly encouraged Wilson to become more anti-Serbian. This played as a sort of duet:

PRESIDENT WILSON pointed out that Montenegro was an older State than Serbia. She could therefore be separate from Yugo-Slavia . . .

M. SONNINO . . . pointed out that Montenegro was a very much older

State than Serbia. She alone had resisted for centuries the domination of the Turks.[56]

This reinforcement of Wilson's mental mapping from the Italian perspective was also perhaps related to the fact that the queen of Italy was King Nicholas's daughter.

In March, Arthur Balfour was still trying to resolve the question of what Montenegrins really wanted, and he wrote speculatively to Colonel House in a letter that was forwarded to Wilson. Balfour thought that, "so far as can be ascertained," most Montenegrins wanted to be part of the Yugoslav state on some terms, whether federated or fully fused, and "so far as our information goes," there did not seem to be a movement for Montenegrin independence or for the restoration of King Nicholas and the Petrovich dynasty. "We are ourselves inclined to feel that any statements which represent such a movement as being in existence emanate from Italian or other anti-Serbian sources," Balfour wrote, though Wilson himself had conceded that it was possible for someone as pro-Serbian as himself to be "anti-Serbian" in the case of Montenegro.[57]

Balfour declared in frustration that "the main conclusion which may be drawn from the above is that we do not actually know the real wishes of the Montenegrin people."[58] What did the Montenegrins really want? The radical uncertainty surrounding this question was almost epistemological. The new Wilsonian peacemaking principles were summed up in November 1918 in an article on "Winning the Peace" in *The Public: A Journal of Democracy*, with an editorial injunction to the victorious allies "to stand true and to express what the peoples want," as "only in this way will it be possible to deal with Eastern Europe, where a multitude of nationalities will flaunt their inexperienced freedom."[59] Wilson himself was, however, discovering in Paris how difficult it was to determine what the peoples of Eastern Europe really wanted.

In May, Wilson received a report from one of his Balkan experts, Yale professor of economic history Clive Day, who thought that it would be "most unfortunate if the American Government did anything to support the claims of King Nicholas who is thoroughly discredited in his own country." Rather, according to Day, "the United States will do most for a fair and lasting settlement of the problem if it throws its influence in favor of a union of Montenegro with the other Jugo-Slavs, but acts as a moderator in repressing the arbitrary and violent measures of the Serbs."[60] Other reports more favorable to the small state from the American explorer Charles Furlong and from Sir John Francis Charles de Salis, former British minister to Montenegro, failed to bring about any reversal of policy. Ultimately, Nicholas would not be restored to his kingdom, and Montenegro would be absorbed into the Yugoslav state, but the case allowed for the emergence of some skepticism about whether a peace settlement on Wilsonian principles could ever provide national satisfaction.

Harold Nicolson, a member of the British delegation in Paris, later reflected, "I knew that it would be better in the long run, for economic and political reasons, were Montenegro in fact to be absorbed by Serbia. . . . Yet I felt extremely uncertain whether such a solution was in fact that desired by the Montenegrin people themselves." Nicolson ultimately came to feel that "it was in connection with this problem of Montenegro that my early faith in Self-Determination as the remedy for all human ills became clouded with doubts and reservations."[61] Wilson himself experienced a conflict in his own sympathies that pointed to an awkwardness in the application of Wilsonian principles.

■ ■ ■

"A slice of the Dobrudja"
While Wilson's presidential friendship and international principles were competitively and importunately claimed by King Nicholas and Crown Prince Alexander, the case of Queen Marie of Romania further suggested the potent implications of royal relations with the American president. The English-born, half-Russian Romanian queen first wrote to Wilson in 1917 from Jassy (Iași), while Bucharest was occupied by Germany and Austria, "as a woman who is at the same time a Queen, a Queen who loves her country and who feels that she must appeal to you on its behalf."[62] Wilson met Queen Marie in Paris in April 1919. "The President and Mrs. Wilson and I called on the Queen of Roumania in her suite at the Ritz Hotel," the president's aide Dr. Cary Grayson noted in his diary,

observing: "The Queen is a tall, well-proportioned, very handsome lady. She is of the blonde type. She was dressed in excellent taste, wearing a gray gown with slippers to match. She wore a beautiful string of pearls, and two beautiful earring pearls, and a pearl ring."[63]

Forty-three years old, the granddaughter of Queen Victoria on one side and of Tsar Alexander II on the other, Marie of Romania had already proved her political importance and was thought to have greatly influenced her husband King Ferdinand to enter the war in 1916 on the side of England, Russia, and France. At the Ritz in 1919, according to Grayson, she was quite sure of herself in conversation with the president:

> She was a very free talker and said to the President: "You are here in a very perplexing and complicated situation, because I realize that everybody wants the impossible, and they look to you to give it to them. And you certainly have my sympathy. . . . They even want you to draw the boundary lines, which I know is a very unpleasant and unpopular task."[64]

The queen kept coming back to the subject of boundaries, hoping to engage Wilson's reciprocal sympathy for Romania's extensive territorial ambitions in Transylvania, Bukovina, Bessarabia, and Dobruja.

The president told the queen self-deprecatingly that "I feel sometimes now that in helping to determine the boundary lines of the states of Europe, I am getting my revenge for the difficulty which attended my study of geography while I was a boy."[65] Wilson born in 1856 would have been a very young child when Romania was first constituted in 1859 and when Italy was united in 1861, but a schoolchild already at the time of the complex Austro-Hungarian compromise of 1867 and Bismarck's unification of Germany in 1871; the Eastern crisis of 1876 and the redrawing of the borders of southeastern Europe at the Congress of Berlin in 1878 coincided with his university years at Princeton. In fact, Wilson's geopolitical inclinations in Paris in 1919 could be seen as a sort of political revenge—or critical revision—against the ways in which the map had been remade during his early life.

Grayson, however, considered Wilson's allusion to his childhood struggles with geography as strategic gamesmanship—indeed chess—as he evaded the queen's diagonal attacks: "The president thus very cleverly edged away from a discussion of boundaries which it was very plain to be seen the Queen had hoped to bring about, probably with an idea in her mind of bringing up the Roumanian situation, and especially the extension of Roumania towards Bulgaria." The queen urged him to make time to see the official Romanian representative in Paris, the prime minister Ion Brătianu: "He is a good man but you will find him a tiresome, sticky and tedious individual." She presumably rated her own charms rather higher and planned to exercise them upon Wilson the next day at lunch. Grayson noted that "as a parting thrust, showing that she realized that she had been sidetracked in her earlier conversation, the Queen said to the President: 'I hope that you will talk international affairs and let me speak of Roumania all during the lunch.'" Wilson, after the meeting, characterized her to Grayson as "a brilliant woman" who was "traveling in high gear this morning."[66] The notion of friendship, or even personal sympathy, did not seem to cross his mind.

Grayson again provided a full account of the lunch the next day to which the queen also brought her two daughters and her sister, arriving twenty minutes late: "The President was most charming and gracious to her but she asked very pointed questions at times, which he always diplomatically evaded. One of the questions she asked was: 'What one individual is causing the greatest obstruction in the Peace Conference?'"[67] It was an awkward question, coming at a moment when Wilson's range of sympathies was becoming gradually complicated by an overlapping set of antipathies, and he assured the queen that he well understood that "it was impossible to establish a just peace that would be pleasing to everyone." When the queen commented that there would be "weeping and gnashing of teeth" by the dissatisfied nations, Wilson responded oddly with a joke about an African American preacher who exclaimed: "And there shall be weeping and gnashing of teeth and them that hasn't teeth will have to gum it."[68] The turning aside of the queen's political comment with a bit of obscure racial humor perhaps suggested that Wilson himself was not inclined to take entirely seriously the conference discontents.

Wilson was rather unreceptive to Romanian self-promotion, and when the queen praised her own husband King Ferdinand as a monarchical opponent of Bolshevism, Wilson replied that "in his opinion the proposition of planting a King on a country where he did not originate was fraught with very serious danger, not only to the King, but to the country itself." King Ferdinand was German by origin, and Wilson later reflected to Grayson that "perhaps I went a little too far in saying what I did as to the transplanting of Kings." Wilson was well aware that he was responding provocatively rather than sympathetically to the queen, and the diary of Edith Benham (social secretary to First Lady Edith Wilson) shed some light on the president's somewhat irritable mood:

> The Queen had come to establish a propaganda for Roumania, a Greater Roumania, and she did the worst thing she could in being nearly twenty-five minutes late. Every moment we waited I could see from the cut of the P.'s jaw that a slice of the Dobrudja, or Roumania, was being lopped off. At one time he threatened to go on and begin luncheon without her.[69]

From Benham's perspective, the relation between the president's sympathies and the geopolitical outcomes of the conferences were—though humorously formulated—certainly plausible, and the map of Dobruja (disputed between Romania and Bulgaria) hovered over the royal luncheon. That day the queen herself was perhaps the "one individual causing the greatest obstruction" in Wilson's mental composure—and his irritation had potential implications for the mental map that he was constantly annotating and amending at the conference.

Four months later, in August 1919 and back in Washington, Lansing noted that "today at my daily conference with the President we were discussing the rapacity of Roumania." Wilson's annoyance at the queen's presumption in April had given way to a full-fledged fury at the whole nation, which sought to aggrandize itself (for instance, by seizing Transylvania from Hungary) at the expense of its neighbors: "The President said that Roumania's conduct was insufferable, that he had for that Government a feeling of contempt and indignation, and that he considered Roumania the most despicable of the Balkan nations. He added that the Roumanians had a German king."[70] Wilson who discovered Eastern Europe through a select group of favored friends would eventually develop a personal ranking of least favored nations, balancing sympathies with antipathies. That he considered Romania to be "Balkan" would have been offensive enough to the Romanians, even without the further disparagement.

Ultimately, Wilson, though sympathetic to the king of Montenegro who greeted him as a friend, had to swallow his sympathy for the smallest of small nations and embrace Serbia as the bulwark of the new Yugoslav state, endorsing the Yugoslav national agenda in opposition to Italy. Likewise, though he was unsympathetic to Marie of Romania, and never warmed to the Romanian national cause, he could not blunt the force of Romanian "rapacity" as long as the peacemakers in Paris stood fiercely opposed to Béla Kun's Bolshevik regime in Hungary. Considering the cases of Romania and Montenegro, Wilson's mapping of Eastern Europe took some of its cues from the colorful trappings of royalty—as in the confusing geography lessons of the schoolroom long ago—but evolved according to a sentimental calculus of friendly (and unfriendly) feeling that shaped, and sometimes challenged, Wilsonian principles.

■ ■ ■

"A new international psychology"
In April 1919, Wilson's press secretary, Ray Stannard Baker, reported admiringly that the president was "standing like a rock on the Italian question." Wilson refused to sign a treaty in which the Italians received Dalmatia or the city of Fiume at the expense of the new Yugoslav kingdom, though northern Dalmatia was promised to Italy by the Treaty of London.

> He has a kind of still determination—sat by the sunny window, where Mrs. Wilson was at work with bits of crochet-pattern—a huge bunch of white lilacs perfuming the room—& talked to me about decisions which may make or unmake the world. . . . I brought along an interesting article by Dr. Pupin, giving an account of the Italian point of view & describing the devotion of the Serbs to the President—one Serbian woman having knit him a pair of socks. I showed it to Mrs. Wilson, who was much amused by it.[71]

Invoked thus, in a sunny room in Paris perfumed by white lilacs, as if in a Renoir painting, the image of the Serbian woman knitting socks for

Wilson appeared as an icon of dedication. Such signs of devotion helped to shape Wilson's mapping of Eastern Europe at the crucial moment when the world was being made and unmade. The remote and anonymous Serbian woman, perhaps metaphorically knitting together the new Yugoslav state, personified the friendship of Eastern Europe for the American president—even if the account appeared comical to Mrs. Wilson. Mihajlo Pupin, who provided the account, was a Serbian American scientist who not only made important contributions to the technology of long-distance telephone communications but also advised the American peace delegation on Serbian matters, in this case contributing to the long-distance operations performed in Paris upon the map of Eastern Europe.

At the very beginning of the year, on January 3, 1919, Wilson was in Rome, presenting his vision of the peace settlement to the Italian parliament. He still believed that the principle of national self-determination would harmoniously reconcile the peoples of Europe, including the Italians and the South Slavs. Baker reflected on Wilson's popularity in Italy, hoping that the president could "impress upon the Italian people the need of the adoption of a positive reconstructive program in order to avert the dangers of an old fashioned get-and-grab peace."[72] In his Rome speech, Wilson articulated a vision of the postwar world organized around the principle of justice—but, even more, the sentiment of friendship. The Balkans, he explained, had previously been rendered unstable by their relation to Austria-Hungary, an instability that Wilson understood in terms of the volatile mapping of repressed emotions, occult influences, and hidden connections: "The great difficulty among such states as those of the Balkans has been that they were always accessible to secret influence. . . . And that north of them lay disturbed populations which were held together, not by sympathy and friendship, but by the coercive force of a military power."[73] Now, however, with the end of the war and the collapse of the Habsburg monarchy, an age of sympathy and friendship might begin with the unification and independence of the Yugoslav kingdom. Friendship for the newly emancipated South Slavs was crucial to the vision that Wilson presented in the Italian parliament:

They must now be independent. I am sure that you recognize the principle as I do that it is not our privilege to say what sort of government they shall set up, but we are friends of these people, and it is our duty as their friends to see to it that some kind of protection is thrown around them, something supplied which will hold them together. There is only one thing that holds nations together, if you exclude force, and that is friendship and good will. The only thing that binds men together is friendship and, by the same token, the only thing that binds nations together is friendship. Therefore, our task at Paris is to organize the friendship of the world, to see to it that all the moral forces that make for right and justice and liberty are united and are given a vital organization to which the peoples of the world will readily and gladly respond. In other words, our task is no less colossal than this, to set up a new international psychology, to have a new atmosphere.[74]

The moment of the tabula rasa was not just one for remaking the map but for establishing a whole new psychological atmosphere. The proclamation of a new "international psychology" coincided with the moment when Wilson himself stood at the ovational center of extravagant expressions of sympathy and friendship.

Wilson's ambassador in Rome, Thomas Nelson Page, who was hoping to sustain Wilson's sympathy for the Italians in spite of the looming crisis over the Adriatic, wrote to Wilson urging that some kind of American-Italian cooperation might be achieved by supporting Montenegro against Serbia. Page reported to Wilson a conversation with Sonnino:

> I asked him why he did not give up his claims to Dalmatia and, accepting the modified programme of others in Italy and elsewhere, try to secure Montenegro's independence and right of uncoerced decision, and bring Italy to act with America in accordance with your principles. He replied that if Montenegro could have the Cattaro and be free it would make a great change for Italy and relieve her greatly from the peril of possible attack in the future from behind the islands on the Dalmatian side.[75]

The appeal to Wilsonian principles was accompanied by a geography lesson for the president, a lesson on the Adriatic relation of the islands of Dalmatia and the gulf of Cattaro or Kotor in Montenegro, facing Italy across the sea. Page was aware that the current moment was fraught with challenges, inasmuch as the map was about to be remade, and that the Adriatic crisis was fundamentally a Wilsonian moment. "The whole world seems to me at this moment to hang on your decision," Page wrote, hoping for "the settlement of the Adriatic problem in such a way as to make the Italian people feel that you are in full sympathy with all their just claims." The transformation of the map called for the projection of Wilson's sympathy among the rival peoples of the Adriatic region, but "full sympathy" was a difficult proposition when there were so many claimants for his favor.[76]

Yugoslav devotion to Wilson was not in doubt, and already in November 1918, House was forwarding to Wilson a secret request from the provisional Yugoslav government for American troops—rather than Italian troops—to occupy strategic points in the contested Adriatic territories. The Slovene leader Anton Korošec conveyed this request: "because he and his countrymen regarded the President as a liberator, and the United States as their second fatherland, owing to the large immigration of recent years."[77] The multiple sympathies of the American immigrant population, of the nascent Yugoslav government, of the South Slavic peoples, and of Wilson himself all converged at this formative moment to render sympathetic the deployment of American troops in the Adriatic region. In fact, the popularity of the American troops was being strategically exploited by the Italians, as Wilson soon discovered, according to Grayson:

> In Rome, the President learned that the one regiment of American troops, which had been assigned to the Dalmatian territory, had been divided by the Italian Commander into platoons and used as a "cover" for the Italian advance into the disputed territory. The President learned that the Italian military chiefs had found when they advanced into the towns of Dalmatia, Albania, and Yugo-Slavia rioting followed the appearance of Italian troops. The Italian commander then adopted the expedient of sending in small bodies of American soldiers. They were received with popular rejoicing. During the night, however, the Americans would be withdrawn and replaced by Italian soldiers. In this way,

the Italian commander had been using the popular esteem for the Americans to advance his own troops far across the armistice line.[78]

The geopolitical implications of Wilsonian sympathy were so potent that American popularity could be craftily manipulated to adjust the contested borders on the new map of Eastern Europe in purposeful violation of Wilsonian principles. Antagonisms could be "covered" by eliciting and channeling alternative sympathies.

When Wilson visited Italy in January, he was popular with both the Italians and the Yugoslavs, but he himself had to maintain a carefully controlled monopoly on the exploitation of his own personal charisma.

> When in Rome, Mr. Page, the Ambassador, told the President that he had a conversation with an Italian, who asked him how much of this territory he thought Mr. Wilson would let Italy have and finished up by saying: "Well I suppose if Mr. Wilson does not want us to have it, we should not get it." This was an indication of the popular confidence which the President had aroused in Italy. At this stage, however, the President was debating, "in his own mind," as he expressed it, how far he could disappoint the Italian popular ambitions and still get through an amicable settlement.[79]

The anecdote was surely intended to appeal to the president's political fantasy of postwar Europe: the Italian who believed that Italy ought not to receive territories that Wilson himself did not want to consign to it. The president was well aware that such moral credit was a limited resource and that, especially when he enjoyed the simultaneous sympathies of rival national claimants, the calculus of disappointment was a function of shifting expectations. The "amicable" settlement based on Wilsonian commitment to principle could be only narrowly obtainable by the finest balancing of sympathies and disappointments.

Wilson wrote the king of Italy, Vittorio Emanuele III, a polite thank-you note on January 8: "The very delightful reception which you and your gracious Queen both accorded Mrs. Wilson and me in Italy will always remain in our hearts as a very delightful and fragrant memory. I tried to express to you when I was with you the sentiments of genuine friendship it had stirred in us."⁸⁰ The note was polite but not entirely perfunctory, inasmuch as "the sentiments of genuine friendship" were precisely the emotional vectors of Wilson's strategic effort to construct a new map imbued with sentiment and perfumed with the "fragrance" of his own evolving sympathies.

Wilson was more purposefully political in writing to Prime Minister Orlando, declaring that the Habsburg monarchy "is prostrate and in such a complete state of disintegration that neither to the North, nor in the Adriatic, need the Italian people dread any further menace." For that very reason Wilson called upon Orlando and the Italians to renounce the Treaty of London with its promise of northern Dalmatia.

> The boundaries proposed in that agreement were laid down as a frontier against the Austro-Hungarian Empire and that Empire no longer exists. . . . In order to hasten the break up, Italy along with all the greater States associated with her in the war, encouraged the Jugo-Slavic peoples to break away from the Empire and assured them of her sympathy with their aspirations for independence and thus herself assisted in radically altering the circumstances which had justified the London agreement. As parts of the Austro-Hungarian Empire the Jugo-Slavic peoples of the Adriatic coast were Italy's enemies. They may now be her friends.⁸¹

The economy of sympathy and friendship pivoted on the tabula rasa created by Habsburg disintegration, with the sympathies that preceded and encouraged that disintegration balanced, in Wilson's conception, by post-Habsburg friendships between nations.

■ ■ ■

"The Slavic world against the Western world"

In February, when Wilson was back in America lecturing in Boston on the virtues of the treaty and the League of Nations, he promised that, by the "new magic" of new ideals, "we are on the eve of a new age of the world, where nations will understand one another, when nations will support one another in every just cause." Yet Wilson now already feared that the United States might be the only "disinterested friend" of the nations of

Eastern Europe, which made the League seem all the more essential. "Do you believe in the Polish cause, as I do?" Wilson asked the Bostonians. "Do you believe in the aspirations of the Czecho-Slovaks and Jugo-Slavs, as I do?"[82] It was a sort of credo of belief in the new Eastern Europe, and Wilson appeared as the high priest of that creed, urging the assembled Bostonians to embrace his own sympathies with the aspirations of these nations, and invoking their extreme vulnerability in the absence of true friends and international guarantees.

In Paris, Chief Territorial Specialist Isaiah Bowman submitted an ethnographic map of northern Italy (created by the Italian geographer Olinto Marinelli) to House and Wilson in April 1919. Bowman wrote to House that "it seems to me that the map should not only receive the closest scrutiny on the part of yourself and the President, but that the President should have it at hand when the Italian questions are discussed." Wilson's note on the back of Bowman's letter suggested the immediate impact of the map on the presidential mind, with ethnographic features fully implicated in Wilson's sense of international relations. He worried that by favoring Italy against the Yugoslavs on the Adriatic, the peacemakers would be committing "the fatal error of making Italy's nearest neighbors on her east her enemies, nursing just such a sense of injustice as has disturbed the peace of Europe for generations."[83] The time to remake the map of Eastern Europe was at hand, and a misstep at that moment could be "fatal," could vitiate the whole future course of the region.

At the conference in April, Wilson made his appeal directly to Orlando and Sonnino: "He urged his Italian colleagues to remember that they were in the hands of true friends. He would not be serving their interests if he consented to their claims to Fiume and Dalmatia." Orlando was perhaps skeptical about Wilson's reassurance, and was, by then, pointedly referring to "my dear friend Colonel House." Wilson's sense of friendship for Italy was certainly conditional and governed by his unprecedented engagement with Europe as a whole: "There had been a time when he had not cared a snap of the fingers what happened to Europe," Wilson admitted in the Council of Four. "Now, however, it was his privilege to assist Europe to create a new order."[84] A week earlier he had had lunch with the queen of Romania; a few days later, he would learn of the Serbian socks being knitted for his American feet. He had a map in his hand and in his head as he pronounced upon the future of Fiume and Dalmatia.

Clemenceau commented that "in listening to President Wilson's speech, he felt we were embarking on a most hazardous enterprise," albeit with the best intentions. The French leader perceived with some concern Wilson's commitment to a complete break with the diplomatic past at the transformative moment: "We were seeking to detach Europe and the whole world from the old order . . . [but] it was not possible to change the whole policy of the world at one stroke."[85] Wilson believed in precisely that comprehensive change of everything at a single stroke. Herron had warned him in 1918 against trying to build illusionary bridges between the old Europe and the new Europe, and now in 1919 Wilson clearly embraced some of this Manichaean spirit. The Treaty of London belonged to an anachronistic order, and its fulfillment would lead backward into the European past, according to Wilson:

> Then two orders would exist—the old and the new. In the right hand would be the new order and in the left hand the old order. We could not drive two horses at once. The people of the United States of America would repudiate it. They were disgusted with the old order. Not only the American people but the people of the whole world were tired of the old system.[86]

Claiming to faithfully reflect American disgust and fatigue with past political arrangements, Wilson affirmed his deep personal commitment to the complete transformation of Europe.

In a somewhat prickly exchange with Lloyd George in the Council of Four, two days later on April 21, Wilson clarified his opposition to the Italian claims:

> WILSON: The Italians cannot accuse the United States of being an interested party.
> LLOYD GEORGE: No, but of taking the side of the Yugoslavs against them.
> WILSON: Our tenet is that the Slavs have the same right to independence and to national unity as the Italians themselves.

LLOYD GEORGE: Yes, but if a word must be said for the Italians, the Slavs must admit that Italy's sacrifices contributed much to their own liberation, and that did not prevent the Croatians from fighting against us to the end. Except for the Czechoslovaks, the Slavs of Austria played a rather questionable role.

WILSON: It is difficult for the rest of us, free peoples, to understand the state of mind of races which have been oppressed and held under terror for a long time.[87]

What Wilson understood to be a matter of American disinterestedness, of American endorsement of equal rights for all nations, others would inevitably perceive as American partisanship, the support of one side against another, and Wilson's politics of sympathy only reinforced this critical interpretation of his own principles.

In Paris in 1919, Wilson increasingly came to generalize his sympathy for individual Slavic nations to the Slavs as a whole—a racial whole, as he conceived it. The disintegration of the Habsburg monarchy helped to produce this generalization by leaving behind the ethnographic entity of "the Slavs of Austria," which became itself the basis for conceiving of a more general ethnographic Slavdom. Lloyd George could thus disparage the Slavs as a whole for failing to fight on behalf of the Allied cause in wartime, while, for Wilson, such disparagement represented a failure "to understand the state of mind" of formerly oppressed races, an understanding that he implicitly claimed to have achieved himself. This was perhaps an awkward claim for Wilson, whose administration did not advance the cause of racial equality in the United States. Still, he saw himself presiding over an emancipatory moment—for Slavs who were suddenly free after centuries of subjection, as Wilson saw it—the moment that would produce the brand new mapping of Eastern Europe.

The next day, on April 22, in further discussions with Lloyd George over the possible cession of some of the Dalmatian islands to Italy, Wilson outlined the full extent of the Slavic presence in Europe, something fearsome even to him because it inevitably involved Russia too:

WILSON: There is a fatal antagonism between the Italians and the Slavs. If the Slavs have the feeling of an injustice, that will make the chasm unbridgeable and will open the road to Russian influence and to the formation of a Slavic bloc hostile to western Europe.

LLOYD GEORGE: I do not think that this sentiment would be provoked by the cession of certain islands.[88]

The ironic comment of the British prime minister was meant to puncture the apocalyptic foreboding of Wilson's geopolitical vision, but Wilson certainly believed that the sensitivity to national injustice at this moment could in fact be stoked even by seemingly insignificant territorial assignments, the smallest and least inhabited Adriatic islands. At this point the ethnographic map that he held in his head was vastly extensive and fearsomely explosive. A misstep at the conference, he feared, could bring into being a hostile Slavic bloc, not Wilsonian but Bolshevik in inspiration, a completely alternative conception of Eastern Europe.

In the Council of Four on April 23, Wilson referred to a report from the Serbian American Mihajlo Pupin, "to convey the impression that the result of a peace unsatisfactory to the Jugo-Slavs would be to drive them into the hands of the Bolshevists," for "they would unite with the rest of the Slav peoples."[89] The maps in Wilson's mind were curiously plastic—reflecting the contemporary international moment of multiple possibilities—and his geopolitical curiosity made him susceptible to proffered impressions and influences. The Russians, he understood, were not only related to the other Slavic peoples of Eastern Europe but geographically adjacent to many of them. While Americans like himself could connect with Eastern Europe through friendship, Russians had the advantage of linguistic similarity and family resemblance, which meant that the small Slavic nations of Eastern Europe were always at risk of being politically dominated, ethnographically absorbed, and ideologically corrupted by their enormous Slavic neighbor. Wilson, who was himself a master of combining Slavic nationalities—Czechs with Slovaks, Serbs with Croats—could all too easily imagine the combinatory pan-Slavic projects that the Bolsheviks might put into play, drawing the peoples of Eastern Europe into Moscow's orbit. Precisely because Wilson recognized the Slavic resemblances between Russia and Eastern Europe, he was all the more determined to keep them separate and distinct on the geopolitical map.

For all his Slavic sympathies, it is important to note that Slavic solidarity, especially in an age of Russian Bolshevism, was something that Wilson found potentially alarming. Similarly, Harold Nicolson, in his conference diary, admitted to "a sneaking sympathy with the Italian case" and a corresponding fear of Slavic solidarity as a geopolitical force: "I also have an uneasy feeling that it would be a mistake to give the Slavs too firm a footing on the Adriatic. What should we do with a Slav block from Vladivostock to Fiume, from Danzig to Samarcand? *Les Scythes ont conquis le monde.* [The Scythians have conquered the world.]"[90]

For Nicolson, "Scythian" implied barbarism and implicitly characterized the Slavic world. Pupin, a scientist, and himself a South Slav, suggested the possibility of something like a chemical reaction in the Slavic inclination to form bonds with other Slavic nations. Wilson cited Pupin as believing that "if the Yugoslavs have the impression that they have not been treated justly, they will throw themselves on the side of the Slavic world against the Western world."[91] This was a hypothetical configuration of postwar Eastern Europe, in hostile opposition, that made Wilson himself uneasy and that he sought to avert.

On April 23, 1919, when Wilson put his case directly to the Italian people, he began by emphasizing once again the fundamental geopolitical fact of 1919: "The Austro-Hungarian Empire, then the enemy of Europe, and at whose expense the Pact of London was to be kept in the event of victory, has gone to pieces and no longer exists." He offered lessons in the geography of the new Eastern Europe, observing, for instance, that "Fiume must serve as the outlet and inlet of the commerce, not of Italy, but of the lands to the north and northeast of that port: Hungary, Bohemia, Roumania, and the states of the New Jugo-Slavic group." The peroration of his message, however, appealed to the emotional matrix of reciprocal friendships that formed the basis of Wilson's own sentimental perspective. In the case of Italy, "it is within her choice to be surrounded by friends; to exhibit to the newly liberated peoples across the Adriatic that noblest quality of greatness, magnanimity, friendly generosity." At the same time, the magnanimity of Italy would be met by a corresponding

American sympathy: "America is Italy's friend. Her people are drawn, millions strong, from Italy's own fair countrysides. She is linked in blood as well as in affection with the Italian people."[92] This fraternity of blood and sentiment, which transcended the Atlantic, might also transcend the Adriatic, shaping a peace settlement based on Wilsonian principles.

The measure of Wilson's sentimental commitment to the Yugoslavs may be judged in part by the reciprocal sentiment that his Adriatic declaration called forth, almost instantly, in a note of April 23 from the Serbian leader Nikola Pašić, who was present in Paris: "Your righteous and divine words have saved from slavery a part of our nation. With your declaration you have revived the faith of all feeble nations that there verily begins a new era of fraternity and equality in rights of all nations. Our nation with three names will eternally praise you as our saviour."[93] Wilson did not need a geography lesson on the three names of the Kingdom of the Serbs, Croats, and Slovenes, for, in fact, he preferred more synthetic categories, however awkward, like "the states of the New Jugo-Slavic group." Rather, it was a moment of religious celebration of the divine Wilsonian words that announced the advent of a new era of emancipation. If the Habsburgs had been hyperbolically castigated as the emperors of enslavement, the lapsing of their empire introduced a transformative moment that was still fraught with the dangers of renewed bondage. Pašić was sensitive to the potency of Wilson's salvific fantasies.

The Italian official reaction confirmed, by its indignation, that Wilson was indeed seen as a partisan of the Yugoslavs. Orlando, departing from Paris in protest, issued a statement of outrage that Wilson would presume to try "to oppose the Italian people to the Italian Government," which the prime minister saw as an insult to "the high degree of Italian civilization"—that is, "treating the Italians as if they were a barbarous people without a democratic government." Wilson's conception was rather the reverse, for he hoped that the Italian people were in advance of their government, ready to advance into the new world of Wilsonian ideals, even if the Italian leaders remained mired in the old politics of self-interest. Yet, "civilization" and "barbarism" were crucial terms for the Italian perspective on the Adriatic question, and the Slavs of the eastern Adriatic were viewed in barbaric counterpoint to the supposedly civilizing role of the Italians. Orlando thus endorsed "the Italian aspirations toward the Dalmatian coast, Italy's boulevard throughout centuries, which Roman genius and Venetian activity made noble and grand."[94] Wilson's principle of the equality of the rights of nations ostensibly overrode such perceived inequalities of civilization, but there were suggestions that he too was susceptible to these hierarchical valuations, a mapping of the nations according to their degree of civilization. It was not just that he proposed to the Italians "that noblest quality of greatness, magnanimity," to be exercised toward "the newly liberated peoples across the Adriatic." Wilson's vision of the potential bonding of the Slavs in hostile resentment toward the West hinted at the menace of barbarous violence.

This was a point on which Wilson and Lloyd George, despite some Anglo-American divergence over the Adriatic question, could partly agree in discussion:

> LLOYD GEORGE: The Slav is a force that one can not control; he can be the instrument of the worst tyranny or the bloodiest anarchy; he can become a terrible danger for the world. Moreover, we must not forget the ties of race which unite the Slavs of Russia and the Slavs

FIGURE 6. The National Theater in Zagreb as centerpiece of Wilsonov Trg (Wilson Square). Before the war it was called University Square. It was Wilson Square from 1919 to 1927. It was subsequently renamed first for King Alexander of Yugoslavia and eventually for Tito. Today it is the Republic of Croatia Square.

> of southeastern Europe. If I were Italian, I would not like to see the Slavs on that coast across from my country . . .
>
> WILSON: What makes the Slav less formidable than the German is that he has not attained the same degree of organization. . . . Germany has a more complete system of education than any other country; if Russia was capable of doing as much, she would be irresistible. But in many respects she is backward. . . . In my opinion, of the dangers which threaten Italy, the most serious would be the discontent of the Slavs.[95]

Both Wilson and Lloyd George agreed that the Slavs constituted a potential threat to Italy, based on their backwardness. If Germany was better organized and educated, and Russia less so, then the Slavs of Eastern Europe who lay in between them geographically might have been mapped onto a civilizational incline of greater and lesser development. On the whole, however, Wilson seemed to believe that the Slavs in general were more closely aligned with Russian backwardness, which, in Lloyd George's political schema, put them all at risk for either tyranny or anarchy, each Slavic state a potentially unstable and volatile element in the geopolitical Wilsonian settlement. The triggering mechanism would be Slavic "discontent," which Wilson now urgently sought to reduce and avert.

Armed with a map (which he had received from Bowman) Wilson attempted to prove to the Italians that the territories they claimed were ethnographically Slavic, not Italian:

> I have before me an Italian map published before the war, that of Marinelli, which would be sufficient to contradict the Italian argument; it shows that, aside from the southern portion of the island of Cherso and the island of Lussino, there are Italian elements only on some isolated points. What discourages me is that, when Italy has made proposals, they dissolve as soon as one tries to be precise.[96]

Wilson with a map in his hand, confident in his own precision, seemingly unaware that his maps were powerfully shaped by his own sympathies, would never understand the Italian perspective on islands like Cherso and Lussino (Cres and Lošinj under their South Slavic names), which he himself was only just now discovering on the map. In 1770, an Italian naturalist, Alberto Fortis, had visited these Adriatic islands and written about them as objects of Venetian imperial administration. Like Herder, Fortis contributed to the Enlightenment's understanding of the wider Slavic world.[97] Wilson was only beginning to understand that mapping the Slavic world, both geographically and ethnograpically, was not necessarily a matter of scientific precision but often existed within the volatile domain of culture and mentality, shaped by a long historical legacy. He did not always understand how his own attempted interventions fit with earlier perspectives on Eastern Europe.

Colonel House in Paris expressed the opinion that "Italy has gone mad," while Herron in Switzerland took a strong public position in favor of Italy—which led to Wilson's renunciation of his impassioned friend: "I am through with him," the president announced to House.[98] If the Italians were no longer Wilson's friends, then the friends of the Italians were also no longer Wilson's friends. "The Italians must realize, furthermore, that they can not have what they want without the consent of the United States," Wilson commented. "If their only preoccupation is to save their pride, they are throwing themselves into an impasse." He insisted that they would have to accept the Wilsonian principle that "one cannot dispose of peoples without their consent," and that "to insist upon the execution of the Treaty of London is absurd."[99] Wilson's position was hardening over what he saw as the facts of the ethnographic map. Insistence on his principles was also a point of pride—that pride which he preferred to attribute to the absurd Italians. Urging the mechanism of plebiscites on the Italians, Wilson told Orlando to his face that "Italy must wholly abandon the old methods and enter into the new world with the new methods." Rejecting plebiscites, Orlando indignantly insisted that "he was not a Shylock, demanding his pound of flesh from the Jugo-Slavs"—and reminded Wilson again that, from an Italian perspective, "there was a different state of culture in Jugo-Slavia from Italy, because there was a different state of civilization."[100] Wilson sometimes also imputed a difference in levels of civilizations, but his sentiments, reinforcing his principles, led him to resist the Italian claims.

The hardening of Wilson's perspective partly reflected a sense that the window for settling the peace and creating the new world was closing, that his millenarian moment was escaping. Even as he forcefully pressured the Italians over the Adriatic question, he was ready to give an ultimatum to the Romanians, who were attacking the Hungary of Béla Kun in the spring of 1919 and extending their border in Transylvania with its mixed Romanian and Hungarian populations. "I favor imposing the frontier that we have accepted on the Rumanians," Wilson said on June 12. "They will scream," Clemenceau commented with cynical interest.[101] The conference returned to the subject the next day on June 13, and Wilson scripted a forceful ultimatum to Romania:

> WILSON: We can say to the Rumanians: "If you do not conform to our decisions, we will stop supporting your claims . . . "
> BALFOUR: You can say that, but, in fact, you will not again put Rumanian populations under Hungarian domination.
> LLOYD GEORGE: No, but in doubtful cases we have always decided in favor of our friends.[102]

Balfour pointed out that Wilson would not want to contradict his own principles of ethnography just to punish the Romanians, but Lloyd George cheerfully admitted that, regardless of principles, the peacemakers, including Wilson, perhaps especially Wilson, were inclined to favor their friends. Since Béla Kun, the commissar of Bolshevik Hungary, was no friend to any of the peacemakers, the comment was really only relevant to the Romanians, and a reminder that the favoring of friends also meant not favoring those who were not friends.

Two weeks later, Wilson reflected with Lloyd George and Clemenceau on the dynamics of friendship as the fundamental problem in their relation to Italy: "What is tragic in the situation is that we are friends of Italy, we want to be such, and it is she who makes that friendship impossible." Wilson thus continued to refuse to countenance Italian rule in Dalmatia or Fiume, and was increasingly distressed by Italian claims to a mandatory role in Albania—with further claims to Rhodes and some part of post-Ottoman Anatolia, where Italian troops were already present. "It is necessary," Wilson declared fiercely, "to refuse to talk with them so long as their troops are where they do not have the right to be."[103] For Wilson it was a matter of reconciling friendship with principle: "The

Government of the United States, in common with its associates, desires to render Italy every kind of assistance that is in its power to render, but it cannot do so at the sacrifice of any of the principles upon which the present negotiations have been conducted."[104] They were his own Wilsonian principles after all.

Of course the Italian reaction to Wilson mirrored his own change of sentiments toward Italy, and when asked at a press conference back in Washington in July about Fiume, he replied "I understand that the street in Rome that they had called 'Via Wilson' has been changed to 'Via Fiume.' That is the latest information I have, which is a practical joke on myself."[105] It was certainly not intended as any kind of a joke, but reports of the change of street names presented a very precise symbolic substitution by which the Italians demonstrated that they too understood the dynamics of reciprocal friendship and its renunciation.

■ ■ ■

"The most avaricious and brutal of the smaller nations"
Taking his case for the treaty to the American public upon his return, Wilson also made the case against Italy in Columbus, Ohio, a city named for the hero of Italian Americans.

> My fellow citizens, I do not think there is any man alive who has a more tender sympathy for the great people of Italy than I have, and a very stern duty was presented to us when we had to consider some of the claims of Italy on the Adriatic. . . . But her people did not live there except in little spots. It was a Slavic people, and I had to say to my Italian friends that everywhere else in this treaty we have given territory to the people who lived on it, and I do not think that it is for the advantage of Italy, and I am sure it is not for the advantage of the world, to give Italy territory where other people live.[106]

This was a story of Wilson's tender sympathy for the Italians—an unreciprocated sympathy, for the Italians refused to accept that Wilson understood the interests and advantages of Italy better than the Italians did themselves.

Wilson now finally did understand that the mixed ethnography of the Adriatic made the region unmappable according to the purest principle of self-determination, as he had once understood it. The president had learned some lessons about the mapping of Eastern Europe which he passed on to the public of Columbus:

> Here are two neighboring peoples. The one people have not stopped at a sharp line, and the settlements of the other people, or their migrations, begun at that sharp line; they have intermingled. There are regions where you can't draw a national line and say there are Slavs on this side and Italians on that. There is this people there and that people there. It can't be done. You have to approximate the line . . . as near to it as you can, and then trust to the processes of history to redistribute, [as] it may be, the people who are on the wrong side of the line. And there are many such lines drawn in this treaty . . . [107]

Wilson thus recapitulated his own frustration at the impossibility of clearly and cleanly mapping the ethnographic boundaries of Eastern Europe; he expressed his wistful regret that he had not been able to say definitively, "there is this people there and that people there."

Acknowledging the difficulty of determining ethnographic borders, Wilson, speaking in Columbus, still presented the Italian claims as absurd:

> I even had to remind my Italian colleagues that, if they were going to claim every place where there was a large Italian population, we would have to cede New York to them, because there are more Italians in New York than in any Italian city. But I believe—I hope—that the Italians in New York City are as glad to stay there as we are to have them. But I would not have you suppose that I am intimating that my Italian colleagues entered any claim for New York City.[108]

This caricature of Italian claims was undoubtedly meant to be humorous, but perhaps the notion that other countries might entertain such claims was also intended to play on the anxieties of Americans who lived in cities with immigrant populations. These anxieties had in fact produced anti-German sentiment in America during the war, when former president Theodore Roosevelt had questioned the loyalty of "hyphenated

Americans."[109] Wilson himself was susceptible to such anxieties about immigrant populations.

Ten days later, on September 15, the chargé d'affaires at the Rome embassy, Peter Augustus Jay, forwarded to Wilson a personal message from King Vittorio Emanuele III. In a reversion to the diplomacy of royal friendship, as also attempted by the king of Montenegro and the queen of Romania, the Italian king had sent for Jay to "ask me to telegraph to the President an appeal coming directly from him, to consent to the proposals in regard to the Italian claims." Vittorio Emanuele cited "the sacrifices of blood and treasure made by Italy in the common cause," lamented the possible loss of Italian populations ("which actually brought tears to his eyes"), and feared that those populations would be treated by the Yugoslavs "with great cruelty." In a peculiar echo of Wilson's rhetorical device of asking whether New York City should be assigned to Italy, the king of Italy now asked Wilson "how the American people would appreciate the American colonies on the border being handed over to the arbitrary rule of the Government of Mexico." According to Jay, "the King was deeply emotional," and wanted above all for this to be received as a "personal appeal to the President."[110] The emotional tone of the message—conveyed even with the report of tears in the royal eyes—was unprecedented, and perhaps appeared eccentric, but it was not inconsistent with the sentimental climate of friendship with which Wilson himself had attempted to invest the peace settlement.

Jay's meeting with the king took place on September 12, which was, coincidentally, the same day that the poet and nationalist extremist Gabriele D'Annunzio seized power for the Italians in the contested city of Fiume, a démarche that preempted the authority of the peace conference. Wilson's message for Jay, sent from the White House on September 28 was emphatic:

> Instruction from the President: Do not allow yourself to be, or even to seem to be, impressed by what is being said to you by members of the Italian Government with regard to the present crisis. It is all part of a desperate endeavor to get me to yield to claims which, if allowed, would destroy the peace of Europe. You cannot make the impression too definite and final that I cannot and will not yield.[111]

After staking out such an uncompromising position, with no concessions to the tears of the king, Wilson had a stroke a few days later on October 2, which in any event limited his capacity to enter into further discussion of the Adriatic issues.

During the summer of 1919, following Wilson's departure for America, Archibald Cary Coolidge had shifted from Vienna to Paris to participate in a sort of academic mop up of remaining issues "on various committees both for Austria and the Balkans, for the larger part of our experts have left for home." Coolidge himself was impatient to be gone, doubted whether his own expertise could resolve the thorniest problems, and began to comment ironically on some of the Balkan issues in particular. "I see no end to Balkan and Turkish questions," he wrote on June 30, "though I do to my willingness to deal with them, for I mean to get back before the next college term begins." He sarcastically dismissed the discussion of "Bulgarian boundaries, and Servian [sic] demands, and whether the communities at Mt. Athos should have special rights, and other such exhilarating subjects." For the professor these subjects now appeared as a kind of pedantry and held no larger political excitement: "Friday I went to an endlessly long lunch given by some Albanians and had to leave before it was over."[112] The urgency of redrawing the map had given way to a kind of comedy of Eastern Europe, perhaps partly because Wilson was no longer in Paris to lend his charismatic authority to American academic expertise. The Paris peace conference itself seemed like an endlessly long lunch hosted by Albanians, and the professor needed to get back to Harvard in time for the beginning of the fall term.

At the beginning of 1920, as the peace conference was finally about to conclude—with Wilson gradually recovering in America from his stroke—France and England agreed to make concessions to Italy, allowing more complete Italian annexation of Istria and protectorate authority in Albania. Belgrade was given an ultimatum to accept the terms immediately, and Wilson in Washington objected so strenuously that he actually threatened to withdraw America altogether from the treaty—a treaty that would anyway be definitively rejected by the Senate in March.[113] Wilson conveyed his refusal to compromise through Lansing, who would probably have been more inclined to make compromises, and then, soon after, the president forced Lansing's resignation for having summoned cabinet meetings during Wilson's recovery from the stroke.

It was Lansing's successor, Bainbridge Colby, who received Wilson's later comments on the Adriatic in mid-November 1920, indeed after the election of Warren Harding as Wilson's successor. Wilson, now a lame-duck president, was no longer at the center of diplomatic discussions but merely reading in the newspapers about the new map of Europe that had ultimately emerged in spite of Wilsonian objections.

> I have been rendered very sad by what I have read in the papers about the alleged Jugo-Slav-Italian settlement. Italy has absolutely no bowels [of compassion] and is evidently planning a new Alsace-Lorraine on the other side of the Adriatic which is sure to contain the seeds of another European war. If it does, and the seeds develop, personally I shall hope that Italy will get the stuffing licked out of her. She has absolutely no conscience in these matters. Of course, however, if the Jugo-Slavs have entered into an agreement voluntarily with the Italian Government and wish it to stand as a settlement, I do not feel that we are obliged to defend them against themselves.[114]

That he was saddened and disappointed by the Yugoslav acquiescence suggested that he was reconsidering his sympathies, wondering if he should have wasted his friendship on those who were not willing to be as principled and uncompromising on their own behalf as he would have been for them. Much more striking, however, was that Wilson, the great peacemaker, was here almost maliciously hoping for a new war in which Italy might be punished for its bad behavior at the peace conference and, in colloquial American style, "get the stuffing licked out of her"—a licking that, judging from the previous war, would presumably involve massive casualties.

In an additional brief message to Colby, Wilson displayed further sentimental petulance concerning the Bulgarians and the Romanians: "Personally, I feel disinclined to appoint a Minister to Bulgaria. I have found the Bulgarians the most avaricious and brutal of the smaller nations that had to be dealt with in the war and in the settlement of the terms of peace, though for a long time my vote was for Roumania in those respects. Being no longer committed to Roumania, I can perhaps transfer my suffrages to Bulgaria."[115] This was very strange humor indeed at the expense of the small nations of Eastern Europe for whom Wilson had once exercised his shepherdship. He was entertaining Colby with a mock competition over which was the nastiest nation in Eastern Europe. In April 1919, he had looked kindly on Bulgaria by mentally awarding her slices of the Dobruja to punish the queen of Romania for her tardiness at lunch, and by August he considered the Romanians to be "the most despicable of the Balkan nations" on account of their unrestrained aggrandizement against Hungary in Transylvania. Bulgarian contestation with Greece over Thrace had brought about a new contender for least favored Balkan nation, with Bulgaria now disparaged for its avarice and brutality. Wilson's sympathies for the small nations of Eastern Europe, sympathies that had sometimes come into ambivalent contradiction with one another at the peace conference, now in November 1920 gave way to rival antipathies as the president sarcastically pretended to award the highest ranking in the category of "the most avaricious and brutal of the smaller nations" in Eastern Europe. He left it to Harding to appoint a new ambassador to Bulgaria in 1921.

To the end of his life, however, Wilson still fondly recalled his cherished friendship for the Czechs. He exchanged letters with a pastor of the church of the Bohemian Brethren in Czechoslovakia, declaring in January 1923, "It makes me proud indeed to know that I am thought to have promoted the liberties of the people of Czechoslovakia. My interest in them can never grow less, and I shall always deem the title 'friend of Czechoslovakia' as one of the most distinguished I could bear." Wilson further praised "the stout little Republic over which your President Masaryk so admirably presides," and proclaimed himself to the pastor as "your sincere friend and the interested friend of all who devote themselves to the welfare and happiness of the people of Czechoslovakia."[116] The epithet "friend of Czechoslovakia" was, in fact, more than an honorary title for Wilson; it was a whole approach to doing diplomatic business as he reinvented the map of Eastern Europe.

In March 1923, Masaryk's daughter Alice wrote to Wilson from Prague urging him to attend a concert of the Prague children's chorus on tour in America, since "there are no better messengers of sincere thanks than singing children," and "you will hear the expression of our determination to prove worthy of the liberty and the freedom which you helped us win."[117] Wilson missed the concert, but replied to the letter, "You may be sure, in any case, that I did not need the gracious assurances of this special message through the children to assure me of the very generous feeling of the people of Czechoslovakia toward me. What I did to assist that stout little nation to gain independence was done with genuine zest." The stout courage of Czechoslovakia seemed to have become proverbial for Wilson, who would not live long enough to observe its tragic destruction in the late 1930s. He sent regards, through Alice Masaryk, to her father—"and beg of him to think of me as a genuine friend of the people over whom he so worthily presides."[118] The reiteration of "genuine"—the genuine friend who had acted with genuine zest—perhaps suggested that other affinities had come to feel strained with the passage of the years.

Placing "stout" Czechoslovakia on the map of Eastern Europe, however, remained for Wilson a "genuine" accomplishment. He wrote to Tomáš Masaryk directly in May 1923 with a letter of condolence on the death of Masaryk's American wife Charlotte (born in Brooklyn), expressing "profoundest sympathy," which followed from the personal and political sympathy that Wilson had felt for Masaryk going back to their first encounter during the war. The letter was addressed to "my dear Friend," signed from "your sincere Friend," and expressed the wish "that there were some touch of friendship by which I could assist in cheering and steadying your spirits."[119] The personal touch of sentimental friendship, which had helped to shape Wilson's political sympathies in Eastern Europe, forging collective friendships for entire nations, now became fondly and nostalgically personal again, with the peace settlement behind him, in the last year of his life.

In the spring of 1923, Sylvester Beach stepped down as the pastor of the Presbyterian church in Princeton and wrote to Wilson, himself a Presbyterian Princetonian, to report on a recent European trip, to let the president know "how ardently you are loved by many of the peoples of eastern and southeastern Europe; and nowhere more than in that sterling and progressive republic of Czechoslovakia."[120] Beach's daughter Sylvia had just published in 1922, at her Paris bookstore Shakespeare and Company, James Joyce's *Ulysses*, a novel that Wilson would probably not have appreciated. He would certainly, however, have been warmed to learn that he was loved in Czechoslovakia.

In November 1923 Wilson received a token of his friendship for Czechoslovakia in the form of a photo album. He wrote to thank Masaryk for "the really magnificent volumes in which you have so thoughtfully had bound photographs of places and objects which citizens of Czechoslovakia have been so gracious as to name for me." He took such namings as a mark of "friendship" of course—the friendship of the entire nation, not just of Masaryk himself—and claimed to feel "intense pride" at having helped to bring Czechoslovakia "into the family of nations."[121] For instance, the train station in Prague—originally named for Emperor Franz Joseph—was renamed for Woodrow Wilson after the war, and a statue of Wilson was erected there in the 1920s.

As Wilson was leaving Paris at the beginning of July 1919 to return to America, this time for good, a letter was sent wishing him well:

> Permit us on the eve of your return to America and in the name of the small nations to express to you the profound impression we have received of your sincerity, disinterestedness and good will. . . . None can attest so truly as we the sympathy and solicitude you have manifested to struggling nations, lifting us from despondency to hope and dispelling the apprehensions and misgivings which have afflicted us in the past.[122]

Notable perhaps was the dwindling number of foreign friends who signed this message: Greece's Prime Minister Elefthérios Venizélos, Czechoslovakia's Foreign Minister Edvard Beneš, Nikola Pašić representing the Yugoslavs, Boghos Nubar Pasha representing the Armenians, and the Zionist leader Nahum Sokolow. Diplomacy had taken its toll on Wilson's sympathies for the nations of Eastern Europe and on theirs for him. Back in the White House, he did not fail to acknowledge the endorsement of his principles by this small circle of admirers representing their small nations: "It moves me very deeply that you should so fully realize the heartfelt sympathy I feel for the cause of Justice, and particularly for the nations which, because they are less strong than the strongest, have hitherto struggled with little hope for the realization of the highest and most legitimate ambitions."[123] This was the underwhelming endpoint of Wilson's long engagement in a programmatic exchange of reciprocal sympathies within the emotional crucible that also produced and propagated his international principles. With the Versailles treaty complete, with Wilson leaving Europe forever, with America destined to remain outside the framework of the League of Nations, with the transformative moment of Eastern Europe finally concluding, and with the crystallization of a new map, five faithful Wilsonian friends greeted him, hail and farewell.

4
National Majorities and National Minorities in Wilson's Eastern Europe

"Indisputably Polish populations"

"Do you believe in the Polish cause, as I do?" Wilson asked rhetorically in his Boston address of February 1919. The Polish cause was his first and most unambiguous commitment to national independence in Eastern Europe, the thirteenth of the Fourteen Points: "An independent Polish state should be erected which should include the territories inhabited by indisputably Polish populations." Yet notably missing from the signatures on the farewell message from national leaders to Wilson in July 1919 was a Polish name, to acknowledge his special sympathy and support for the Polish nation.[1] The new Poland was very prominent in Wilson's conceptual remapping of Eastern Europe, as were Czechoslovakia and the Yugoslav state, and the absence of a Polish name on the farewell letter perhaps reflected a fraying of reciprocal sympathies between Wilson and Poland from the time of the Fourteen Points speech in January 1918 to his departure from Paris in July 1919. The phrase "indisputably Polish populations" which may have been intended as an affirmation of Poland in January 1918 had, over the course of 1919, raised a series of challenges to the territorial mapping and ethnographic definition of the new state. Speaking in Kraków in December 1918, with reference to the mixed Polish and Ruthenian population of Eastern Galicia, the Polish geographer Eugeniusz Romer posed the problem of how to understand the word "indisputably" (*niewątpliwie*), and skeptically asked, "What is meant by this weighty word in the new world order that Wilson heralds?"[2] Persistent questions about the German, Ukrainian, Lithuanian, and Jewish populations implicated in the territorial delimiting and political framing of the new Poland eventually caused Wilson extreme frustration in dealing with Polish affairs, embittering the original spirit of fervent friendship.

The Lippmann-Cobb memorandum, presented to Wilson by Colonel House on October 29, 1918, as the war was about to end, annotated the Fourteen Points to attempt to address the complexities of remaking the map. The imminent end of Austria-Hungary meant that it was no longer the Czechs whose autonomy had to be advocated—they would have independence—but rather the situation of the German populations who would find themselves in Czechoslovakia: "Its territories include at least a million Germans for whom some provision must be made."[3] In fact, there would be three million Germans in interwar Czechoslovakia, out of a total population of thirteen million. The Lippmann-Cobb memorandum put Wilson on notice that this was going to be a problem. When Wilson wrote to congratulate Masaryk on October 18, ten days before receiving the Lippmann-Cobb memorandum—"I need not tell you with what emotions I read the Declaration of Independence put out by the National Council of the Czecho-Slovaks"—those emotions certainly did not include anxiety over the situation of the Germans who would find themselves living in the new state. Sailing to France in December 1918 on the USS *George Washington*, Wilson is supposed to have exclaimed, "Three million Germans in Bohemia! That's curious! Masaryk never told me that!"[4] Germans in Czechoslovakia would not become a major issue at the peace conference—and Hitler would take up their cause with a vengeance during the Munich crisis of 1938.

With the dissolution of the Habsburg monarchy in November 1918, the Habsburg province of Galicia was appropriated by Poland, but already in October the Lippmann-Cobb memorandum observed: "Western Galicia is clearly Polish. Eastern Galicia is in large measure Ukrainian (or Ruthenian) and does not of right belong to Poland."[5] The memorandum, offered a complicated new geography and ethnography of Eastern Europe that went well beyond anything anticipated in the Fourteen Points. "Poland" was not a well-defined term—nor could it have been, given that no Polish state had existed since 1795. Even "Galicia" was a term that had to be considered by halves, with a population of Ukrainians, also identified as Ruthenians. The memorandum laid down as a principle that

"Poland should receive no territory in which Lithuanians or Ukrainians predominate"—though that in itself would not be simple to determine in Poland's eastern regions. Furthermore, the reassignment of territories from Germany to Poland would create new minorities in Poland's western regions: "if Posen [Poznań] and Silesia go to Poland, rigid protection must be afforded the minorities of Germans and Jews living there, as well as in other parts of the Polish state."[6] The Inquiry thus acknowledged that the creation of new nation-states in Eastern Europe would create "minorities" that would inevitably be politically vulnerable to the predominant national majority. The peace conference would, therefore, have to contemplate the international imperative of minority protection.

■ ■ ■

"Poland, immature, inexperienced, as yet unorganized"

For Wilson, who had been hailed one year earlier by Paderewski as "the foster-father of a chiefless land" and "Poland's inspired protector," the ethnographic complications posed by the Lippmann-Cobb memorandum on October 29, 1918, intruded awkwardly upon the simpler mental mapping derived from his own sentimental affinities.[7] On November 7, four days before the armistice, the concerns of the memorandum were amplified by a letter from the civil rights lawyer Louis Marshall, president of the American Jewish Committee, writing to Wilson to outline the Committee's concerns about the three million Jews in newly independent Poland. Marshall, who had played a role in publicizing the persecution of Jews in the Russian empire, and who would also attend the Paris peace conference, was worried about Jews' civil and religious rights in Poland as a minority. "The American Jewish Committee has long sympathized with the aspirations of the Polish people for independence," Marshall wrote. He now drew the president's attention, however, to the fact that, alongside Paderewski, one of the leaders of the Polish National Committee was Roman Dmowski, founder of the National Democracy (ND; Endecja) movement and a notorious anti-Semite who advocated "a most virulent economic boycott" of Jews in the Polish lands. Although the Polish National Committee was officially committed to equal rights for "Polish citizens, without distinction as to origin, race or creed," Marshall doubted that Jews would be considered "Polish citizens" in the new state; more likely, he thought they might be treated as foreigners and denied civil and political rights, as in prewar Romania.[8] Wilson, in fact, knew very well who Dmowski was, since the president had met with him in the White House in September 1918 to discuss Polish independence.[9]

Marshall believed that Dmowski's National Democracy was pursuing a "policy of extermination" toward the Jews of Poland, and would lead to "unspeakable evil"—"unless the Constitution of the new Poland shall contain guarantees adequate for the protection of the Jewish inhabitants." Those guarantees, enumerated in Marshall's letter to Wilson, would have to include: citizenship for all inhabitants, equal rights for all citizens, no discrimination on account of race or religion, no restriction on the use of Yiddish or Hebrew language, autonomous management of Jewish religion and education, and the right to work on Sunday for those who observed the Jewish Sabbath on Saturday.[10] Marshall had actually met personally with Dmowski in New York on October 6, 1918, before the end of the war, and had perhaps offered an implicit deal in which Jews might endorse postwar Poland if Dmowski ended the economic boycott of Jews and renounced anti-Semitism. Paderewski was reportedly anxious about Dmowski's meeting with Marshall, fearing that the former's programmatic anti-Semitism would antagonize the latter and create political problems for the future of Poland.[11]

In a letter to Wilson of November 16, Marshall asked the president for a public statement of support for Jewish rights:

> Although I fully realize the practical difficulties presented by the extraordinary conditions which now exist in eastern Europe, I am strongly persuaded that a public announcement by you, which will unquestionably be heeded by all the world, in which you would give expression to your abhorrence of these outbreaks of religious and racial prejudice, will go far to thwart the plans of those who may seek to profit, politically or otherwise, by these wanton attacks upon the Jews. Poland and Roumania are seeking to enlarge their boundaries and to secure political independence. To accomplish that end they must rely on the good-will

of our country, as represented by you, and on that of our co-belligerents. Hence any intimation that persistence in anti-Semitic activity will be regarded as creating an obstacle to the giving of the recognition desired, cannot fail to make a deep impression.[12]

The moment of creation of a new map of Eastern Europe, with independent national states seeking enlarged boundaries, was also the moment of the invention of "minority rights"—implicit in the work of rearranging the map on the basis of self-determination, but not something that Wilson had initially anticipated. What Marshall helped Wilson to see was that minority rights could only be applied at the moment when the map was being remade, that such a moment offered the opportunity both for pressuring nascent states and shaping new constitutions.

Marshall not only fingered Dmowski as an outspoken anti-Semite, but also, uncomfortably for Wilson, associated him with Paderewski (referring to "the party which they, Messrs. Dmowski and Paderewski, represent"), the president's favored Polish friend. Marshall understood very well that Wilsonian sympathy was the political currency of the moment, and suggested that it might be strategically offered and conditionally withheld:

> Would it not be a practicable thing to let these gentlemen understand that their aspirations for a new Poland cannot receive sympathetic consideration until they first give evidence that they are possessed with that spirit of justice and righteousness which is essential to the establishment of a free and independent government? . . . Only then can the world regard the establishment of the new State without misgivings; for it is inconsistent with the grant of the political independence that one part of the inhabitants of a State shall be the victims of the hate, prejudice and intolerance of a majority.[13]

Five days later on November 21, a murderous pogrom began in Lemberg (Polish Lwów; present-day Ukrainian Lviv), carried out largely by Polish forces who had gained the upper hand in the civil struggle against local Ukrainians, and who now turned against the city's Jews, just as Marshall had feared and predicted. Presenting the Jews of Poland as the imminent victims of the hatred of the Roman Catholic Polish majority, Marshall introduced Wilson to a new way of thinking about the ethnographic map of Eastern Europe, not as compact blocs of territory in pursuit of self-determination but, rather, as territories in which every triumph of self-determination produced excluded ethnographic communities who did not belong to the succesful independent majority.

In January 1919, when Masaryk telegraphed triumphant New Year's greetings to Wilson from Prague Castle, Paderewski in Warsaw was feeling less secure in his American connections. He wrote to Colonel House on January 12, somewhat petulantly, that "I have telegraphed you several times, but evidently not one of my messages has reached you." The Polish-Soviet war was about to begin, and Paderewski, pleading for military assistance, cast Poland as the victim of Soviet aggression, Ukrainian violence, and German defamation:

> Contrary to the rumors originated by the untiring pro-German propaganda, the Poles have been nowhere the aggressive party. Though claiming most legitimately the exclusive possession of Dantzig [Gdańsk] as an indispensable condition for their political, commercial, and economic life, they all rely with unshaken confidence on the results of the peace-conference and do not intend to surprise the delegates by any *fait accompli*. But could anyone ask them to remain quiet when brutally attacked and not to defend themselves? Surprised by the murderous Ukrainian Bolshevik army, the women and children of Lemberg took up arms and defended the city. At the present moment a force of 80,000 Ukrainians, armed and equipped by the Germans, led by German and Austrian officers, under the command of the Austrian Archduke, Wilhelm of Habsburg, is at the gates of Lemberg . . . [14]

While The Inquiry had already noted for Wilson that German, Jewish, and Ukrainian minorities were at risk in independent Poland, Paderewski countered by affirming that German propaganda, Habsburg intrigue, and Bolshevik aggression were preparing to victimize Poland while pretending to vindicate Ukrainian national rights in Eastern Galicia.

Petitioning House for food and arms, as well as diplomatic support, Paderewski depicted a Europe poised between civilization and barbarism, for Bolshevik victory would mean that "our entire civilization may cease to exist," and, consequently, "the war may only result in the establishment of barbarism all over Europe." For Paderewski the postwar transformative moment was fraught with the possibility of a new barbarism, originating in Eastern Europe but undermining the peace settlement in all of Europe. "Kindly forgive this chaotic writing," Paderewski concluded, though the threat of chaos was precisely what he wanted to evoke.[15]

On January 21 Lansing was notified by Paderewski that he had formally become prime minister and foreign minister of the provisional Polish government. Wilson was acknowledged as "the first to proclaim the resurrection of Poland." Paderewski continued: "Free at last thanks to the generous efforts of the United States and the Entente Powers, Poland aspires to cooperate as one of the Allied nations in the great task of all civilized democracies in the suppression of anarchy the greatest enemy of civilization."[16] What Paderewski understood as the suppression of anarchy and defense of civilization—most obviously in resisting Soviet Bolshevism—would be understood by the peacemakers in Paris as seizing opportunities to extend the Polish borders. This came up in the discussions of the Allied Supreme War Council the very next day, on January 22:

> Mr. Balfour expressed the opinion that among the many difficulties the greatest would be to get the Poles to accept a restricted programme. He felt that this would have to be imposed upon them. The Poles were using the interval between the cessation of war and the decisions of the Peace Congress to make good their claims to districts outside Russian Poland, to which in many cases they had little right.[17]

This interval between the end of the war and the conclusion of the peace was fraught with frustrations for the peacemakers who saw themselves at risk of losing control of the map. The Poles appeared to be redefining borders in Eastern Europe according to their own priorities.

Wilson himself was anxious about the Poles, and worried that if Polish troops in France were sent to assist the Polish government in Warsaw, those troops would then occupy territories whose ultimate sovereignty ought to be determined by the peace conference. He drew a comprehensive map of what such military moves would mean for Eastern Europe as a whole:

> With the object of sending Polish troops into Poland we were going to prejudge the whole Polish question. This question, moreover, should not, he [Wilson] thought, be isolated from all others. Many other questions resembled it. The Roumanians, for instance, were taking action of a similar kind. The Serbians also were behaving towards Montenegro in what appeared to him to be a questionable manner. The Hungarians also were trying to bring about a *fait accompli* before the termination of the Peace Congress. If we were to say to the Poles, "You must hold your hand," the same must be said to the rest. They must all be told that they prejudiced their case by premature action.[18]

Thus, from Poland to Montenegro, across the entire domain of Eastern Europe, Wilson was now aware that national self-determination was going to be a competitive game, and that the application of his principles to the blank slate of the map was a barely sustainable fantasy that depended upon pure intentions, national restraint, and neatly interlocking claims. The *fait accompli* represented, inevitably, the vitiation of the blank slate, the disruption of the Wilsonian remapping of Eastern Europe. The president, whose sympathy had been so famously engaged by the "aspirations" of the small nations of Eastern Europe, now believed that those aspirations had to be comprehensively restrained in the hope of achieving some sort of national justice for the entire region.

Wilson was willing to put in a good word for Paderewski ("President Wilson pointed out that M. Paderewski, in his letter, had undertaken not to surprise the Powers by a *fait accompli*, or attempt to obtain one in Dantzig"), but he certainly did not embrace Paderewski's assertion that Polish arms were the only thing that stood between Europe and anarchy.[19] Lansing wrote that same day to Paderewski recognizing the new Polish government "with that spirit of friendliness which has in the past animated the American people in their relations with your countrymen"—but the spirit of friendliness was already being qualified with reservations that followed from Wilson's new awareness that Polish independence was less straightforward than it had originally seemed at the time of the Fourteen Points.[20]

At the beginning of February a delegation from the Jagiellonian University of Kraków came to Paris to award Wilson an honorary degree—but without a proper diploma, since there was no parchment available; the delegation promised to send the diploma "as soon as they could get some parchment."[21] Wilson went back to the United States without his diploma in February, and continued to affirm his support for Poland, asking his audience in Boston, "Do you believe in the Polish cause, as I do?" He followed this, however, with another rhetorical question to the Bostonians: "Are you going to set up Poland, immature, inexperienced, as yet unorganized, and leave her with a circle of armies around her?"[22] He pleaded for a military guarantee of the peace settlement "by the united forces of the civilized world," including America. Yet the characterization of Poland as "immature, inexperienced, as yet unorganized" would hardly have sounded flattering to the Poles, and even seemed implicitly to exclude them from the "civilized world" that would have to guarantee the settlement.

■ ■ ■

"The unhappy status of the Jews of Eastern Europe"
In 1918, an American Jewish Congress was established, representing a broader constituency of immigrant Jews than Louis Marshall's American Jewish Committee. The Congress represented American Jews from Eastern Europe, while the Committee was more related to the world of German Jews in America. In March 1919, Rabbi Stephen Wise, one of the founders of the Congress, sent an appeal to Wilson—"we respectfully direct your attention to the unhappy status of the Jews of Eastern Europe"—and submitted a memorandum that discussed under successive headings "The Present Status of the Jews of Eastern Europe," "The Effect upon the Jews of the Organization of New and Enlarged States in Eastern Europe," and "The Guarantees Required by the Jews to Secure for Them Fundamental Human Rights."[23] The Congress memorandum offered a particularly powerful mapping of the domain of the future peace settlement, inasmuch as the case of the Jews offered Wilson a very general geographical

characterization of the region, transcending national boundaries—"the Jews of Eastern Europe"—thus helping to define for the president the vast and blank space of Eastern Europe which was about to be reconstituted as a domain of new national states with Jewish minorities.

Wilson was considered generally sympathetic to Jews in America; in 1916, he had appointed the first Jewish Supreme Court justice, Louis Brandeis. The president's perspective, however, was not uncomplicated or fully informed. When Wilson discussed Jews with his wife Edith and with Colonel House—"how ubiquitous Jews were; one stumbled over them at every move"— the president guessed that there might be a hundred million in the whole world, and was surprised to learn from the almanac that there were only thirteen million.[24] His interest in the numbers prepared him to receive representations on behalf of the Jews as a minority in need of support and protection, and the counting of the Jews could also be correlated with his interest in the ethnographic mapping of Eastern Europe.

The "Jews of Eastern Europe" appeared as a religious and ethnographic community that could be counted across national boundaries: "They constitute in the aggregate seven million souls, more than one-half of all of the Jews of the world," the American Jewish Congress memorandum noted. "They and their ancestors have resided in the lands which they now inhabit for centuries." When touched by the secular state, however, "they have been subjected to discriminatory laws and regulations and have been regarded as occupying the status of an inferior people."[25] The creation of the new states of Eastern Europe thus offered an opportunity for emancipation but also presented the danger of new discrimination.

In Romania, Jews had been systematically denied citizenship ever since independence in 1878, as the Congress memorandum observed. In the case of Poland, the memorandum focused on the record of Roman Dmowski who, together with Paderewski, would represent Poland at the peace conference: "The political organ of Mr. Dmowski has unceasingly denounced the Jews as aliens and foreigners, taking precisely the same position as that of the Roumanians." The memorandum therefore called for equal rights for Jews in the new states, focusing especially on Poland and Romania, but using these to generalize also across "the entire Eastern

European territory."[26] That the Polish National Committee promised such rights for all "Polish citizens" was simply a "loophole for evasion," inasmuch as it did not specify that all residents would be citizens, while at the same time "Roumania has promulgated a decree which, while pretending to emancipate the Jews, is couched in such phraseology as to make the grant practically valueless, because of the proofs required to establish the nativity of the Jews of Roumania."[27] The national claims that were being laid out for the establishment or enlargement of the states of Eastern Europe were, according to the memorandum, cynically calculated to deprive Jewish residents of their rights within the newly emerging political frameworks.

"If the age-long sufferings and legal disabilities of the Jews are to cease and of all the people of the earth they are not to be the only ones to be deprived of freedom," the Congress memorandum argued, "it becomes the bounden duty of the Peace Conference to emancipate them and to give to them a charter of liberty." Like the American Jewish Committee, the Congress focused on the need for all residents to be recognized as citizens and all citizens to hold equal rights, while protecting the rights of Jews to use the Yiddish language, work on Sundays, administer their own religious and educational institutions, and obtain "minority representation" in the new political constitutions.[28] It was observed that "national rights" in Eastern Europe involved "certain rights, which may be called cultural or communal for want of a better term," and which pertained to Jews in a manner that went beyond the strictly religious sense—and most notably in "the conditions which prevail in Eastern Europe, where many nationalities are intermingled, where religion and life are interwoven." Citing the analogous case of the Ruthenians (or Ukrainians) as a minority in Poland, the memorandum insisted that "account must be taken of the newly formulated and intense desire of all of the various ethnic minorities in Eastern Europe to preserve their cultural identity."[29] The Congress thus identified the Jews of Eastern Europe in a highly modern and theoretically secular sense as an ethnic minority seeking to preserve its cultural identity, indeed the most pervasive ethnic minority in Eastern Europe as a whole, even as ethnic majorities were seeking to create and consolidate national states.

The prospective establishment of national majority states on the new map of Eastern Europe—in accordance with the Wilsonian principle of self-determination—thus became the moment for creating and defining minority rights, according to the Congress memorandum:

> The peoples of Eastern Europe are all of them suppliants for political rights. Poland, Roumania, Czecho-Slovakia, and Jugo-Slavia are suing for sovereignty and for enlarged boundaries. Nobody will begrudge them the realization of their dreams. The Jews of Eastern Europe also come to present their cause for adjudication. They are not seeking sovereignty or specific privileges, but merely justice. . . . They behold in the Peace Conference their last opportunity to secure those rights which are conceded to all other men. . . . Unless they now secure what they have so long sought, in terms which cannot be evaded, they will be the only people living in supposedly civilized lands who would be deprived of the simplest, and yet the most precious, of human rights—civil, political, and religious liberty.[30]

The American Jewish Congress presented Wilson with a highly comprehensive mapping of the new field of geopolitical operations in Eastern Europe, comprehensive precisely because the Jews of Eastern Europe did not belong to a sharply defined political domain. The covering of the map of Eastern Europe with claims for sovereignty based on self-determination concealed a more complicated and submerged map of "Eastern Europe, where many nationalities are intermingled"—and where the national triumph of majorities simultaneously defined the minorities who would not participate in the new national sovereignties. Eastern Europe thus became, potentially, the terrain of the "supposedly civilized lands"—as the peace conference created states that would be sovereign but not necessarily civilized.

In a separate memorandum, the American Jewish Congress endorsed the Zionist movement, affirmed that "Palestine is the historic home of the Jews," and applauded the Balfour Declaration of 1917. This memorandum also recognized, however, that "Palestine is not large enough to contain more than a part of the Jews of the world," and most would therefore remain "where they now abide," that is, in Eastern Europe, and in need of the guarantee of equal rights.[31] The Zionist leader Chaim Weizmann had already written to Wilson about Palestine in January 1919, expressing appreciation on behalf of the Zionist organizations in Warsaw, which cherished the implications of Wilsonian principles for Jews in Poland. They expressed gratitude to Wilson for "giving to all oppressed nations the possibility to live and develop freely." Wilson was thus saluted by the Jews of Poland (looking to "the accomplishment of your sublime programme") even as he was lobbied by American Jews on behalf of the Jews of Eastern Europe.[32] Like other immigrant American communities, Jewish Americans looked to their own political presence in the United States to shape the president's mental map.

The American Jewish Congress warned Wilson that the peace conference presented a window that would otherwise slam shut on "the last opportunity" for Jews to achieve national justice:

> It is inconceivable that any State shall be permitted to reduce to practical slavery or to a state of helotism any part of its population. It would be a travesty upon justice and a sorry awakening from that spiritual exaltation which has won this war in the cause of humanity, if the Jews of Eastern Europe, the descendants of the oldest of the civilized races, were to be the only ones who would have no lot or part in a regenerated world.[33]

The Wilsonian conception of the moment emphasized emancipation and regeneration, but the rights of minorities became one of the awkward issues that marred, and ultimately deflated, the heightened sympathies of spiritual exaltation that Wilson channeled into his new mapping of Eastern Europe.

■ ■ ■

"The Polish state of mind"
In March 1919, Lansing and House, joining together with two other members of the American delegation, General Tasker Bliss and Henry White, wrote to Wilson about the need to appoint a diplomatic minister to the Polish government "as a demonstration to the Polish people of the friendship and support of the United States." It was noted that recent developments

"have unavoidably produced the impression in Poland that the Allies and the Associated Governments are indifferent or even unfriendly to the Polish cause, and a widespread and insidious campaign has been carried on from certain quarters to spread the idea that our Government in particular has altogether changed its attitude towards Poland." It was therefore essential "to dispel such impressions or to refute such slanders through the presence of an American Minister in Warsaw," especially since "the Polish Government is in need of friendly counsel, and it is particularly disposed to defer to the advice of the United States."[34] The need for such a broadly signed joint letter to the president suggests that Wilson himself was seen by his advisers as part of the emerging problem in Polish-American relations, and, in fact, Wilson's perspective on Poland was evolving in the direction of more critical complexity in some contrast to the seemingly unqualified enthusiasm of his wartime advocacy. Lansing and House were rightly concerned about a perceived change of American attitude, and therefore urged the continued cultivation of Polish-American friendship. Hugh Gibson, who had been working with Herbert Hoover on war relief, was appointed Envoy Extraordinary and Minister Plenipotentiary to Warsaw in April.

In discussion with Lloyd George at the conference on March 19 Wilson expressed his sympathy for Poland as a matter of "anxieties" over minority populations.

> President Wilson said that it must be realised the Allies were creating a new and weak state, weak not only because historically it had failed to govern itself, but because it was sure in future to be divided into factions, more especially as religious differences were an element in the situation.... The desire might arise among the Germans to rescue German populations from Polish rule, and this desire would be hard to resist. It was a question of balancing antagonistic considerations.[35]

The application of the principle of national self-determination, Wilson had learned, was rarely straightforward, but would always involve antagonistic considerations of relating majority to minority.

Even as Eastern Galicia, with its largely Ukrainian population, was being claimed by the new Poland, Wilson communicated with Lansing, also on March 19, about the prospect of meeting with a Ukrainian representative in Paris: "He [Wilson] hesitates to receive Mr. Sidoresko [Grigory Sydorenko] . . . because so far as he remembers our government has not recognized the Ukrainian Republic, and yet it would seem that to see these gentlemen would afford a useful opportunity to give them a warning about Lemberg."[36] Since Sydorenko served under Symon Petliura's government in Kiev, he was presumably to be warned against trying to extend Ukrainian sovereignty to the Galician lands claimed by Poland, but Wilson was also aware that the Ukrainians had a plausible ethnographic claim to those lands.

Lansing advised Wilson not to meet with Sydorenko and had already "referred the entire matter to Professor Lord, the member of the American Mission who has recently returned from Warsaw and Lemberg."[37] Lord was Archibald Cary Coolidge's Harvard protégé, and the referral of the Ukrainian matter to his academic expertise would inevitably lead to a more complicated view of the ethnographic circumstances. After evading a presidential meeting with the Ukrainian representative, Wilson asked Lansing to "find means to communicate to the groups of gentlemen representing Ukrania and Poland here in Paris the whole purpose and temper of the discussion yesterday with regard to Lemberg."[38] It was Lord who was assigned to make that communication, since it was his expertise that would evaluate the rival claims to Galicia.

On March 31, General Tasker Bliss wrote to inform Wilson of a truce in the fighting between Poles and Ukrainians around Lemberg, noting that "with those 'cranky' people fighting may be resumed at any moment."[39] Bliss obviously expected Wilson to recognize the Poles and the Ukrainians as truculent and "cranky"—with some suggestion of an immature, childlike temperament. This was certainly not the language of reciprocal sympathies, but rather suggested a distinctive emotional vocabulary for discussing the peoples of Eastern Europe. A few days later in the Council of Four, Wilson remarked, "It seems that our disagreeable friends the Poles raise a new difficulty about the truce which they must conclude with the Ukrainians."[40] He had been consulting with Lord about what sort of admonishing telegram should be sent to the Poles, and the oxymoron of "disagreeable friends" seemed to have acquired some casual currency in the circle surrounding the president.

In the Council of Four, Wilson was now leaning toward the idea of Danzig as a free city, separate from Poland, but warned the other three leaders that "when I earlier mentioned to M. Dmowski the hypothesis of Danzig as a free city, he hit the ceiling." The Poles were presumed to be entirely temperamental, and Wilson, on April 1, had come to believe that, in spite of the principle of self-determination, the Poles themselves should not necessarily be consulted about their own sovereignty issues, as in the case of Danzig.

> CLEMENCEAU: We cannot take a definite decision on this subject without the presence of the Poles.
> WILSON: No, but we can agree among ourselves beforehand.
> LLOYD GEORGE: I believe that it would be vain to hope to satisfy the Poles.
> WILSON: They must accept the solution that we judge reasonable.[41]

The cranky and disagreeable peoples would not necessarily determine their own borders, nor even be fully consulted; they would receive those borders from the reasonable arbiters of the peace conference.

Such were the wages of crankiness in the Wilsonian settlement, and Poland, initially the most favored of Wilsonian causes, was now regarded with considerable reserve. "We must not allow ourselves to be influenced too much by the Polish state of mind," Wilson commented. "I saw M. Dmowski and M. Paderewski in Washington, and I asked them to define for me Poland as they understood it, and they presented me with a map in which they claimed a large part of the earth."[42] No one was readier than Wilson to discuss maps, but he now also understood that national mapping existed altogether as a "state of mind," and that considerations of ethnography could be governed by a hyperbolic perspective. Dmowski and Paderewski, in spite of Wilson's special fondness for the latter, were linked together in their extravagant mappings according to a communally Polish state of mind.

■ ■ ■

"One of those indentations in the drawing of the frontiers"
Archibald Cary Coolidge was determined to consider the engineering of new frontiers in relation to the creation of new national minorities. In his March 1919 memorandum on "The New Frontiers in Former Austria-Hungary," he argued, with mathematical reference to Czechoslovakia, that "many Germans will have to be citizens of the new Bohemia in any event, but the number should be cut down wherever this can be done without subtracting a considerable number of Czechs from the population."[43] On April 1, Coolidge summed up the whole theoretical problem for Wilson with a "Memorandum on the Rights of National Minorities," in which he declared that "it is urgent that some understanding should be reached and proclaimed by the Conference as to what constitutes at least the minimum of these rights, political, linguistic, religious." He stated frankly that the incorporation of minorities, as in the case of the Germans of Czechoslovakia, was, in some sense, a violation—even if seemingly necessary—of the principle of self-determination. He used Czechoslovakia as his example, even though the case of Poland was creating even more controversy at the conference. "There are today many millions of people who are about to be handed over to or left under the rule of others with whom they are at present in deep enmity and from whom they can see no reason to expect generous treatment in the future," Coolidge observed, and he actually proposed that each country's claims should be weighed partly with reference to the guarantees given for minority rights.[44]

The peacemakers, Coolidge suggested, needed to issue a declaration that "will tranquillize apprehensions and will serve as some sort of guarantee." He called for "a statement of the broad principles of human rights which should and must prevail in assuring the new national minorities the life, liberty and pursuit of happiness to which they are entitled and which now seem so gravely menaced."[45] The principle of minority rights was thus invoked to remedy complications in the application of Wilsonian principles to the map of Eastern Europe, inasmuch as the sympathetic furthering of some national aspirations frustrated others. The moment of peacemaking, therefore, had to balance the national principles of self-determination and minority rights. In his April 1919 memorandum to the Italians Wilson urged them to avoid the "fatal error" of claiming the eastern Adriatic coast and making the South Slavs into enemies, He offered the assurance that any Italian minority in the Yugoslav state would be secure: "The pledges under which the new states enter the family of nations will abundantly safeguard the liberty, the development, and all the just rights of national or racial minorities."[46] The peacemaking moment was precisely the moment when it was possible to fall into the sort of "fatal error" that would eventually destroy the entire new order, but it was also the moment when, as Coolidge suggested, it was possible to build into that system the safeguards that would secure minority rights and therefore stabilize the system itself.

The issue of minority communities took a vivid and unusual form at the end of March, when an embassy of goatherds from the Tatra Mountains arrived in Paris to plead in person that their districts be assigned to Poland. The mountain districts of Orawa (Orava) and Spisz (Spiš), like the Silesian Teschen region, were disputed between Poland and Czechoslovakia. The Tatra population included Polish and Slovak elements, but also mountaineers who had probably not hitherto contemplated their national identity until this historical moment of constituting national states. The Tatra embassy in Paris made its first impression upon the nose, as Ray Stannard Baker noted:

> I came into my office & found it smelling like a sheep-pen—two peasants from northern Czecho-Slovakia in their home-spun natural wool peasants' clothing—a Polish chaplain was there to interpret. Here is the account: A quaint petition in boots reached Paris today in the form of a party of Polish peasants from the Orawa and Spisz Districts of Northern Hungary [Slovakia]. They object to the proposed plan of annexing them to Czecho-Slovakia and are seeking an audience with President Wilson. . . . The Delegation, wearing suits of thick, white wool felt, gayly [sic] decorated with red embroidery, and high cossack caps of black shaggy fur, attracted much attention when they arrived at the Crillon and sought an audience with the President.[47]

The question of whether these mountaineers belonged to Poland or Czechoslovakia was a diplomatic dilemma, but their smell and their apparel placed them clearly on the mental map of Eastern Europe. There was a powerful proximity of animal life, from the smell of the sheep or goats to the white wool felt and black shaggy fur, while the folkloric ornamentation of the red embroidery emphasized an aspect of traditional identity.

The mountaineers presented an image so quintessentially of Eastern Europe that Baker's account could barely conceal its comical perspective on the subject ("a quaint petition in boots"), enjoying the humorous incongruity of such a delegation in Paris with its grand hotels like the Crillon. Baker even quoted in a comical pidgin English one of the visitors "who once lived in Ironton, Michigan, and has forgotten most of his English [and] said: 'We go feet two days, then two weeks train to see your President. Tell him I got boy thirty years old in United States. I like America. I think she help us if she only know.'"[48] There were actually two returned American immigrants in the delegation, identifiable as Piotr Borowy and Wojciech Halczyn. They both participated in a Polish committee defending the Polish claim to the disputed Tatra region. Although the committee chair was the famous turn-of-the-century poet of "Young Poland," Kazimierz Tetmajer, it was the mountaineers Borowy and Halczyn who were sent to make the case to Wilson in Paris. They were accompanied by a Catholic priest, Ferdynand Machay.[49]

The mountaineers were received by Wilson on April 11. According to Machay's account, Borowy stroked Wilson's hand at length through the meeting, while Halczyn said, "We know well that you can do it, and it only depends on you."[50] They understood it to be Wilson's prerogative to decide whether they would be assigned to Poland or live as a minority in Czechoslovakia. The president's aide Cary Grayson offered his own account of the meeting:

> At 10:00 o'clock this morning the President received two Galacian [sic] Peasants, who were accompanied by a Polish priest and Polish astronomer who had taken them in charge. The two men were goat-herds and came from a small mountain community in Galacia, south of the Polish border. They represented two little colonies of Poles, who were desirous of having the boundary line of Galacia, changed so that their homes would be in the new Republic of Poland. These two men were

picturesquely garbed in a native mountain costume, which had not been washed since they first put it on, and they smelled very strongly of their herds of goats that they had left in their native hills. They deserved a great deal of credit. They had heard that the President was in Paris, so they set out each separately from his own little village and met on the highway. They were walking toward Warsaw and they met the astronomer, who accompanied them and who showed them the way by the stars at night in their long walk. At Warsaw the Polish authorities took them up and arranged for them to come to Paris, but they defrayed the cost of their trip from their own savings. The Bishop interpreted their remarks for the President, and the President thanked them for coming so far to see him. Their meeting with the President was one of the most touching scenes I have ever witnessed. They said they had come to ask the President—the biggest man in all the world—to see that they were turned over to Poland and not to Cheko-Slovia.[51]

Their origin in the Tatra mountain range, within the Carpathians, was here designated as Galicia which was itself misspelled as "Galacia," the most vaguely imaginable place for Grayson who envisioned a mapping of Poland that could only be primitively negotiated on foot and according to the position of the stars. For all the implied comedy of the circumstances, as described by Grayson and Baker, there was also no doubt that the presence of such a picturesque delegation offered a sentimental affirmation of the bond of sympathy between Wilson and the peoples of Eastern Europe.

What made the meeting with the mountaineers so striking, however, was the encounter between the odorous reality of Eastern Europe and the abstract principle of self-determination that Wilson almost embodied. He appeared to them as the arbiter ("it only depends on you") of their possible political futures, Poland or Czechoslovakia, union with their chosen national community in a common national sovereignty or consignment to national minority status in their remote mountains. That same afternoon Wilson would have lunch with Queen Marie of Romania, who came late and infuriated him, coloring his map of Eastern Europe in quite a different way.

Wilson spoke of the goatherds the next day, on April 12, in the Council of Four when discussing the conflicting claims of Poland and Czechoslovakia:

> I must tell you how moved I was yesterday by a visit of a group of Polish peasants who came from their country, having traveled 60 kilometers on foot to the nearest station, and whose villages had furnished them the funds necessary for the trip. They begged me to see to it that the line of the frontier unites them to Poland, their country, and not to make them subjects of the Czechoslovak Republic. Their simplicity and passion were touching. This is a case of one of those indentations in the drawing of the frontiers about which it is so difficult for us to decide.[52]

Just as his rage at the tardy Romanian queen made him imagine lopping off slices of the Dobruja for Bulgaria's benefit (before Bulgaria was dubbed "the most avaricious and brutal of the smaller nations"), so his emotional response to the goatherds made him ready to contemplate indentations on the map at the point where his principle of self-determination intersected with his sentimental sympathies.

The interplay of principles and emotions was on display in the Council of Four that same day, as the peacemakers discussed the Marienwerder region of West Prussia, surrounding Danzig at the mouth of the Vistula River.

LLOYD GEORGE: It would be contrary to all our ideas to leave within the Polish State a territory so obviously German, and which has always been a part of ancient Prussia.

CLEMENCEAU: You cannot imagine Paderewski's emotion; it went even to tears.

WILSON: Yes, but you must take account of his sensitivity, which is very lively.

LLOYD GEORGE: After all, the Poles are assured of independence after a century and a half of servitude. If they do not believe themselves capable of surviving because we refuse them a small territory which contains 150,000 Germans!

WILSON: I would favor giving M. Paderewski a declaration signed by us, explaining our motives, in order to make the Poles understand that we have acted without any desire to favor their enemies, but on the contrary, in order to preserve them from future danger.[53]

Regardless of whether Paderewski's "sensitivity" was supposed to be that of a great musician or the political sensitivity of a Polish nationalist leader, there was something implicitly patronizing about Wilson's suggestion of a declaration to "make the Poles understand" that the judgment of the conference was for their own good.

Lansing wrote to Wilson the next day, after seeing Paderewski, that "in connection with the Teschen situation I suggested that Poland and Bohemia should attempt to reach a friendly settlement between themselves if possible as it would leave a much better feeling than if it was settled by others." The secretary of state also worried that dissensions were being exploited by the French, who sought to present France as "the ultimate arbiter between the new states of Eastern Europe," and "who are making all sorts of promises to the various nationalities."[54] Lord, the academic expert on Poland, focused on the issue of arbitership in a memorandum of April 13, anticipating the cessation of Polish-Ukrainian hostilities in Eastern Galicia and the imminence of a geopolitical settlement:

> This final settlement is now close at hand; but in beginning their deliberations upon the future political status of Eastern Galicia, the Allied and Associated Governments more than ever feel it necessary that the present hostilities should cease. For they cannot permit the interested parties to attempt to anticipate their decision by creating *faits accomplis*.[55]

The continuation of fighting—between Poles and Ukrainians over Galicia, between Hungarians and Romanians over Transylvania—compromised the peacemakers' capacity to impose their principles freely upon the map of Eastern Europe.

Lord, though generally friendly to Poland, was persuaded, and sought to persuade Wilson, "that the Polish High Command should at once agree to confine itself henceforth to a purely defensive attitude pending the conclusion of the armistice." He noted that the Allies should have considerable credit with the new Polish state (created with their support) and that Poland was peculiarly dependent upon the good will of the peacemakers, and therefore should feel "the importance, particularly at such a moment, of maintaining the utmost harmony between Poland and the Allied Powers."[56] For Lord, the problem of Polish claims also came up in his earlier memorandum on the Baltic countries of Estonia, Latvia, and especially Lithuania—where Poles and Lithuanians claimed some of the same territory, including the city of Vilnius (Polish Wilno), just as Poles and Ukrainians both aspired to govern Lemburg (as either Lwów or Lviv). Concerning the Baltic nations, Lord affirmed that "the peoples in question, being distinct and non-Russian races, are as much entitled as Poland to separate consideration" and should therefore be able to make their cases at the peace conference.[57]

Wilson was focused on the danger of a Slavic bloc dominated by Russia, while Lord, the professor, was identifying the non-Slavic elements that would appear on the new map of Eastern Europe. Under the principle of national self-determination, the Baltic peoples—in this case, the Lithuanians—were not to be included in either a Russian or Polish state. Paderewski had once told Wilson that the president of independent Poland should also bear the title of "king of Lithuania," thus recalling the former Polish-Lithuanian Commonwealth, but Lord, who had written his doctoral dissertation on the partitions of the Polish-Lithuanian Commonwealth, was skeptical about the reconstitution of such a union. If anyone at the peace conference was a friend of Poland, it had to be *nasz Lord*, "our Lord," as Eugeniusz Romer called him. Friendship for Poland and sympathy for the Poles was, however, giving way more and more to the need to discipline those "disagreeable friends" whose national territorial aspirations threatened to jeopardize the comprehensive peace settlement in Eastern Europe.

■ ■ ■

"The State of _____"

On May 1, the Council of Four discussed "New States. Conditions to be accepted by them. Protection of Jews and religious minorities." This subject had been clearly outlined for Wilson by Marshall and then by Wise, representing Jewish American organizations, and just a month before, in April, Archibald Cary Coolidge had submitted his memorandum on national minority rights to the president. Wilson, however, embarked upon the subject in a spirit of understated naïveté: "President Wilson said it had been brought to his attention that the Jews were somewhat inhospitably regarded in Poland."[58] He then proceeded to offer prepared statements of commitment for possible incorporation into imminent treaties, referring unspecifically to "the State of _____," which stood in for any of the new states of Eastern Europe, though he specifically mentioned Poland, Romania, and Czechoslovakia. These statements would charge each state to "accord to all racial or national minorities within its jurisdiction exactly the same treatment and security, alike in law and in fact, that is accorded the racial or national majority"—while also making them promise not to infringe upon freedom of religion and not to permit any member of a religious minority to be "molested in life, liberty or the pursuit of happiness."[59] These were such general principles that the state in question was to be designated by filling in the blank, and therefore particularly appealing to Wilson, who certainly saw himself as a man of general principles. Yet the whole comprehensive structure was clearly modeled on the particular case of Poland, and the emphasis on religion suggested that the minority rights of Jewish populations ("inhospitably regarded") were of particular importance for framing these principles. That the principles were American in inspiration was self-evident from the odd quotation from the principles of the Declaration of Independence, stressing the rights to life, liberty, and the pursuit of happiness.

While the principles remained abstract, the discussion immediately lifted the veil of abstraction and specified not only particular places and peoples but even personalities. Wilson and Lloyd George both claimed to know something about Jews in the Polish lands, while Clemenceau, who had once actually visited Galicia and had written stories about Galician Jews, could lay claim to more direct and concrete knowledge.

> LLOYD GEORGE said that Paderewski had made to him a very able defence of the attitude of Poland towards the Jews, and had pointed out that the Jews had themselves to blame to a considerable extent.

> PRESIDENT WILSON said that the reason the Jews had caused trouble was because in those countries they were not really welcome citizens.... They were only disloyal in countries where they were not treated properly.
>
> LLOYD GEORGE and M. CLEMENCEAU said that the Jews were very good citizens in their countries.
>
> LLOYD GEORGE said that in Poland he understood the Jews were really more efficient men of business than the Poles.
>
> CLEMENCEAU said that in Poland a Pole who wanted to carry out any transaction—for example, to buy a horse—would send for a Jew.[60]

In this remarkable exchange, the Big Three moved from Wilson's abstract statement on the rights of minorities to the general question of whether Jews could be loyal citizens. For Wilson, the issue of "hospitality" and "welcome" were central to procuring "proper treatment"—were indeed questions of sympathy that could only be awkwardly mandated by treaty. By emphasizing hospitality Wilson even seemed to imply that the Jews really were a foreign element within Poland.

Wilson felt strongly that the peace treaty with Germany, which would cede large German populations to the new Polish and Czechoslovak states, would provide the appropriate framework for a guarantee of minority rights. Yet, the peacemakers were not in full agreement as they confronted the relation of majorities to minorities:

> WILSON: A detailed text was prepared on the status of the citizens of Poland.... This plan was drafted after consultation with the representatives of the minorities. What I do not like is that they demand a sort of autonomy for the national minorities.
>
> LLOYD GEORGE: This is a claim of the Jews, who wish to form a sort of state within the state. Nothing would be more dangerous.
>
> WILSON: The reason why I ask that the general stipulations which I just indicated be included in the treaty with Germany is that Poland is incorporating several million German subjects into her territory.
>
> LLOYD GEORGE: In any case, these stipulations must be imposed upon the Poles. There is obviously something to say to justify the hostile feeling of the Poles against the Jews. M. Paderewski told me

that, during the war, the Jews of Poland were by turns for the Germans, for the Russians, for the Austrians, and very little for Poland herself.

WILSON: It is the result of a long persecution. The Jews of the United States are good citizens.

LLOYD GEORGE: It is the same in England.

CLEMENCEAU: And in France.

WILSON: Remember that, when the Jews were outside the law in England, they acted as people outside the law. Our wish is to bring them back everywhere under the terms of the law of the land.[61]

On the one hand the need to protect German minorities had become inextricably tangled with the need to protect Jewish minorities. On the other hand, some open hostility to the Jews (on the part of Lloyd George, for instance) was balanced by the conviction that minority guarantees "must be imposed upon the Poles." Wilson himself was ambivalent: on the one hand, he was opposed to the persecution of Jews, and on the other hand nervous about minority demands for autonomy, which might compromise state sovereignty in the new states of fill-in-the-blank.

David Hunter Miller, the legal adviser to the American delegation, wrote to Wilson on May 3 on behalf of the Committee on the Rights of Minorities, insistent that "provisions binding Poland to an agreement in these matters is essential in the Treaty of Peace."[62] Wilson, in discussion with the representatives of the committee, worried that "anti-semitism in Poland is very sharp; I remind you on this subject of the personal attitude of M. Dmowski." Miller replied with brutal frankness: "You will make Poland sign what you want, provided you ask her for it before the signing of the treaty which gives her her frontiers and her international status." Lloyd George unreservedly embraced this point of view: "I repeat that we have a grip on the Poles as long as the treaty with Germany is not signed."[63] The quid pro quo would be the concession of minority rights in exchange for enlarged borders in the treaty.

This would be the peacemakers' hold on Poland, with its minorities of Germans, Jews, and Ukrainians, over Czechoslovakia with its German minority, and even over Romania, which had such a bad reputation for denying citizenship to its Jewish population and was about to acquire a large Hungarian minority in Transylvania. Romania had been recognized as an independent state since the Congress of Berlin in 1878, but Miller reported in 1919 that "I asked the President whether Romania was considered as a new State for the purposes of our Committee, and he said, 'Yes.'"[64] Romania counted as a new state only because it was acquiring new territories on the new map of Eastern Europe. As the signing of the treaty came closer, Wilson could see clearly that the window was closing, that the new states could only be compelled to conform to his vision as long as their new borders remained unconfirmed by the treaty, that only until then did "we have a grip on the Poles," as Lloyd George frankly remarked.

A few days later, when discussing the peace treaty concerning Austria-Hungary, which would now have to be settled by separate treaties with Austria and Hungary, Wilson was all the more certain that the treaties had to be as comprehensive as possible:

> President Wilson pointed out that once peace was made with Austria and with Hungary, and once these countries had been made separate, and the Treaties of Peace with them had been completed, the present Conference would have no further authority. To leave it to the component parts to arrange matters between themselves would cause very serious trouble.[65]

All the "component parts" of the geopolitical and ethnographic map had to be coordinated and controlled. Wilson had only to contemplate "the personal attitude of M. Dmowski" to understand that, without the guiding intervention of the peacemakers, other forces could easily come into play. In Wilson's mental mapping, Eastern Europe was the domain of "component parts" that could be artfully rearranged ("the State of _____"), the metamorphosis pertaining to the disposition of those components which remained flexibly in play, subject to Wilsonian principles and sympathies, right up until the signing of the treaties, when the interlocking parts would be locked in place.

The presentation of the treaty to the Germans took place on May 7 at Versailles, though it would not be formally signed until June 28. The treaty was, of course, humiliating for the defeated Germans, but, oddly,

NATIONAL MAJORITIES AND NATIONAL MINORITIES

the occasion was made into one of incidental mockery of Paderewski, who committed the mortal Wilsonian sin of being late. Colonel House described his entrance: "Everyone was seated in the room where the Treaty was to be presented promptly by three o'clock except Paderewski, who, as usual, came late. He evidently can not get it out of his head that he is not giving one of his great concerts in which the audience is always supposed to be seated before he enters."[66] The frustrations of trying to discipline the new Polish state, in its territorial ambitions and in its relation to internal minorities, were closely associated with the writing of the German treaty, and it was telling that Paderewski was still being singled out for his tardiness at the ceremonial presentation. His sense of self-importance was perhaps part of what Wilson called "the Polish state of mind" in which

FIGURE 7. This map, probably from late 1918, showed the different parts and pieces of Europe in play, whether claimed or promised, for the peace settlement, also illustrating some of the Wilsonian "points" (like access to the sea for Poland and free navigation of the Dardanelles). The map showed the interlocking parts that had to be puzzled together to create the new Eastern Europe.

Poles claimed not only center stage, like Paderewski, but "a large part of the earth" for themselves.

Cary Grayson offered another account of Paderewski's belated entrance, again interpreted as dramatic posturing:

> As soon as all the delegates had been seated Paderewski, the Polish President, living up to his dramatic training in the United States, attempted a spectacular entry. He stalked through the door at the end of the room, throwing his gray head far back, and essaying a dignified and diplomatic walk. The performance fell flat. Not two people in the room saw him, because just as he came through the door the German newspaper correspondents were escorted through the back entrance, and they proved more of an attraction than did the former pianist. Paderewski endeavored to save the situation by making an elaborate bow toward the front of the room, but even this did not carry inasmuch as at that very particular moment Clemenceau was telling a story to the President and Lloyd George that apparently amused them inasmuch as they smiled broadly. Meanwhile, Paderewski settled down in his seat with a look of utter chagrin covering his features.[67]

In April 1919, Harold Nicolson had seen Paderewski bowing to the public at the Paris Opera and noted with similar condescension: "Paderewski bows and smiles. Not a presidential bow: a concert-platform bow. His wife looks like hell in orchids."[68] Now in May at the peace conference Paderewski's bowing was again perceived as excessively theatrical.

Paderewski had been Wilson's most important Polish national interlocutor going back to the wartime period, and the supposition of friendship between them had been fundamental to Wilson's redemptive friendship for Poland as a whole. Yet the frustrations of the peace conference, which had produced the Wilsonian notion of "our disagreeable friends the Poles" had so thoroughly strained American affection for Paderewski that now he was mocked for his staginess—not a national hero but a "former pianist"—and for the failure of his performance. While it was not actually stated that Clemenceau's funny remark that so entertained Wilson and Lloyd George was at Paderewski's expense, it was casually implied and would not have been out of character.

At this moment, as the treaty was about to be achieved, and the transformative moment approached, Paderewski was consigned to "utter chagrin," a man without a friend. While "not two people saw him," his embarrassing entrance was recorded by at least two people, and he was allowed to "represent" Poland by being rendered ridiculous. The Americans in Paris, and Wilson especially, had clearly decided that the honest representation of Poland belonged to the goatherds from the Tatra Mountains and not to the world-renowned concert pianist who so stagily sought to impose himself upon the attention of the peacemakers,

■ ■ ■

"As if to the Hottentots"

In May 1919, a Polish-Ukrainian war was being fought for possession of Eastern Galicia, and the peacemakers in Paris demanded that Poland cease hostilities and let the conference address the issue of the future frontier. Wilson, though he claimed to have confidence in Paderewski, was inclined to affirm the prerogatives of the conference, and was ready to issue an ultimatum to the Polish government. The president contemplated the possibility of making the Polish representatives withdraw from the conference, and even hinted at refusing food relief to Poland through Hoover's American Relief Administration. Back in 1917 Paderewski had declared to Wilson that "the spelling of your name has been the only comfort and joy of a starving nation," and that "millions of people have been feeding on you." Now in 1919 Wilson hesitated to condemn Paderewski in particular:

> MR. LLOYD GEORGE said that M. Paderewski ought to be supported, as he was a very honest and loyal man. He should be given an intimation that if the orders of this Council were not carried out, no further support would be given...
>
> PRESIDENT WILSON said it was important not to give even a superficial idea that M. Paderewski was not being supported. He had played the game straight throughout. The message ought to be sent, not to M. Paderewski, but to General Piłsudski, the Head of the Polish State.[69]

That Paderewski had played the game "straight throughout" did not allay concerns that he had been, in fact, outplayed in Polish politics by such figures as Józef Piłsudski with his military campaign in Ukraine and Dmowski with his militant anti-Semitism. Wilson preferred not to embarrass Paderewski at home by seeming to censure him from Paris, even as Paderewski embarrassed himself by his stagy conduct at the Paris peace conference.

On the same day, May 17, the Council of Four reviewed the report of the Committee on New States for the protection of minority rights in Poland. There was general agreement on guarantees of citizenship, religious freedom, free use of minority languages, and even education in the minority language in particular districts—with future right of appeal to the League of Nations. These guarantees were generally applicable to all minorities, but the committee also found that it needed to include some specific guarantees for Jews, because they were both a religious and an ethnic minority, because they lived all over Poland rather than in particular districts, and because of the alleged intensity of Polish anti-Semitism, which made special safeguards necessary. Most controversial was the question of whether the observance of the Jewish sabbath on Saturday should be guaranteed by treaty as a minority right.[70] David Hunter Miller, addressing himself to this particular issue, felt the committee's recommendations "do not go as far as the American Jews desire, but in my judgment go further than any such treaty has ever gone before"—thus acknowledging that the concerns of American Jews played a fundamental role in shaping the recommendations, not just on Jewish rights, but on minority rights in general.[71]

Wilson himself drew attention in the Council of Four to the controversial proposal concerning the protection of the Jewish sabbath, that is, the particular clause that would forbid Poland from holding elections on Saturday lest Jews feel unable to cast a ballot—"which otherwise would amount to a virtual disenfranchisement of the Jews." This had been endorsed by the British delegation, with the support, among others, of the Polish-Jewish emigrant to England Lewis Namier, eventually to become a famous historian of British electoral practices. Wilson, a serious Presbyterian, seemed to worry, however, that Christians might have to vote in

Sunday elections. It is also possible that Wilson, as a Virginian president in an age of poll taxes and literacy tests, might not have been shocked by the various forms of disenfranchisement. Lloyd George, approaching the sabbath issues from the point of view of a Liberal Party leader, worried that a minority guarantee "to allow Jews to work on Sunday would be regarded as an unfair advantage against the Christians"—which happened to be "the feeling in England, as regards the opening of Jewish shops."[72] Both Wilson and Lloyd George worried over the possibility that minority guarantees could actually privilege minority populations over the national majority.

Wilson remained inclined to make concessions to Jewish concerns, however, and not only because of pressure from Jewish American organizations: "President Wilson said he not only had a friendly feeling towards the Jews, but he thought it was perfectly clear that one of the most dangerous elements of ferment arose from the treatment of the Jews. The fact that the Bolshevist movement had been led by the Jews was partly due to the fact that they had been treated largely as outlaws."[73] Wilson's "friendly feeling" for the Jews, his supposed personal sympathy, was balanced, as in the case of the Slavs, by his political anxiety over Bolshevism, a fear that the Jews (like the Slavs with their ethnic relation to Russia) might be drawn into a broad and menacing Bolshevik coalition of peoples. Minority guarantees for the Jews, like the Adriatic settlement for the Yugoslavs, would be partly focused on managing the postwar transformation in such a way as to tilt the balance of sympathies in Eastern Europe toward the Western agenda of the peacemakers. The Jews and the Slavs were crucial ethnographic elements in Wilson's mental mapping of the balance between Eastern Europe and Western Europe.

In May 1919, one year after he helped found the American Jewish Congress and one year before he helped to establish the American Civil Liberties Union, the Harvard law professor Felix Frankfurter forwarded for Wilson's inspection ("I wonder if this is not a letter that the President would like to read") a report from Warsaw decrying the anti-Semitic persecutions allegedly taking place. "There are more than a million Jews in the New Poland being starved and persecuted to death," Frankfurter's unnamed correspondent in Warsaw wrote. He described the "horrors" of Jewish life, facing starvation, disease, persecution, and murder, thus marking with new emphasis Wilson's mental map of the "New Poland" that was coming into being. The Warsaw correspondent, presumably with Frankfurter's endorsement, demanded minority rights guarantees for Jews in Poland, and, further, declared that "the Polish Government must be bullied and brow-beaten into quitting its policy of extermination and persecution."[74] Frankfurter, who had been born in Habsburg Vienna before emigrating to the United States, and who was also present in Paris in 1919 as a representative of the Zionist movement, was naturally attuned to the legal aspects of defining minority rights in Eastern Europe.

A simultaneous letter to Wilson from Louis Marshall reinforced the message of Frankfurter's Warsaw correspondent. While Marshall was focused on the situation of the Jews in Poland—and described pogroms and murders in Pinsk and in Vilnius—he also generalized the Jewish instance as an issue of Wilsonian sympathy and minority rights across Eastern Europe.

> The hopes of all minority groups of Eastern Europe rest upon that whole-hearted sympathy that you have unfailingly evinced for the oppressed. It is, therefore, that I venture to call your attention to the atrocities to which the Jews of Poland and Galicia have recently been subjected—even at the very moment whilst the Peace Conference is engaged in bestowing sovereign powers and extensive territories upon Poland.[75]

Marshall very well appreciated the significance of the present moment of geopolitical plasticity, when the map of Eastern Europe was being remade, and the problem of what it meant to be a vulnerable minority was highlighted against the emerging contours of majority national government.

A few days later Marshall followed up with a second letter to the president, extending the domain of concern from Poland to Ukraine, Lithuania, Estonia, and Latvia, as the sites of recent pogroms: "Those familiar with these lands and with the forces now in operation there, are agreed that unless the Great Powers, as a condition of the official recognition of any new government therein, whatever it be, shall effectively protect the Jewish and other minorities, there will unquestionably result horrors unprecedented in the annals of human atrocities."[76]

Marshall thus focused on the imminent moment of official recognitions attending the new map of Eastern Europe. In addition to general minority guarantees, he further proposed that every new government should be required to give "the pledge that no pogroms shall take place" within its borders, thus imposing upon the governments "absolute responsibility" for pogroms: "whether committed by a mob or otherwise." The governments would represent the majority peoples of Eastern Europe, consistent with the principle of national self-determination, but this representation also implied official responsibility when the majority persecuted a minority. The pledge against pogroms was therefore supposed to mark the foundational moment for the establishment of new governments in Eastern Europe.

While Wilson was being pressed to acknowledge the importance of addressing Polish anti-Semitism at the conference, Vittorio Orlando, on the same day in May that Marshall prophesied unprecedented atrocities, defended Italy's claims before the Council of Four by saying that "he was not a Shylock, demanding his pound of flesh from the Jugo-Slavs."[77] Even among the peacemakers it was possible to speak the language of implicit anti-Semitism. When Harold Nicolson went to Budapest in April 1919, he reported that the communist leader Béla Kun (himself a Jew) was accompanied by "a little oily Jew."[78]

Paderewski, on May 31, wrote to Wilson to protest indignantly on behalf of the Poles, affirming his government's "broad and tolerant views" toward Jews in Poland, and insisting that "Polish tradition has at all times been resplendent of the virtue of tolerance, at times when this virtue was unknown in many other countries."[79] Indeed, in Shakespeare's time the leading role of the Roman Catholic Church in the Polish-Lithuanian Commonwealth was qualified by different degrees of tolerance for its Protestant, Orthodox, and Jewish inhabitants. Now Paderewski claimed that "in most cases the provocative attitude of a fraction of the Jewish population was responsible for these [anti-Semitic] incidents in Poland." While blaming the victims, he also boldly invited Wilson to send an investigative commission, insisting that Poland had nothing to hide: "I appeal to you, Mr. President, to put an end to this unworthy activity, by sending a special mission to Poland in order to investigate and report on the true state of things, thus dispelling the accusations, under which my country is labouring."[80] The appeal was well calculated to engage Wilson's determination to make himself fully informed about the ethnographic map of Eastern Europe, and the work of the Morgenthau commission later in 1919 would partly vindicate the Polish perspective that accusations of anti-Semitic atrocities were overstated. For Paderewski, in May, it was still a matter of attempting to channel what remained of Wilson's attenuated sympathy for Poland. In another context, Eugeniusz Romer fiercely objected to the conference sending investigative commissions to Poland, "as if to the Hottentots."[81] The international monitoring of minorities, to be sure, would always involve some condescending assumptions about the superior civilization of the monitors.

In June, the Council of Four looked beyond the treaties to consider a report on "empowering the Council of the League of Nations to deal with any infraction of the obligations undertaken by Poland for the protection of racial, religious or linguistic minorities."[82] The guarantee of minority rights was to be imposed in making treaties and establishing new states, but enforcement would necessarily go beyond that. The only plausible enforcer was the future League of Nations, and Wilson took the view that any member of the League should be able to bring the charge of infractions against any other. He envisioned a future in which the new states of Eastern Europe would achieve a certain interlocking equality of rights with respect to one another even as they acknowledged the rights of their minorities:

> The Jews in the United States of America, Great Britain, France or Italy were treated just the same as anyone else. The Jews who were likely to disturb the peace of Europe did not reside in these States, but in Eastern Europe. Supposing Poland did not keep her covenants in regard to the Jews, a Roumanian representative would have the right to call attention to it, and vice versa. By this means equality would be established between the different States.[83]

In fact, Romania was perhaps the least likely country to protest over Poland's mistreatment of its Jewish population.

Wilson's conception was based on a sweeping mental mapping of Western and Eastern Europe with respect to Jewish minorities. He suggested that Western Europe and America were in no way susceptible to anti-Semitism, because Jews there were treated "just the same as anyone else." His perhaps inflated sense of benign equality in Western Europe produced, by contrast, an even more emphatic conception of anti-Semitic victimization in Eastern Europe. This was not simply a humanitarian concern, but also a new awareness of the political volatility of national minorities: "the Jews who were likely to disturb the peace of Europe," perhaps by turning to Bolshevism. The Jews of Eastern Europe thus became a matter of concern for the future peace, and the guarantee of minority rights had to disarm that concern without provoking the sensitiveness of the majority populations of the new states.

On May 31, Wilson addressed a plenary session of the peace conference, declaring that "I should be very sorry to have the impression lodged in your minds that the Great Powers desire to assume or play any arbitrary role in these great matters, or presume, because of any pride of authority, to exercise an undue influence." It was simply that the Great Powers would have to provide a military guarantee of the final settlement, and, therefore, "we cannot agree to leave elements of disturbance unremoved, which we believe will disturb the peace of the world." In particular, he cited the rights of minorities: "Nothing I venture to say, is more likely to disturb the peace of the world than the treatment which might in certain circumstances be meted out to minorities." He then made very clear that this was a matter to be inscribed particularly upon the map of Eastern Europe: "I beg our friends from Roumania and from Serbia to remember that while Roumania and Serbia are ancient sovereignties the settlements of the Conference are greatly adding to their territories."[84] Technically, Romania and Serbia were not "new states" but by their enlargement at the transformative moment of the conference they became, for Wilson, new states of the new Eastern Europe.

Wilson responded by name to the objections of Ion Brătianu, the Romanian prime minister who headed Romania's delegation to the peace conference:

> Mr. Bratiano [sic]—and I speak of his suggestions with the utmost respect—suggested that we could not, so to say, invade the sovereignty

of Roumania, an ancient sovereignty, and make certain prescriptions with regard to the rights of minorities. But I beg him to observe that he is overlooking the fact that he is asking the sanction of the Allied and Associated Powers for great additions of territory which come to Roumania by the common victory of arms, and therefore we are entitled to say: "If we agree to these additions of territory we have the right to insist upon certain guarantees of peace. I beg my friend Mr. Kramar, and my friend Mr. Trumbitch, and my friend Mr. Bratiano to believe that if we should feel that it is best to leave the words which they have wished to omit in the Treaty, it is not because we want to insist upon unreasonable conditions, but that we want the Treaty to accord to us the right of judgment as to whether these are things which we can afford to guarantee."[85]

Naming the names of the Czechoslovak, Yugoslav, and Romanian representatives—Karel Kramář, Ante Trumbić, Ion Brătianu—Wilson fitted together the interlocking elements of the map of Eastern Europe, a map that had to be nationally balanced between majorities and minorities, and conceived as a whole at the defining moment of the treaties—for the final map would then be definitive, subject to military guarantee for the long-term future of Eastern Europe. If the new states would guarantee the rights of minorities, the Great Powers would guarantee the borders of the new states. Wilson felt a little bit abashed about presenting himself so frankly as the master of the map, and even declared that "I sometimes wish... that I were the representative of a small Power"—so that he might not be suspected of pride or presumption.[86] He was aware that Lloyd George took some satisfaction in claiming that he, as a Welshman, could well understand the perspective of small nations.

While Wilson was explaining his perspective to Brătianu and Kramář, however, the armies of Romania and Czechoslovakia were invading the territories of Hungary, which was now under the communist government of Béla Kun. Romania and Czechoslovakia were thus crossing the armistice lines and taking the determination of borders—in Slovakia and in Transylvania—into their own hands, and the Council of Four was determined somehow to make them desist.

LLOYD GEORGE: Should we not see M. Brătianu and M. Kramář or M. Beneš about this matter?
WILSON: I do not like to play with ammunition dumps; that can produce explosions.⁸⁷

Wilson's metaphor envisioned the map of Eastern Europe as a terrain covered by potentially explosive sites. Lloyd George's own ethnographic summation of Eastern Europe was similarly volatile: "They are all little brigand peoples who only want to steal territories."⁸⁸ Even as a Welshman, his sensitivity to the concerns of small nations had some limits.

The peacemakers in Paris were ready to try to preserve the borders even of communist Hungary, which also meant preserving their own hegemonic prerogatives.

LLOYD GEORGE: Do not forget that the Hungarians are a proud people and have a great military tradition. Let us summon M. Brătianu.
CLEMENCEAU: I prefer that we settle this question among ourselves. I have had enough of giving advice.
LLOYD GEORGE: The time has come to impose our orders.⁸⁹

The time had come for the peacemakers to impose, not just their orders, but their prescribed order, upon Eastern Europe. Wilson proposed to tell the Romanians: "If you do not observe our terms, which alone make possible a settlement of your own affairs, we will refuse you all assistance from this time on."⁹⁰ As the peacemakers, including Wilson, felt the conference losing its power to shape the new Eastern Europe, they began to think in terms of ultimatums.

Meeting with Brătianu, Kramář, and Beneš the next day, Wilson and Lloyd George insisted that the Romanian and Czechoslovak invasions of Hungary were further consolidating Hungarian support for the Soviet government of Béla Kun. Brătianu responded by affirming a regional knowledge that excluded the Great Powers: "There are questions that we know better than you do, because we are closer."⁹¹ Knowledge about Eastern Europe—its politics and history, its geography and ethnography—became one of the contested issues of the peace conference.

Now that the conference was embarked upon the question of minority rights, every territorial incursion—like those of Romania and Czechoslovakia against Hungary—had to be viewed as creating dangerous new imbalances between majorities and minorities. It was at this important moment in June 1919 that Paderewski offered Poland's protest against minority guarantees. He insisted on the importance of the conference providing by treaty "the confirmation of the sovereignty and independence of the Polish State," and argued that minority guarantees compromised that sovereignty. It was again a question of "we know better than you do, because we are closer"—with Paderewski insisting that current "discord" (that is, anti-Semitism) was provoked by the Jews themselves who "on many occasions sided with Poland's enemies" in the past. This would no longer be possible with Poland becoming definitively independent: "The reconstruction of the Polish State, which must be admitted by the Jews as an established fact, will allow the Polish nation, whose existence will no longer be imperiled by their hostility, to return to her ancient principles respecting the Jewish question." Paderewski, claiming a better knowledge of Polish history, reminded the Western peacemakers that Poland had once been "a refuge to the Jews banished from the West."[92] Above all, Paderewski objected to the idea that any treaty "should admit the intervention of the Chief Powers in her internal affairs," noting that Poland had already experienced the "nefarious consequences" of foreign interference in the age of the partitions. He protested that the whole future development of the Polish constitution would be dependent upon the approval of the League of Nations, overseeing the minority guarantees, thus permanently compromising Polish sovereignty.

Paderewski's objections led to some puzzled conversation among the peacemakers, with Lloyd George feeling that Hebrew (a respectable ancient language) should be taught in Poland, but more skeptical about Yiddish ("as every effort ought to be made to merge the Jews of Poland in Polish nationality, just as the Jews in Great Britain or France became merged in British or French nationality"). Sonnino wondered what sorts of hardships would be caused for Jewish communities if Yiddish were not taught in Polish schools, and Wilson, when asked "what was done in New

York," hazarded a guess that "teachers were appointed, who understood Yiddish, and they gave their instruction in Yiddish."[93] In fact, the New York City public schools offered English language instruction to children from Yiddish-speaking immigrant families. The American literary critic Irving Howe, on his first day of school in the 1920s, was laughed at for speaking Yiddish: "That afternoon I told my parents I had made up my mind never to speak Yiddish to them again."[94] American public education would not have offered a useful model for the guarantee of minority languages in interwar Poland.

For Wilson, however, the chief issue was not the details of the minority guarantee but the simultaneity of that guarantee with the peace treaty, the merging of minority considerations into the transformative moment that would produce the new states of Eastern Europe. Both Henry Morgenthau and Louis Marshall wrote to Wilson on this point, with Morgenthau worrying that if a Polish treaty with minority guarantees were not "signed simultaneously with the German treaty . . . then it may never be signed in its present shape, and minorities will again be exposed to the tyranny and injustice of majorities."[95] The creation of a new map of Eastern Europe compelled Wilson to reflect on the relation of majorities to minorities within the framework of national self-determination.

■ ■ ■

"Something is being done about Ruthenia"
While Wilson's early advocacy of the restoration of Polish independence in the Fourteen Points was complicated by his later recognition of the circumstances of the Jewish minority, the fraying of his sympathetic relation to Poland was no less conditioned by his discovery of the Ukrainians on the map of Eastern Europe. In a meeting of the Council of Four in May 1919, discussing the Polish-Ukrainian war in which Polish armies effectively conquered eastern Galicia with its Ukrainian majority population, Wilson remained persuaded that only Paderewski had the will to desist from conquest and allow the conference to adjudicate the disputed border. He believed that the Polish Sejm (parliament) had opposed itself to Paderewski, now prime minister, and had rejected his pacific inclination. Wilson's reaction was emphatic: "if Poland

continued fighting, he thought that the representatives of Poland ought to be asked to withdraw from the Peace Conference."⁹⁶

Paderewski sent a confidential message to the president from Warsaw on May 14, attempting to shape Wilson's political and ethnographic conception of the Ukrainians. "The Ukrainians are far removed from being what they have pretended," Paderewski wrote, claiming to have heard reports of "the contamination of the Ukrainian Army by Bolshevism." He ingenuously suggested that he himself, like Wilson, was trying to become better educated about the Ukrainians in Galicia:

> Desirous of meeting your wishes, and the wishes of your colleagues, I looked thoroughly into the situation, and I found that the whole of the East Galician country is unanimous in a demand for decisive and energetic action, owing to the numerous crimes which the Ukrainians daily commit in East Galicia, massacres and slaughters which can only be compared to the Turkish crimes in Armenia. . . . The Government is now rendered powerless by the excitement throughout the country. . . . It is not possible to ask quiet and patience of a people at the same moment they are being murdered ruthlessly by Ukrainian soldiers who have turned against their own chiefs, by bandits organized in the hope of plunder, with whom Poland is asked to negotiate as with equals.⁹⁷

Paderewski clearly knew Wilson well when he characterized the Ukrainians not only as Bolsheviks but even as Turks—which certainly would have resonated with the president's Gladstonian affinities and his long-standing sense of an "Eastern Question" characterized by horrors and atrocities. Calling the Ukrainians "bandits," furthermore, fit perfectly with Lloyd George's sense of the "little brigand peoples" of Eastern Europe.

Yet Paderewski's characterization of Ukrainian plunder and massacre of Polish victims resembled nothing so much as the reports that Wilson was hearing simultaneously about Polish plunder and massacre of Jewish victims. These concerted efforts to color (in blood) the president's mental map of Eastern Europe were further intensified, in Paderewski's appeal, by a strong sense of civilizational inequality, of barbarous Ukrainians, with whom one could not negotiate as equals. He offered Wilson his resignation as prime minister, as if Wilson (and not Piłsudski) were the Polish head of state ("I am willing to tender at any moment the resignation of my Government"), while assuring Wilson that this would certainly not halt the military campaign. Paderewski claimed to have confidence in "your sure insight, based on your sublime sense of justice"—but clearly understood that Wilson's insight would be influenced by his ongoing education about the ethnographic mapping of Eastern Europe.[98]

Before the end of May, Wilson was supplied with a report forwarded by Lord from a military observer, Lieutenant Reginald Foster, on the spot in Eastern Galicia. Foster visited the towns of the contested Polish-Ukrainian region, including Chyrów (Khyriv), Sambor (Sambir), Drohobycz (Drohobych), Borysław (Borislav), Strij (Stryi). "In the various towns [we] talked with Ruthenians and Jews as well as Poles," Foster reported. "In Sambor we made a tour by automobile of the surrounding villages, Ruthenian and Polish, and in Boryslaw met the Ruthenian and Jewish representatives on the newly elected town council."[99] It was the sort of detailed information that The Inquiry had been created to acquire, back in 1917, and that Lord, a member of the team under Coolidge, could now produce in a less strictly academic fashion, based on reports from local observers in Eastern Europe. Observation could also offer subjective impressions and partisan conclusions, however, as in this case when Lord's observer Lieutenant Foster reported that, after the allegedly harsh requisitions of the Ukrainian authorities, the Ukrainian peasants were now peacefully tilling their fields and "bore no hostile feelings toward the Poles and expressed themselves glad that they had come to establish order again." Foster further noted that the new Polish authorities would be able to get the oil fields at Borysław working again.[100]

Foster's sympathy for the Poles made him politically skeptical about the Ukrainians or Ruthenians: "It is hard to understand after what I have seen in the last few days how much faith can be put in the ability of these Ruthenian people to govern themselves." He even questioned whether "this Ukrainian movement was really a national movement." Foster offered a radical rereading of the map in which the Ukrainians were ethnographically erased as an illusionary national movement, invented by Germany and Austria as a political expedient—"the backbone of the Ukrainian army was clearly stamped 'made in Germany' with a touch of Austria." Foster was so notably partisan that he ended on an exclamation point: "The fact that the Ukrainians accepted this help showed a sympathy that one does not find in these other newly created countries. And yet we treated them on the same basis as the other countries!"[101] The report was thus aimed precisely at Wilson's conception of the newly created countries on the newly redesigned map of Eastern Europe. This reaffirmation of sympathy for the Poles countered some of the indignant disapproval of the peacemakers as they contemplated the Polish-Ukrainian war. Although Eastern Galicia clearly did not meet Wilson's criterion of "indisputably Polish populations," the conference would ultimately have to accept the military outcome of that war and recognize all of former Habsburg Galicia as part of Poland, albeit with concern for Ukrainian minority rights.

Coming to Paris to speak before the Council of Four in June, Paderewski offered his own convoluted lessons in ethnic geography: "There is some misunderstanding concerning Ukrainia and Galicia. There are two Ukrainias and there is only one Galicia. The people in Galicia pretend to be Ukrainians on account of the similarity of their language with the real Ukrainian people. These people are not Ukrainians."[102] They were Ruthenians, according to Paderewski. He claimed to have done everything he could to cease hostilities, including offering his own resignation, but, in the face of Ukrainian aggression he could not restrain the spontaneous Polish reaction: "We could not keep back those boys of twenty years of age. They went on. They simply marched like a storm." It was Lloyd George who dominated the exchange in the Council of Four, but Paderewski's replies were aimed at Wilson's ethnographic concerns:

> LLOYD GEORGE: Does Poland claim the whole of Galicia? . . .
> PADEREWSKI: We have given autonomy to this country. We claim the whole of Galicia. We claim it for the simple reason that it is absolutely impossible to define ethnographically this country.[103]

Paderewski thus offered an implicit conceptual refutation of the principle of national self-determination, suggesting that some territories might actually be too ethnographically complicated to define for geopolitical purposes.

Lloyd George, however, was intent upon mounting a rhetorical indictment of Poland, which was perhaps also intended for Wilson's benefit:

> Here is Poland that five years ago was torn to pieces, under the heel of three great powers, with no human prospect of recovering its liberty.... Now, you have got at the very least, even if you took every one of these disputed parts away—you have got twenty millions of Poles free, you have got an absolutely united Poland. It is a thing which no Pole could have conceived as possible five years ago; and in addition to that, they are claiming even populations which are not their own.... The Poles had not the slightest hope of getting freedom, and have only got their freedom because there are a million and a half of Frenchmen dead, very nearly a million British, half a million Italians, and I forget how many Americans.[104]

Wilson may not have liked this last piece of forgetfulness, but the thrust of Lloyd George's remarks were intended to set Wilson's own principles as the standard for scolding Paderewski. If Poland felt the pressure of the peacemakers, it was because Poles had failed to acknowledge the gratitude owed to the Allied armies. "If that is what Poles are like, then I must say it is a very different Poland to any Poland I ever heard of," Lloyd George declared, framing a new and jaundiced conference perspective on Poland.[105]

Following this scathing indictment, Lloyd George proceeded to lecture Paderewski on the subject of small nations:

> LLOYD GEORGE: You know I belong to a small nation, and therefore I have great sympathy with all oppressed nationalities, and it fills me with despair the way in which I have seen small nations, before they have hardly leaped into the light of freedom, beginning to oppress other races than their own. They are more imperialists, believe me, than either England and France, than certainly the United States....
>
> PADEREWSKI: I beg to protest emphatically against the accusation that we are imperialists.... We are not imperialists, and we do not want to annex any country or any people. We have never imposed upon any nation or foreign language. We never persecuted any religion. We never imposed upon the people different customs, and the proof

of it is this, that after six hundred years of common life with primitive people, like the Lithuanians, like the Ruthenians, even like the Ukrainians, these people are still existing.[106]

Lloyd George particularly relished the affinity between Wales and Lithuania as small nations ("It is really like setting up Wales as a separate republic—exactly the same population—2,200,000"), and he can not really have liked to hear the Lithuanians dismissed as a "primitive people."[107] For Wilson the characterization of small nations as primitive was similarly problematic, inasmuch as it was the supposed equality of small nations which shaped his peacemaking principles.

In the Council of Four, Lloyd George articulated the dilemma of fraying friendship: "I ought to say that you and I have been very good friends, Mr. Paderewski. I don't want to have any dispute with you. What I mean by imperialism is the annexation of peoples of a different race against their will, or even a people of the same race against their will."[108] Lloyd George was perhaps unsure about whether Poles and Ukrainians should be considered to belong to the same or to different races. For Paderewski, Poles were of different "blood" from Ukrainians, and he emphasized this point as he continued to confront the peacemakers over the Polish-Ukrainian encounter:

> PADEREWSKI: You must find it natural that we try to protect people of our own speech and our own blood if they are attacked, if they are murdered, if they are slaughtered, by Ukrainia and by these people under the Bolshevist regime.
>
> LLOYD GEORGE: They are making the same accusations against your troops. I only saw a Ukrainian once. The only Ukrainian I have ever seen in the flesh was upstairs. I haven't seen another. It is the last Ukrainian I have seen, and I am not sure that I want to see any more. That is all I know about it.
>
> PADEREWSKI: On the day I left Warsaw a boy came to see me, a boy about thirteen to fourteen years old, with four fingers missing on his hand. He was in uniform, shot twice through the leg, once through the lungs, and with a deep wound in his skull. He was one of the

defenders of Lemberg. Do you think that children of thirteen are fighting for annexation, for imperialists? . . .

LLOYD GEORGE: Lemberg, I understand, is a Polish city. They were undoubtedly fighting for a Polish city.[109]

Lloyd George, like the other peacemakers, was discussing the map of Eastern Europe on the basis of abstract and speculative knowledge: "Lemberg . . . I understand . . . undoubtedly." His knowledge of Ukraine and Ukrainians was very limited, as he himself jokingly explained by referring to the only real Ukrainian he'd ever actually met—in Paris at the peace conference—as if it were somehow a comically unsettling encounter which would be better not to repeat. Paderewski responded with graphic and direct knowledge of the people of Eastern Europe, a famous pianist reporting on a boy without fingers.

The contested map of Eastern Europe thus emerged as a problem of speculative and conceptual uncertainty in which the graphic reality of real individuals—wounded children—intersected with the political projection of peoples whose very existence was subject to denial. "The people in Galicia pretend to be Ukrainians," Paderewski declared, claiming intimate knowledge of their identity. To the extent that ethnography was supposed to underlie the application of the Wilsonian principles of national self-determination and minority rights, the peacemakers—like Lloyd George who had only once met a real Ukrainian—found themselves baffled by the projection of phantoms and abstractions. Paderewski's ethnographic entangling of Galicians, Ukrainians, and Ruthenians pointed toward a nihilistic subversion of the Wilsonian principles of self-determination and minority rights, and suggested that greater knowledge of the map of Eastern Europe did not necessarily lead to greater clarity. At the end of June, Wilson was asked at a press conference, "What about Ruthenia?" to which he replied, "Something is being done about Ruthenia, but I am ashamed to say I don't remember what."[110] Possibly the question referred to Carpatho-Ruthenia, adjoining eastern Galicia, and about to be joined with Czechoslovakia, but Wilson would also have heard about Ruthenians in discussions concerning Poland and Ukraine. "Ruthenia" would remain confusedly abstract for him—like

"Ukrainia"—marking the eastern limits of what he could assimilate into his mental mapping of Eastern Europe.

■ ■ ■

Plebiscite in Upper Silesia

Wilson's friendship with Paderewski and sympathy for Poland was complicated by the issue of minority rights with reference to both Jewish and Ukrainian populations as the new Polish borders expanded to their definitive postwar limits (including some five million Ukrainians and three million Jews in a total population of thirty million). In the case of the Ukrainians, the issue was, very crudely, how much territory the Polish armies would occupy, thus determining the size of the Ukrainian minority, and those eastern armies lay, to a large extent, outside the control of the peacemakers in Paris. The peacemakers did, however, have much more to say about the size and extent of the German minority in postwar Poland, and especially with regard to the future sovereignty of the province of Silesia, with its mixed population. Conquered from the Habsburg monarchy by Frederick the Great of Prussia in the 1740s, Silesia offered important coal resources for nineteenth-century German industrialization, and became a territory of disputed interest following the war, given its complex population.[111] Lower Silesia (to the northwest) had a largely German population and would remain with Germany, while Upper Silesia (to the southeast) was divided between German and Polish populations and was contested accordingly. Teschen Silesia, adjoining Upper Silesia, was disputed between Poland and Czechoslovakia as Cieszyn or Těšín. Furthermore, at the peace conference Silesia became one of the speculative laboratories for applying the political technology of the plebiscite to the elaboration of the Wilsonian principle of self-determination. In theory, nothing should have been truer to Wilsonian principles than the process of allowing people to vote for their national sovereignty, and Wilson, at least initially, was fully enthusiastic about this method of determination.

American Progressivism, which had shaped Wilson's political career, frequently looked to voter referendums, state by state, as a means of progressive reform, and Wilson would have recognized sovereignty plebiscites in Europe as a mechanism closely related to the voter referendum in America and a fundamental exercise in the practice of democracy. On May 21, 1919, in the Council of Four, he contemplated the Adriatic dispute between Italy and Yugoslavia and urged that "in the case of the [Dalmatian] islands the only way to settle the question of which population predominated was by a plebiscite since the official statistics were disputed both by the Italians and the Jugo-Slavs."[112] The idea that there could be a higher and more transparent ethnographic truth than statistics was of interest to Wilson; the plebiscite, in principle, could enable a population to produce, on the spot, its own statistical self-representation.

In the Council of Four, the possibility of a plebiscite for the disputed Adriatic territories was discussed alongside that of a plebiscite for Silesia and, analogously, for Anatolia with its mixed Turkish and Greek populations. Wilson was particularly interested in the ways that plebiscites might work as a uniform technique across the evolving map, from Silesia to Dalmatia to Anatolia, and he even came to acknowledge the unanticipated possibility that national self-determination might not correspond perfectly to national identity, that people might vote for a sovereignty that did not correspond to their own personal sense of nationality:

> His [Wilson's] idea was the same as Mr. Lloyd George had suggested in a conversation with him just before the meeting in regard to Silesia, where Mr. Lloyd George had suggested doubts as to whether the population was Polish in sentiment. There might be cases where the preference of the population was stronger than the nationality. For example there might be people in Silesia, who, though Polish in origin, preferred to remain German. The same principle might apply to the Adriatic. On the coast of Asia Minor on the Aegean littoral there was a considerable Greek population. . . . To illustrate this, President Wilson brought out an ethnographical map of Turkey.[113]

Ever the man for maps, Wilson regarded the plebiscite as the potentially ideal corrective to the ethnographic map, while acknowledging that ethnography was a politically malleable, rather than absolutely objective, basis for national self-determination. On May 21, 1919, Wilson was excited about the wide-ranging possible applications of the plebiscite for refining the map of Eastern Europe.

The very next day, however, on May 22, he was compelled to entertain his first doubts about the universal feasibility of the procedure. Even as the Council of Four was preparing its ultimatum to Piłsudski on ceasing hostilities in Galicia, Wilson received a report on Carinthia with its disputed territories between Austria and Yugoslavia. A group of Americans chaired by Colonel Sherman Miles and including Inquiry scholar Robert Kerner had "conducted an investigation in Carinthia to determine the political will of the people in the southeastern corner of that province," to ascertain their preferences for future sovereignty:

> We had a unique opportunity to apply the principle of self-determination practically in the field. For ten days we covered the district, visiting towns and hamlets unexpectedly and talking to people of all classes. We had with us one representative of each of the two sides, and were ourselves able to question the people both in the German and Slovene languages. We found that the majority of the people in the disputed district, though Slovene by blood, called themselves "Wendish" and desired to remain under Austrian rule.[114]

In this case self-determination meant sending a team of Americans to determine what the populations of Eastern Europe really wanted from the political settlement. Having found the Carinthians unexpectedly pro-Austrian rather than pro-Yugoslav, Miles noted: "I understand that the present intention is to permit the people of the disputed area to express their will by a plebiscite five years hence. I believe that this should be done. But the question now is under which Government (Yugo-Slav or Austrian) should the disputed area rest during the next five years?"[115]

Miles meant to suggest that the plebiscite itself might well be influenced by the occupation, whether Yugoslav or Austrian. Since Carinthian "self-determination" in this case had already been established through the informal survey conducted by the American committee, a future plebiscite could only run the risk of making the wrong decision under the influence of the intervening occupation. When the conference eventually accepted that Eastern Galicia would be part of Poland, it was done with the stipulation of a plebiscite for Poles and Ukrainians to be held twenty-five years in the rather remote future.

Postponement was one way of acknowledging that the instrument of the plebiscite was not absolutely reliable in itself but capable of being influenced by the circumstances in which it was held. Wilson worried that the continued German administration of Upper Silesia would prevent the presumed Polish majority from winning a plebiscite. "I have thought about the question of Silesia," Wilson observed in the Council of Four on June 3. "It appears to me difficult to hold a plebiscite in that region. It would be necessary to begin by making all the German officials leave." Furthermore, he objected that "all of Upper Silesia is in the hands of fifteen or twenty German capitalists," and that they would influence the outcome of the vote. Plebiscites, he now realized, would not function freely and produce ethnographically reliable outcomes unless the political and economic circumstances were neutral. "My advisers say that it will not be possible to obtain a truly free and genuine vote from a population which has been so long in a state of vassalage," he said of Silesia.[116] The problem of the ideal plebiscite—uninfluenced by powerful authorities—emerged as an obstacle to holding an actual plebiscite which could only be held under prevailing social and political conditions.

Lloyd George took a different view, insisting that a plebiscite had to be held in Upper Silesia and reassuring Wilson that the Poles would probably win it. For Lloyd George, the plebiscite was above all a matter of legitimizing the decisions of the peace conference, demonstrating that national self-determination was not actually an arbitrary determination made by the peacemakers in Paris on behalf of the populations in Eastern Europe.

> LLOYD GEORGE: Silesia has been detached from Poland for 700 years. All that I ask is that the population have the right to speak for itself on the fate of the region.
>
> WILSON: Exactly; can it do it?
>
> LLOYD GEORGE: It is possible that we would have to occupy the territory during the plebiscite.
>
> WILSON: In this case, the Germans will say that the vote took place under the pressure of our bayonets.

LLOYD GEORGE: That matters little if we ourselves have good reason to think that the vote took place freely. I know what intimidation by great landowners is like; I had some examples of it in Wales.[117]

Wilson could hardly have been more skeptical about whether it was possible to hold a free plebiscite in Silesia, or one that would be perceived as free. He would not allow Lloyd George's special knowledge of the power of great landowners in Wales to pass without a response, and Wilson claimed to understand even better how power and influence could vitiate a free vote. "I have myself lived in a region subject to capitalist influence," he replied, "and I have worked to destroy it; but I can assure you that even today capitalists still dominate the electorate in Pittsburgh."[118] Wilson chose Pittsburgh as his example of a city where self-determination would be impossible—though, ironically, it was the city where, in May 1918, expatriate Czechs and Slovaks had reached the agreement on joint self-determination to create Czechoslovakia.

The jostling between Wilson and Lloyd George now turned a little more hostile as the latter seemed to question the former's commitment to self-determination, with stinging comments about Wilson's reliance on Lord's expertise.

LLOYD GEORGE: No one has proclaimed more forcefully than you have the principle of the rights of peoples to self-determination. It means that the fate of peoples must be determined by the people themselves, and not by a Dr. Lord, who thinks he knows better than they what they want. I am doing nothing but adhering to the Fourteen Points; why, after having decided that there would be plebiscites in Danzig, in Klagenfurt, in Fiume, in the Saar Basin, must we rule out that solution in Silesia?

WILSON: I hold as much as you do to the principle of the right of peoples to self-determination. What I want to avoid is that a Polish population be called upon to make a decision under the influence of Germany and under the aegis of German officials.

LLOYD GEORGE: That is more or less what M. Orlando says when he asserts that a plebiscite in Dalmatia would be worthless because of the pressure exerted by the Yugoslavs.

WILSON: I cannot allow you to say that I am not for the right of peoples to self-determination. That is absurd. What I want to obtain is the true expression of popular sentiment.[119]

This exchange was pointedly antagonistic. Lloyd George knew that Wilson would feel offended at being compared to the Italian prime minister, who refused to accept plebiscites if he feared an unfavorable outcome, and he clearly believed that Wilson was setting such a high standard of purity for the principle of self-determination as to rule out real self-determination in practice.

Wilson now found himself aligned with Paderewski, who also rejected the Silesian plebiscite as untenable, for fear that the Poles might lose. On June 5, the same day that he discussed Galicia with the Council of Four ("we claim the whole of Galicia"), Paderewski was also closely questioned about the disputed territory of Upper Silesia, which, if assigned to Poland, would add significantly to the German minority under Polish government. Wilson noted the value of "the slight redrawing of the boundary so as to leave as many Germans outside of Poland as possible," and explained to Paderewski, "We have been considering a plebiscite under international supervision and under such rules as an international commission should set up, to get the German troops out and any German officials who might be interfering with it."[120] Wilson was now convinced that plebiscites were susceptible to corruptive interference, and he envisioned therefore conditions of hypothetical purity—the blank slate of the transformative moment—when German troops and officials might be removed so that populations could freely express their identities and political choices. Paderewski replied humbly, at first, that "the destiny of my country is entirely in your mighty hands, and you could have very well disposed of it without notifying me about these intentions"—and he was grateful for the notification.[121]

Again, the details of the map remained a Wilsonian preoccupation, and since "the ethnographic map which they were awaiting had not yet arrived," the American president sought further information about Silesia from Paderewski. The Polish leader explained that the German Catholic clergy were particularly influential in parts of Silesia, led by the archbishop of Breslau (Wrocław)—"and the influence of that clergy is most dangerous for us, because those people rule absolutely our people, and in the case of a plebiscite, they would, even in spite of our majorities, amounting in many districts to ninety per cent and more—they would decidedly follow the orders of that German clergy. From that point of view a plebiscite is absolutely impossible."[122] Papal suasion was one of the disturbing forces that Wilson worried about in Eastern Europe, and Paderewski played upon that concern to powerful effect, for while it might be possible to displace German soldiers and officials, the influence of the clergy would be subtler. "We could not really—if we were asked—agree to a plebiscite," declared Paderewski.[123] Clemenceau pressed him on this: "About the plebiscite: Let us suppose that we wouldn't ask for a plebiscite immediately and that in the meantime the country would be occupied by troops of the Entente—suppose Americans, we should say—don't you think that then in that country there would be a great chance to have a fair vote?"[124] Paderewski absolutely did not think so, of course, and his insistence on the impossibility of a fair plebiscite compelled the peacemakers, including Wilson, to consider whether the plebiscite might be a flawed mechanism for self-determination.

A memorandum by Lord, submitted that same day, June 5, acknowledged that "in view of the extraordinary intermixture of population in the eastern parts of Germany and the jagged and sinuous character of the linguistic frontier, it has been impossible to propose a frontier between Poland and Germany which would not contain considerable numbers of Germans." Sympathetic to the Polish cause, Lord rebutted the German objections to the eastern border delineated in the treaty and expressed confidence that the minority rights provision would protect the Germans in Poland.[125] The issue of minorities rendered the application of the principle of self-determination unexpectedly problematic; for Lord, as for Paderewski, some things appeared simply "impossible." The borders that could be inked upon a map would never capture the "jagged and sinuous" commingling and overlapping of populations.

Lord also sent Wilson another memorandum arguing that "a plebiscite in Upper Silesia would not be fair under the present circumstances." The long history of Prussian rule, dating back to the age of Frederick the Great, and involving the presence of German administrators, landowners, industrialists, and clergy, would inevitably condition the outcome of the plebiscite: "the inhabitants of Upper Silesia, although they have been able to maintain their Polish character through six centuries of political separation from Poland, and in spite of the very clear national sentiment of which they have already given proof, would not be able thoroughly to express their aspirations." It might eventually be possible "to make a plebiscite genuinely fair," but only by sweeping programmatic removal of all of the German authorities in every sphere so as "to free the Polish population from all the shackles upon it."[126]

According to Lord, there would have to be a military occupation by Allied armies in Upper Silesia "until the establishment of a definitive new regime." In the meantime "it would be necessary to transform the political administrative, and religious organization of Upper Silesia, to assure to the Poles, by prolonging the new regime for a considerable period, the time necessary to form a free and mature decision about their future."[127] Thus, peculiarly, a new regime would have to be created and maintained in order to reach the point where it might be possible to establish a definitive new regime. It would be necessary to reduce German influence to zero in order for the unshackled Poles to express themselves freely in a plebiscite. This memorandum submitted by his own academic expert compelled Wilson to recognize that the ideal conditions for implementing his ideal principles would be exceptionally elusive—if, indeed, not actually "absolutely impossible," as Paderewski claimed.

■ ■ ■

"Loading the dice"
Plebiscites were held in Carinthia, Schleswig, and East Prussia in 1920, determining the German border at different points. The Upper Silesian plebiscite of 1921 was, however, a disaster from the Wilsonian perspective. This territory with a seemingly Polish-speaking majority voted in favor of Germany, the plebiscite taking place while irregular forces from both sides were fighting against each other, notwithstanding the presence of English, French, and Italian occupation troops. (In June 1919, Wilson had already found "it was very difficult for him to send United States troops

to occupy Upper Silesia during the plebiscite."[128]) Ultimately, the border was determined by the battling of the paramilitary forces rather than by the plebiscite results, and Upper Silesia was divided between Poland and Germany according to the standing of the respective forces on the ground. The prolongation of the transformative moment utterly failed to produce conditions in which self-determination could be neatly derived from a plebiscite vote. After World War II, Lower Silesia was punitively assigned to Poland, along with Upper Silesia, and, in a very un-Wilsonian manner, the German population was simply expelled.

At the Paris Peace Conference in 1919, Wilson was already aware of some of the problematic issues that might make plebiscites unreliable instruments of national self-determination, but on June 11, in the Council of Four, he spoke in favor of a Silesian plebiscite, allowing for an appropriate postponement to erase past prejudicial influences:

> WILSON: (after study of the map): I consider it settled that we adopt the system of the plebiscite after a period of at least one year and two years at most. Dr. Lord has just told me that he had recently received a report from an American who visited Upper Silesia. This witness says that all classes of the population want the plebiscite. Since Dr. Lord personally opposes it, it is in a spirit of objectivity that he transmitted this information to me.[129]

The president's study of the map appears in the transcript as an almost irrelevant gesture—a stage direction—for the crucial information was conveyed, not by the map, but by Lord's informant in Upper Silesia. Yet Wilson, throughout the conference, was a man with a map in his hand. Lord considered a fair plebiscite to be almost impossible, and Wilson understood that it would be at best problematic; nevertheless, self-determination seemed to require a plebiscite.

The question of Silesia was still on the minds of the peacemakers a few days later when they considered plebiscites in relation to the payment of reparations. On June 14, Lloyd George raised the question of whether territories that were German during the war, and might be separated from Germany after the war, should have to make payments to the victorious Allies—that is, make contributions to the enormous sum of German reparations, which

John Maynard Keynes was about to denounce as economically disastrous in *The Economic Consequences of the Peace*. "For example," Lloyd George wondered, "were Dantzig and Upper Silesia, both very wealthy states, to bear no part of the burden of the reparation?" Clemenceau, promptly and predictably, "said that they ought to pay." Wilson commented vaguely that "whatever views anyone might hold about Poland, the Polish people had been compelled to fight for the Central Powers," and "their territory had been devastated by Russia as well as by Germany." Therefore, it would be unfair to require the new state of Poland (though it included former territories of Germany and Austria) to pay reparations.[130]

Lloyd George, however, thought that, given Silesia's mineral wealth, "if any part of Upper Silesia went to Poland, there should be a joint consideration between Germany, Poland, and the [Reparations] Commission as to how much of the burden of reparation was to be borne."

> MR. LLOYD GEORGE said that . . . it was not just to say to Silesia that if she voted [herself] out of Germany, she would escape a payment of perhaps 500 million pounds. This was loading the dice against Germany.
>
> PRESIDENT WILSON protested strongly against the use of this term [loading the dice]. He pointed out that he was not obliged under the Armistice to agree to a plebiscite in Upper Silesia at all, as No. 13 of the 14 points was perfectly clear on the subject. He had only conceded the plebiscite to meet Mr. Lloyd George's principles. . . . As the population [of Silesia] had been ground down under the landowners, it would not be loading the dice to make it exempt from sharing Germany's burden of reparation.
>
> M. SONNINO pointed out that the effect of no share of reparation being taken by Upper Silesia, would be to offer the rich proprietors of the land and of the mines a strong inducement to use their influence to the utmost to vote against Germany.
>
> MR. LLOYD GEORGE said he must make a strong protest against the release of Upper Silesia from taking any share of the reparation. He did not feel that he could withdraw the suggestion that it was loading the dice, although, of course, this had no personal application.

PRESIDENT WILSON said that nevertheless he must strongly demur to the use of this term.[131]

The intolerable insinuation was not simply that the circumstances of the plebiscite could be influenced, but that they could be strategically gamed, and that Wilson himself, pious Presbyterian and son of a Presbyterian minister, was not just gambling on the plebiscite but actually loading the dice to produce the desired result. It would have been impossible to offend his principles with more purposeful aim than to suggest that self-determination was susceptible to dishonest manipulation and that Wilson himself was attempting to fix the game and win his bet. Wilsonian sympathy for the Poles was represented as the cynical inclination to arrange the political circumstances for Poland's advantage.

Lloyd George persisted in demanding reparations from Upper Silesia, even if it voted to join with Poland, saying, "Upper Silesia is a great industrial region where the capital is German." Wilson pleaded that Poland needed all the capital it could manage to conserve: "We are establishing a Poland almost without capital. Are we going to take from her what little she has?" For both men it was becoming increasingly clear that a plebiscite could not serve as a straightforward mechanism of national self-determination as long as the political context could influence the sovereignty preference of the voters, but they could not agree on what constituted a neutral context. On the subject of reparations Lloyd George rudely returned to the phrase that Wilson found most offensive.

> LLOYD GEORGE: It does not seem to me fair to tell the Poles that they will be assured of a pecuniary advantage if they vote in the way that we wish; that amounts to loading the dice.
> WILSON: I call to your attention that, according to the thirteenth of the Fourteen Points, concerning Poland, I did not commit myself to instituting a plebiscite in Upper Silesia.
> LLOYD GEORGE: As for us, we never understood, when the right of peoples to self-determination was mentioned, that that meant that we could dispose of them without consulting them.
> WILSON: I do not believe that it would be cheating to take away from

people who oppressed a country for a long time an argument that they would use to maintain their domination.

LLOYD GEORGE: I cannot take back what I have said; that is called loading the dice.

WILSON: I hope that you will not keep on using that expression.

LLOYD GEORGE: Yet, it expresses the fact.[132]

Each insisted that it was the other who would be unduly influencing the outcome of the plebiscite, whether by demanding or forgiving reparations from Silesia; their disagreement underlined the problematic nature of the plebiscite itself and the difficulty of establishing purely neutral conditions for carrying it out. Wilson defensively clung to what remained of his Polish sympathies, while Lloyd George damningly wondered what was meant by self-determination if not the consultation of the people involved. Self-determination seemed to necessitate the conditions of the blank slate that belonged to Wilson's ideal conception of the moment but remained ever elusive in real historical time and on the actual map of Eastern Europe.

On September 8, in Omaha, Wilson campaigned for the peace treaty and, on the assumption that Nebraskans were farmers, he attempted to explain the European settlement in terms they would understand. If there was any doubt about property lines in Nebraska, "all the farmers would be sitting on their fences with shotguns," and, for that reason, to preserve the peace, the Versailles treaty sought "to settle the land titles of Europe . . . on the principle that every land belongs to the people that live on it." Wilson then pursued this conception with reference to Poland:

> I know there are men in Nebraska who come from that country of tragical history, the now restored Republic of Poland. And I want to call your attention to the fact that Poland is here given her complete restitution. . . . Take what in Europe they call High Silesia, the mountainous, the upper portions of the district of Silesia. The very great majority of the people in High Silesia are Poles. But the Germans contested the statement that most of them were Poles. We said: "Very well, then, it is none of our business; we will let them decide. We will put sufficient armed forces into High Silesia to see that nobody tampers with the processes of the election, and then

we will hold a referendum there, and those people can belong to either Germany or Poland, as they prefer, and not as we prefer."[133]

Wilson's sympathy for Poland, as of old, was on display in Omaha, as he pitched his speech at a possible presence of Polish Nebraskans in the public and advertised the restoration of Poland on the map of Europe.

The thirteenth point authorized the Polish state on lands with "indisputably Polish populations," and, therefore, lands with mixed or disputed ethnography required adjudication by the mechanism of the plebiscite. Yet, Wilson himself became skeptical about the validity of such plebiscites, was not certain that the Poles would win in Upper Silesia, and had been accused of trying to load the dice on their behalf. The plebiscite was, in theory, such a perfectly apt mechanism for supporting the principle of national self-determination that Wilson in Omaha partly rewrote his own role at the peace conference, returning to a moment when his sympathy for Poland was more whole-hearted and his enthusiasm for plebiscites less qualified. Both had been seriously attenuated in the Council of Four as Wilson tried to envision the uncorrupted neutral circumstances in which national self-determination could redesign the map of Eastern Europe.

On September 13, 1919, Wilson spoke at the Tacoma Stadium Bowl looking out over Puget Sound, and then gave a second speech at the National Guard Armory. Addressing the armory audience he recalled his encounter with an almost angelic figure, embodying his sympathetic connection to Poland:

> When I was at that wonderful stadium of yours a few minutes ago, a little child, a little girl in white, came and presented me with some kind of a paper—I have not read it yet—from the Poles. I dare say that it is of the sort that I have received a great many of—just an expression of a sort of childlike and pitiful thanks that America assisted to free Poland. Poland never could have freed herself.[134]

The conjured image of the little girl in white spoke voicelessly for Poland to the American public with a mute expression of gratitude. It was not necessary to read the written message in order to interpret the sentiments that her presence conveyed. As a child she perfectly incarnated the youth of the newly independent Polish state, and her innocence offered to Wilson an image of that state in a morally and spiritually idealized condition, as he himself might once have conceived it on his own mental mapping of Eastern Europe.

Now, in Tacoma, far from Europe—two weeks before the stroke that would partly incapacitate him for the rest of his presidency—Wilson apostrophized the Poles one last time: "You could not free yourselves, but we believe in liberty. Here is your own land to do with as you please." In fact, the issue of minority rights had imposed some treaty limitations on Polish liberty to do what they pleased within their newly independent country, and, consequently, there would be some discontent with the treaty in Poland. Wilson, however, was most concerned with those who opposed the treaty in the United States and especially in the Senate: "I wish that some of the men who are opposing this treaty could get the vision in their hearts of all it has done. It has liberated great populations."[135] After his return from the peace conference Wilson had to campaign for the Wilsonian settlement across America, but he also wished that the liberated peoples of Eastern Europe themselves, and perhaps especially the Poles, would better acknowledge his commitment to their liberation. Throughout the conference he had repeatedly experienced what he saw as disagreeable ingratitude on the part of the Poles, who failed to appreciate what he had done for them out of friendship. Accordingly, he now summoned the figure of the little girl in white, supposedly offering "childlike and pitiful thanks" on behalf of her nation.

CONCLUSION

The Dynamics of Wilsonian Mental Mapping

"A somewhat unusual amount of deity"

No American president has ever been as interested in Eastern Europe as Woodrow Wilson, no president has ever immersed himself so fully in the political, social, and religious factors that shaped the region, and no president has ever had such a profound personal impact on its geopolitical character. Wilson was born in 1856, the year the Treaty of Paris concluded the Crimean War, limiting Russian power and influence in Ottoman southeastern Europe and paving the way for the principalities of Wallachia and Moldavia to emerge as the national state of Romania. Wilson was a student at Princeton in 1876, when Bosnian and Bulgarian risings in the Ottoman empire led to international war, involving Russia, Serbia, and Montenegro, focusing new attention on the Eastern Question, and producing a revised map of emerging national states at the Congress of Berlin in 1878. Wilson was elected president of the United States in November 1912—one month after the First Balkan War broke out in October, and a few weeks before Albania declared its independence from the Ottoman empire. The election was fought over issues of tariff policy, certainly not about Eastern Europe, and it could hardly have been foreseen just how large Eastern Europe would loom in the second term of Wilson's presidency, after America entered World War I.

Wilson never visited Eastern Europe, but from 1917, with the assistance of Colonel House's Inquiry team of scholars and intellectuals, the president made a very quick study of the lands and peoples of Eastern Europe to prepare himself for a peace settlement whose most radical geopolitical innovations would occur in that region. It was fundamentally Wilson's mapping of Eastern Europe into national states that prevailed upon the map of Europe across the twentieth century from the 1920s to the 1990s. The statues of Wilson and the eponymous Wilson streets, stations, and squares that covered Eastern Europe after 1918—from the Prague train station to the most prominent square in Zagreb—testified to his postwar popularity. Such popularity in Eastern Europe would not be rivaled by another American president until Ronald Reagan launched the final phase of the Cold War in the 1980s, and he too has been memorialized with statues and namings from Poland to Bulgaria, many of them established just at the same moment that Wilson's name and image were being brought back in Eastern Europe after the collapse of communism. In fact, Reagan's famous denunciation of the Soviet bloc as an "evil empire" in the 1980s echoed the moral rhetoric of Wilson denouncing the Habsburg and Ottoman empires. Ironically, the end of the Cold War would lead to the radical revision of the Wilsonian map of Eastern Europe, bringing about the disintegration of Yugoslavia and Czechoslovakia, the two most notable creations ratified by the Paris Peace Conference following World War I.

Though Wilson's role in the war and at the peace conference is most often associated with the end of the Habsburg monarchy, with the new states created in the post-Habsburg spaces of Eastern Europe, and with the creation of independent Poland, his earlier interest in the displacement of empire was, in fact, much more powerfully associated with the Eastern Question and the Ottoman empire. It was his youthful interest in Christian Gladstonian politics, and the anti-Ottoman perspective associated with Gladstone and the "Bulgarian Horrors," that shaped Wilson's evolving wartime perspective on the Habsburg monarchy, rather than the other way around. From his flippant private comment "There ain't going to be no Turkey" in 1912 right through to his jokey public remark in St. Louis in 1919 that "we can at any rate postpone Turkey until Thanksgiving," Wilson showed himself ready to dismiss the Ottoman empire—to imagine its abolition, especially in Europe—well before he had any thought of dissolving or dismembering the Habsburg monarchy.[1]

For the Habsburg peoples, he initially prescribed only "the freest opportunity to autonomous development" in Point Ten of the Fourteen Points speech of January 8, 1918, without specifying that the "freest" condition might be some sort of post-Habsburg independence. It was not until October 19, 1918, one day after the Czechoslovak declaration of independence and three weeks before the armistice, that Wilson informed the Habsburg government that America was "no longer at liberty to accept the mere 'autonomy' of these peoples as a basis of peace."[2] Over the course of 1917 and 1918, based on the parallels he drew between the Habsburg and Ottoman empires—with both empires urged to concede "autonomous development" in the Fourteen Points—Wilson gradually translated his long-standing antipathy to sultanic government in Constantinople into a parallel antipathy to imperial government in Vienna.

In 1917, after entering the war against Germany but before declaring war on Austria-Hungary, Wilson was reported to have surmised that "the races forming the Austro-Hungarian agglomeration would wish to be emancipated."[3] In March 1919, in a speech at the Metropolitan Opera House in New York, Wilson invoked "the indescribable agonies of being governed by the Turk," and set the Habsburg and Ottoman peoples alongside each other as having "called out to the world, generation after generation, for justice, for liberation, and for succor."[4] In San Diego in September 1919, he took this rhetoric a step further and spoke of a war to liberate "enslaved" populations, declaring that "enslaved peoples ought to be freed."[5] The rhetoric of enslavement and emancipation ultimately permitted Wilson to assume the mantle of Lincoln in relation to the Habsburg nationalities, and Czech national spokesmen understood this readily when they addressed the president in 1917 to say: "Like the voice of Lincoln . . . so your voice gives new strength to millions of oppressed."[6] Wilson's eventual commitment to the destruction of the Habsburg monarchy would be cloaked in a sense of Lincolnesque mission.

The extent of Wilson's engagement with Ottoman affairs was reflected in his lively responsiveness to the possibility of creating American mandates for Armenia and for Constantinople. He knew that it would be difficult to obtain Senate approval, and these mandate plans disappeared into the counterfactual historical universe along with American participation in the League of Nations; even if achieved, any mandate for Constantinople would certainly have been overturned by the Turkish military campaigns of the early 1920s. Yet it remains striking (and somewhat unremarked) that Wilson really did contemplate such an American engagement at Constantinople, hypothetically imagining the mandate as the basis for a long-term American presence in the post-Ottoman domain of southeastern Europe. Discussing the proposed mandate in the Council of Four, Wilson declared himself to be "quite disinterested," for certainly the role of mandatory was implicitly imperial and might be seen as compromising his commitment to self-determination and his principled refusal to treat peoples and places as "chattels and pawns."[7] For Wilson there was a delicate balance between personal "interest" in Eastern Europe as the object of his diplomatic principles and the American "disinterest" that absolutely denied any pursuit of advantage in the region. The statue of Wilson erected at the Prague train station was supposed to be a tribute to Wilsonian magnanimity of principle; it did not signal an American political presence in Czechoslovakia.

Wilson did not invent the idea of Czechoslovakia or the idea of Yugoslavia, let alone the idea of independent Poland, but he certainly invested his moral and diplomatic authority in those geopolitical projects, and helped to shape the territorial borders and ethnographic balances of the new states as they emerged, creating a radically new map of postwar Eastern Europe. The Wilson papers offer little evidence that Wilson ever thought about these places and peoples before World War I. If at the beginning of the war, Wilson still possessed a very limited knowledge of Eastern Europe, and associated the region principally with voting American immigrant groups, by the time the United States entered the war in 1917, he was already accruing new associations that would constitute his mental map of Eastern Europe. Lloyd George was probably no better acquainted with Eastern Europe than Wilson, though, as a Welshman, he claimed a special affinity with small nations. Wilson was considered a great friend of Poland, and Lloyd George was seen as less sympathetic, if not actually hostile, but of the "Big Three" in Paris, the one who had some personal knowledge of the Polish lands was Clemenceau. He had traveled to Galicia in 1897 and published stories about the Jews of Galicia in 1898 (with illustrations by Toulouse-Lautrec) at the height of the Dreyfus Affair in France.[8]

Colonel House's creation of The Inquiry in 1917 was crucial for providing Wilson with reports and maps of the region, and Wilson, himself

FIGURE 8. After World War I the Prague Train Station, formerly named for Emperor Franz Joseph, was renamed for Woodrow Wilson. On July 4, 1928, a statue of Wilson (shown above) by Czech-American sculptor Albin Polasek was unveiled at the station. Wilson's name and statue were removed from the station by the Nazis during World War II, and it was not until 2011 that a new Wilson statue was erected at the station in Prague.

an academic, certainly appreciated the sort of academic expertise that was exercised by Archibald Cary Coolidge concerning Eastern Europe, assisted by his junior academic protégés Robert Howard Lord (for Poland) and Robert Kerner (for Czechoslovakia and Yugoslavia). The founding of the School of Slavonic Studies (today the School of Slavonic and East European Studies) in London in 1915, involved both R. W. Seton Watson and Masaryk, and thus preceded the summoning of The Inquiry in 1917; together these scholarly efforts contributed to the establishment of the Anglo-American academic study of Eastern Europe. One generation later, with the coming of the Cold War to Eastern Europe after World War II, there would already be an institutional network of scholars in America and Britain engaged with the issues of the region.

Wilson's mental mapping of Eastern Europe was sentimentally conditioned by his personal connections to individual statesmen, and, during the final years of the war, most especially by his friendly contacts with Tomáš Masaryk (a distinguished professor) and Ignacy Jan Paderewski (a celebrated musician); the three men were roughly contemporaries (Masaryk born in 1850, Wilson in 1856, and Paderewski in 1860). In the emotional nexus of their personal and political encounters Masaryk and Paderewski were able to reflect back to Wilson their own national causes as fully consistent with his international principles, and both Czechoslovakia and Poland thus established themselves in the presidential consciousness in forms that he could recognize and approve. Personal friendships like these would be emotionally and rhetorically amplified to become Wilsonian friendships for entire nations, transmitted to him as the collectively friendly sentiments of particular peoples in Eastern Europe. "I shall always deem the title 'friend of Czechoslovakia' as one of the most distinguished I could bear," Wilson declared toward the end of his life. In another letter from this same period, he described his personal dependence on friendship, writing, "My friends grow more and more indispensable to me. . . . I must see my friends or starve." According to Alexander George and Juliette George, in their classic study of Wilson's friendship with Colonel House, Wilson always "sought relief from inner stress through comforting friendships," which soothed his ego.[9] This also applied to Wilson's sense of international relations, conditioned by friendships with foreign national leaders and, in the case of Eastern Europe, presumed friendships for whole nations.

A sort of sentimental metonymy played a part in this amplification of friendship, and it did not require the participation of an eminent national leader. The Serbian woman who knitted socks for Wilson conveyed the fabric of Yugoslav friendship, while the goatherds from Orawa and Spisz, who came to Paris to meet with Wilson as "the biggest man in the world," offered a folkloric enhancement of his mental map of Eastern Europe. They also tested his conflicting friendships for Poland and Czechoslovakia, and allowed him to experience a gratifyingly popular encounter with ordinary people from the region.[10] Some aspects of this encounter recapitulated the implicitly patronizing aspect of Wilson's magnanimous role as the friend of entire nations, and might also have chimed with some of his earlier condescension, in his *History of the American People*, toward American immigrants from Eastern Europe. In wartime, however, Wilson argued for an "instinctive sympathy" on the part of Americans for the small nations of Eastern Europe, based on the presence of immigrant communities in the United States: "We believe in them . . . and say, 'These people are of the flesh and blood of mankind, and America is made up out of the peoples of the world.' What a fine future of distinction and glory is open for a people who, by instinctive sympathy, can interpret and stand for the rights of men everywhere."[11] The instinctive sympathy of the American people was thus conceived as analogous to the personal affinity of Wilsonian friendship.

It is not necessary to take the psycho-biographical approach of Freud and Bullitt, writing about Wilson in the 1930s, to observe that the gratifications to Wilson's ego inevitably colored his map of Eastern Europe. "There was a somewhat unusual amount of deity in the character of Woodrow Wilson," Freud and Bullitt wrote. "His Super-Ego demanded that he should accomplish God-like achievements, his passivity to his father found outlet through submission to God and through identification with Christ."[12] Wilson was supposedly revered in Eastern Europe, and since he never visited any country in the region to experience that reverence directly, the presumption of apotheosis was never tested by any direct encounter. His conception of the peace settlement did focus on a formative moment of genesis, when the previous map of empires was null and void, when Eastern Europe appeared as a blank slate, a geopolitical vacuum, and when he could partly play the role of the creator in designing and defining a new map with new borders. His mental mapping of the region was precisely focused on this metamorphosis, when the former map had become an anachronism, an antique, and the new map was articulated and affirmed through the authority of the peace conference, guided by his own leading role. It was crucial that the interlocking parts of the map should be cut to order for a lasting and legitimate settlement, and he addressed himself to the pieces and parts of Eastern Europe in relation to one another.

The Habsburg monarchy had been "broken into pieces," according to Wilson, and those pieces could be recombined to create a new geopolitical map.[13] The whole settlement was a puzzle to be constructed out of these interlocking pieces, and the crucial thing was to have everything fit together logically and coherently. Wilson observed the geographical relation of the parts to one another: "And south of Poland is Bohemia, which we cut away from the Austrian combination. And below Bohemia is Hungary, which can no longer rely upon the assistant strength of Austria, and below her is an enlarged Rumania. Alongside of Rumania is the new Slavic kingdom."[14] Wilson studied the parts attentively so that he could operate upon the map of Eastern Europe: "We are carving a piece of Poland out of Germany's side; we are creating an independent Bohemia below that, an independent Hungary below that, and enlarging Rumania, and we are rearranging the territorial divisions of the Balkan states."[15] This process of carving, creating, enlarging, and rearranging produced the peace settlement and the new map, but the operations occurred in Wilson's mental mapping of the region, which conditioned the settlement on the ground.

Even as the president received academic reports from The Inquiry, his reactions could be entirely personal and emotional, as when his outrage at the lateness of Queen Marie of Romania had him (according to an observer) rearranging the map in favor of Bulgaria: "Every moment we waited I could see from the cut of the P.'s jaw that a slice of the Dobrudja, or Roumania, was being lopped off."[16] His coloring of the map would change completely one year later, after the peace conference, when he declared: "I have found the Bulgarians the most avaricious and brutal of the smaller nations . . . though for a long time my vote was for Roumania in those respects. Being no longer committed to Roumania, I can perhaps transfer my suffrages to Bulgaria."[17] Wilson was capable of being ironic about his own mood swings as he shifted his allegiances and antipathies, but he nevertheless invested the map with his own emotional energies.

The whole peace conference was emotionally roiling for Wilson in this regard. He arrived in Paris with his sentiments of personal friendship and principles of international politics in neat alignment, only to have the principles prove conflicting, the friendships start to fray, and the alignment become seriously disrupted. "Three million Germans in Bohemia!" he supposedly exclaimed on the ship to Europe in 1918. "That's curious! Masaryk never told me that!"[18] With the conflict in principles that followed from competing claims of sentiment, Wilson discovered on the ethnographic map of Eastern Europe something that he had not anticipated, along with the three million Germans in Bohemia: the new problem of minority rights. It was the flip side of national self-determination, which was the politics of the majority, and for Wilson it began, not with the Germans of Czechoslovakia, whom Masaryk had neglected to mention, but with the minority populations of interwar Poland, whom Paderewski had likewise failed to bring to the president's attention.

American Jewish leaders like Louis Marshall and Stephen Wise led the way in informing Wilson about the poisonous anti-Semitism of Paderewski's close associate Roman Dmowski, whom Wilson had met with in the White House in September 1918. As the conference proceeded in 1919, and Poland became embroiled in a struggle with the Ukrainians of Eastern Galicia and then in war with the Soviet Union, Wilson and the peacemakers had to sacrifice some of their Polonophile sympathies to the minority concerns of Ukrainians or Ruthenians, Lithuanians, and even Germans within the new Polish state. In fact, from Danzig/Gdańsk on the Baltic to Constantinople/Istanbul on the Bosphorus, Eastern Europe became for Wilson the region of complex and mixed ethnographic mappings that could not easily be sorted into national states based on the principle of self-determination. The Poles ended up in Wilson's ambivalent sentimental lexicon as "our disagreeable friends," and it was frustratingly difficult for him to try to modify the preoccupations of "the Polish state of mind." That Polish state of mind could be located phenomenologically in relation to Wilson's own state of mind, his mental mapping of Eastern Europe, in which Poland appeared endlessly expansive: "I saw M. Dmowski and M. Paderewski in Washington, and I asked them to define for me Poland as they understood it, and they presented me with a map in which they claimed a large part of the earth."[19]

Woodrow Wilson with a map in his hand is the iconic and crucial figure of the peace settlement. In May 1919 at a meeting of the Council of Four, he "produced an ethnographic map of Anatolia"—for it was the job of The Inquiry to make sure that Wilson had plenty of maps available to him. Maps, of course, do not provide strictly objective information, even for geography but especially for ethnography; they always reflect the cultural perspectives and priorities of the mapmakers, and this was especially true for the maps that circulated around the Paris Peace Conference. Yet Wilson seemed most sure of himself when he was holding a map in his hand. The Inquiry supplied over a thousand maps, and the geographer Isaiah Bowman played a leading role on Wilson's team at the peace conference. Bowman had a map for Wilson to prepare him to address the conflicting claims of the Italians and the Yugoslavs: "It seems to me . . . that the President should have it at hand when the Italian questions are discussed," Bowman wrote to Colonel House.[20] Wilson did indeed have the map at hand, and proudly declared, "I have before me an Italian map published before the war"—so that now he could identify such arcane cartographical points as the Adriatic islands of Cherso and Lussino (Cres and Lošinj).[21] Harold Nicolson described a scene from Paris with President Wilson as a kneeling celebrant at the altar of cartography: "Clemenceau and Ll. G. sit side by side on a sofa. P. W. takes a map, spreads it on the carpet in an alcove-room, and kneels down. We all squat in a circle around him . . . He explains what has been decided downstairs about the Jugo-Slav frontier. He does this with perfect lucidity: Princeton returns to him."[22] Wilson on his knees offered an image of pious genuflection before the map as a sacred icon, but, as Nicolson suggests, the map also then inspired in Wilson the lecturing Princeton spirit of professorial self-conviction.

Though he had some confidence in his own evolving geographical erudition, Wilson also came to realize the limits of cartography: "The one people have not stopped at a sharp line, and the settlements of the other people, or their migrations, begun at that sharp line; they have intermingled. There are regions where you can't draw a national line and say there are Slavs on this side and Italians on that. There is this people there and that people there. It can't be done. You have to approximate the line."[23] The imprecision of mapping produced for him a powerful sense of the complexity, sometimes impossibility, of mapping Eastern Europe, which sometimes led to frustrations at the conference and, ultimately, some reluctance to embrace the messy details: "Something is being done about Ruthenia, but I am ashamed to say I don't remember what."[24]

At the same time, his advocacy of the Yugoslav position against the allegedly self-aggrandizing Italians helped to consolidate his sense of a more general ethnographic mapping between Eastern and Western Europe: "There is a fatal antagonism between the Italians and the Slavs. If the Slavs have the feeling of an injustice, that will make the chasm unbridgeable and will open the road to Russian influence and to the formation of a Slavic bloc hostile to western Europe."[25] This very powerful ethnographic conception of Eastern Europe as susceptible to Russian influence through its Slavic affinities suggests the ways in which Wilson's map of the region could also be shaded dark. Russia was largely excluded from Wilson's reimagining of Eastern Europe as a system of new national states, but he offered a powerful, even Manichaean sense of polarizing struggle between Russia and the West for the Slavic souls of the new states. Wilson and Lenin offered rival conceptions of national self-determination, and the Leninist Comintern, founded in 1919, would become the ideological antithesis of the Wilsonian League of Nations.

The absence of a map could also shape the agenda of the conference, as when Wilson "asked Mr. Paderewski to begin with Silesia, as the ethnographic map which they were awaiting had not yet arrived."[26] The map could even appear as a sort of stage direction in the accounts of the conference: "WILSON (after study of the map): I consider it settled that we adopt the system of the plebiscite."[27] The plebiscite and the map were, in fact, supplementary, inasmuch as the plebiscite was supposed to constitute the most direct form of self-determination in circumstances where the ethnographic map was confoundingly indeterminate. As an American Progressive, Wilson believed in the mechanism of the democratic referendum, but he experienced gradual disillusionment with the tool of the plebiscite for mapping Eastern Europe, coming to believe that plebiscites could only work in a neutral political environment that was unlikely to exist in the real world. He almost lost his temper at the peace conference in 1919 when Lloyd George accused him of trying to "load the dice." In fact, Wilson wanted a plebiscite in Upper Silesia only if it seemed likely to confirm his own sentimental affinities, in this case for the Poles. As far back as 1917, Paderewski had saluted him as Poland's dearest friend, saying: "You are the foster-father of a chiefless land. You are Poland's inspired protector. For many a month the spelling of your name has been the only comfort and joy of a starving nation."[28] Even as his sympathy for Poland was fraying in 1919, it was natural for him to hope that the Poles would win the plebiscite in Upper Silesia—and even to try to load the dice.

■ ■ ■

"Nearer and dearer than ever to every Polish heart"
At a meeting between the Allied Supreme War Council and representatives of the Weimar Republic in the Belgian town of Spa in July 1920, in addition to discussions about German reparations and disarmament, there was also some adjudication of Poland's borders. The Spa conference coincided with a successful Soviet offensive in the Polish-Soviet war, and the American minister in Warsaw, Hugh Gibson, wrote to the Secretary of State Bainbridge Colby (appointed after Wilson dismissed Lansing in February) to ask for some friendly intervention from Wilson on Polish issues. "The situation in Eastern Europe has reached a phase where I believe a few words from the President would have a very helpful and steadying influence," wrote Gibson. While admitting that there had been "Polish mistakes" in pursuit of Poland's territorial ambitions, Gibson worried that "the spirit of the Poles is being rapidly undermined, partly through military reverses but more particularly through a feeling that Poland has been abandoned by her friends and Allies." Gibson described the Polish perspective:

> Their friendship for the United States is at the same high pitch of enthusiasm as in former times. This feeling for the United States is chiefly sustained through unwavering faith in the President and his friendship. They do not forget that he was the first to demand the resurrection of Poland and that his unfailing support has been infinitely precious to them. I do not believe that anyone who has not been in daily contact with the Poles can realize quite how deep this feeling is or how helpful it has been to the Poles. I cannot but feel that this implicit belief in the President can be turned to great advantage at this time. I am confident that there is nothing better calculated to steady the situation now than a message from him re-affirming his consistent friendship for Poland, and assuring the Polish people that in this critical time they may count upon American sympathy and such support as we can give. Any counsel that the President might care to give to the Polish people would be received not only with respect but with a desire to profit by it. He might be disposed to say a few words of caution on the subject of military adventures or aggression.[29]

Gibson well understood the foundational rhetoric of friendship and sympathy upon which the Wilsonian conception of Polish independence rested, and was aware that Wilson might even presume to appeal beyond the Polish government directly to the Polish people with a message of friendship that also included warnings against aggression and aggrandizement.

The "daily contact with the Poles" that Gibson claimed as the vindication of his perspective was of course precisely the intimacy that Wilson had never been able to establish except in the most abstract and vicarious terms. Paris was as close as Wilson ever came to Warsaw. And now, as he attempted to manage the waning months of his presidency in a condition of compromised medical incapacity, he renounced even the rhetorical politics of friendship and sympathy, writing to Colby: "I hesitate to comply with Mr. Hugh Gibson's suggestions because I think the time has passed when personal intervention on my part or suggestion with regard to foreign politics would be of service, though I am deeply interested in everything that affects Poland."[30] The fraying of friendship at the peace conference left Wilson both self-conscious and reticent about the deployment of his once-celebrated personal sympathies.

When Wincenty Witos, the leader of the Polish peasant party (Polskie Stronnictwo Ludowe) formed a new Polish government later in July 1920—with the Polish-Soviet war ongoing and the Red Army approaching Warsaw—he promptly wrote to Wilson to stress Poland's "deep and sincere gratitude for America's generous help and continuous sympathy" and to acknowledge Wilson personally as "the most staunch promoter and defensor of Polish Independence" and "at this hour of [the] country's greatest need nearer and dearer than ever to every Polish heart."[31] Wilson, however, indifferently turned over the reply to Colby—"for I am sure you can frame it as well as I could"—and Colby actually reproved Poland for its aggression against Russia.[32]

In early September 1920, as Wilson's presidency drew to a close, Stephen Wise wrote to the president's secretary Joseph Tumulty to offer his own perspective on the Polish-Soviet war. According to Wise's cable informant, the war had become the occasion for Polish anti-Semitic persecutions: "Most reliable information treatment Jews Poland shocking. Soldiers rob, beat, tear beards." Wise in New York, like Gibson in Warsaw, was looking for a statement from Wilson. "It has occurred to me," he wrote to Tumulty on September 9, "that it would be of the very greatest moral value if the President might see fit, as I think he ought, to send some message which would of course have instant currency throughout the world, especially wherever Jews dwell, giving expression to his own hope that the terrible sufferings of the Jews may and ought to cease without delay." In fact, Wise hoped to have the letter almost immediately—in three days—in time for the Jewish New Year, when it might be expected to have maximal impact. Wise even wrote that "in the event of the President being unwilling or unable—and he ought to be neither—to write to me in these terms, it would be of importance if the same kind of communication might come to me from Secretary Colby." Wise took the liberty of proposing a text for Wilson's statement of support.[33]

Wilson did not delegate this assignment to Colby, however, but wrote to Wise the very next day with the solicited letter, which then appeared in the *New York Times* on September 12, the day before Rosh Hashanah, under the headline "President Urges Justice for Jews." Wilson, following Wise's proposed text, declared himself to be "deeply moved by the reports which you send me of the trials and sufferings endured by your fellow Jews throughout Eastern Europe." The statement formulated America's relation to anti-Semitic persecution, once more and definitively, as a matter of special sympathy for the Jews: "No American, whatever his racial origin or religious creed, can fail to feel the deepest sympathy with the Jews of Eastern Europe," who suffered "unenlightened and unjust treatment at the hands of governments and peoples." Those governments and peoples were not specifically designated, but Wilson hoped that the unnamed governments would respect Jewish rights "as provided for by the minority clauses of the Peace Treaty"—a treaty to which the United States was no longer party.[34]

At the conclusion of the president's statement, Wilsonian principles were garbed in the rhetorical style of utopian fantasy: "I should greatly rejoice to learn," Wilson wrote, "that there has come about an amelioration of the status of the Jews in Eastern European lands. This government most earnestly desires that Jewish persecution be ended in all lands and for all times."[35] The one thing that Wilson clearly refrained from doing was to condemn Poland by name, for the persecution of the Jews was in this statement associated with Wilson's broader geopolitical sense of Eastern Europe as a whole. The Jews of Eastern Europe were embedded as a minority population—the quintessential minority population—in a newly confirmed mapping of Eastern Europe.

In October 1920, the *Jewish Tribune*, a bimonthly "Organ of the Jews of Russia" published in English in Paris, responded gratefully to Wilson's September statement in the *New York Times*, and offered a lavish tribute to the American president's now concluding political career. "For the first time one heard in the acts of state the heart beat and those beatings accompagnied [sic] a human thought clear and pure as a crystal," effused the writer (S. L. Poliakoff-Litovtzeff), suggesting the synchrony by which the Wilsonian heart could beat in time with other sympathetic hearts, indeed the collective hearts of whole peoples. The tribute claimed that Wilson's language "reminds us of the divine language of the Bible"— the Hebrew Bible presumably, in this case, though Wilson's religious sensibility derived from his father's Presbyterianism. If Wilson appeared as biblically prophetic, it was in part because his prophesies had not yet been achieved: "Wilson would not be Wilson if he were the hero of the sorry epoch we are living through. No, he is the hero of the future."[36] In fact, American politics was already turning away from Wilson, and no one could prophetically have foreseen the eventual collapse of the Wilsonian settlement in Eastern Europe during World War II.

On November 3, 1920, the day after Warren Harding was elected president (a victory for the Republicans and a rejection of Wilson's Democrats), Wilson wrote to Lloyd George urging greater attention to "the aspirations and rights of the Albanian people" in the context of the Adriatic question, but offering no such affirmation of the Polish people: "I believe we are in substantial accord as to the folly of the Poles, I have been fearful that their enthusiasm following temporary military successes may lead to insistence upon territorial arrangements which will be a source of future trouble."[37] Wilson may have been in a bitter mood the day after the U.S. presidential election, conditioning his unsentimental dismissal of Polish folly, but even at that moment, he managed to express concern for the Albanians.

Wilson, out of office in 1921, was perhaps not altogether effusive in his response to the Polish honorary doctorate bestowed on him by the Jagiellonian University in Kraków. It had been announced in Paris in February 1919, at a time when his sympathy was crucial, but could not be formally awarded then because of the scarcity of parchment for a diploma. At that time, Wilson had been told by a representative of the university that just as Copernicus (a Jagiellonian alumnus) had brought order to the heavens, so Wilson was bringing order to the earth. Eugeniusz Romer, who was present on that occasion in February 1919, was very aware that the doctorate was purposefully intended to consolidate Wilson's favor for Poland.[38] Now in 1921 the Jagiellonian diploma was finally delivered: "in recognition of your distinguished services to mankind and as a testimonial of the gratitude of the Polish people for the supreme aid rendered by you in the restoration of the Polish State." The Polish ambassador in Washington, DC, Kazimierz Lubomirski, hailed Wilson as Poland's "great friend" and declared hyperbolically that "the gratitude of Poland to you is immortal."³⁹ To this, Wilson replied somewhat laconically that "nothing connected with the Great War interested or concerned me more profoundly than the question of Poland, and it is very delightful to me to receive any evidence of the confidence and friendship of the great Polish people."⁴⁰ The words "any evidence" suggested that perhaps too little had been forthcoming.

Two years out of office, in November 1922, he wrote in a similar spirit to the Polish diplomatic representative in Washington, "It is a matter of peculiar pleasure and gratification to me to learn in any way of the approbation and friendship of the Polish people and their Government. It will afford me peculiar pleasure therefore to receive at your hands the symbol of the order of the White Eagle."⁴¹ Perfectly polite, there was still perhaps a hint of ironic surprise to learn that the old spirit of friendship was still extant in Poland. Paderewski, Wilson's original Polish friend, also ceased to play a political role in 1922, when he left his position as Polish envoy to the League of Nations, and resumed his international musical career as a pianist. He was in New York on December 27, 1923, the day before Wilson's sixty-seventh birthday and sent a birthday message that nostalgically invoked the spirit of their former mutual engagement: "Always remembering your great and noble deeds, always aware of my country's unredeemable indebtedness to your generosity, always thanking God for the priceless privilege of knowing you."⁴² Wilson would live for barely more than another month, and Paderewski's birthday salute already had a valedictory character. Wilson's death at the age of 67 in 1924 followed from the precipitous decline in his health that dated back to 1919, when he was struck by flu in Paris at the peace conference, later when he collapsed from exhaustion during his American speaking tour on behalf of the League, and, finally, when he suffered his severely incapacitating stroke at the beginning of October in the White House.

■ ■ ■

"Have someone look into the matter and rectify the frontier"
In Paris, in June 1919, Wilson's aide and physician Cary Grayson was accompanied by his family, including two little boys, and the children

were entertained by a pair of French wind-up toys: a mechanical tiger that "crouches back, turns his head menacingly, growls, and then suddenly leaps forward in a way to send delicious chills down the spine of any little boy" and also "a gray elephant which waggled its ears and walked in ponderous elephantic style about the floor." According to Baker's diary, on June 26, 1919, two days before the signing of the Versailles treaty with Germany, Wilson's staff had the "sudden inspiration" of using these wind up toys to surprise and divert the president, so that the tiger growled and leaped at Wilson. "The President laughed heartily," Grayson reported, "and yet, as one could feel, not without restraint. He unbends with the greatest difficulty! And he is tired."[43] There had perhaps been too much growling and lunging over the course of the negotiations for Wilson to find these toys entirely comical—too many unexpectedly hostile antics from favored nations, indeed pet nations, that the president had once presumed to consider as friendly, docile, reasonable, and grateful.

At a Paris press conference on June 27, he spoke about "what we have accomplished here: we have liberated peoples that never had a chance of liberty before—Poles, Jugoslavs, Czechoslavs." On June 28, after signing the treaty, he whispered to Lansing, "I did not know I was excited until I found my hand trembling when I wrote my name."[44] Wilson was tired, and in poor health—but if he trembled as he signed, it was also from consciousness of the weightiness of the moment just concluded with his signature. There would be further treaties to be concluded—Saint-Germain, Neuilly, Trianon, Sèvres, Lausanne—with or without American participation; there were plebiscites pending, geopolitical adjustments still to come. The remapping of Eastern Europe was now passing into history, however, with the new pieces of the reimagined map puzzled together in their newly determined and interlocking forms. Central to this remapping was the reconception of Eastern Europe in its twentieth-century national aspect, supposedly shaped by the will of the peoples themselves, but Wilson's trembling hand surely betrayed some of the uncertainties that he had experienced in the year and half since the solemn proclamation of the Fourteen Points.

There were many issues concerning the settlement of Eastern Europe that he might have regarded with misgivings in Paris on June 28, which was also the fifth anniversary of the assassination of Franz Ferdinand at Sarajevo, a pointed reminder of the extreme fragility of geopolitical circumstances. Wilson, however, lingered over the sentimental bonds of friendship that had inspired his deepest emotional attachments to the map of Eastern Europe. On June 28, he found time to write to Edvard Beneš to thank him for the award of an honorary doctorate from the Charles University in Prague: "It will always be a matter of pride to me that I have received this evidence of the friendship and confidence of my colleagues—if I may call them so—of the University of Prague. It is delightful to be associated in this way with the affairs of a university which will henceforth ornament the scholarship of a great and independent people."[45] A personal sense of friendship remained fundamental for Wilson—a matter of pride and delight—as he placed the "Czechoslavs" (as he oddly denominated them at his press conference) on the map of Europe as an independent people.

On June 28, that momentous day of the treaty signing, Wilson articulated only one last misgiving about the new map of Eastern Europe, a misgiving that emerged from his sudden remembering of a forgotten detail related to a deeply sentimental encounter. Wilson wrote to Lansing:

> The simple peasants whose pictures are enclosed walked some forty or fifty miles to a railway station in their mountain country, and came all the way to Paris to beg that their little mountain pocket might be attached to Poland, and as I am clearing up my papers I am deeply chagrined to find that I forgot to pay attention to their claims at the proper time. If it is not too late, as I sincerely hope it is not, will you not be kind enough to have someone look into the matter and rectify the frontier as they plead it may be rectified, so as to include them in Poland.[46]

These were the Tatra mountaineers, Borowy and Halczyn, who had been granted an audience with Wilson at the Hôtel de Crillon in April: "a quaint petition in boots," according to Ray Stannard Baker, while Grayson had observed that "they smelled very strongly of their herds of goats that they had left in their native hills." Still, Grayson had found that "their meeting with the President was one of the most touching scenes I have ever witnessed"—and Wilson had found himself deeply "moved" and "touched" by their "simplicity and passion."

He completely forgot them, however, and only remembered on June 28—assisted by a photograph that must have evoked their folkloric quaintness—prompting the plea for a last-minute adjustment. No need for a plebiscite. Nothing could have more powerfully illustrated for Wilson the meaning of his own principle of self-determination, of peoples choosing their own sovereignties, than the mountaineers who had traveled all the way to Paris in folk costume to make their voices heard—heard by the American president, "the biggest man in all the world," as they supposedly said in awkward English. Clearly, Wilson's last-minute remembering of the goatherds' delegation was symptomatic of his larger anxieties about the new mapping of Eastern Europe that came into being with the signing of the peace treaty.

In fact, after much dispute between the new states of Poland and Czechoslovakia, a final settlement of the Tatra districts and of Teschen Silesia was determined at the Spa conference of July 1920. That settlement was maintained until September 1938, when Poland took advantage of the Munich agreement and Hitler's seizure of the Sudetenland to launch a Polish occupation of the long-disputed Teschen (Cieszyn) area (with its important railway junction), thus participating in the dismemberment of the Czechoslovakia that Wilson had helped to create. The Tatra districts remain divided today between Slovakia and Poland.

At the Paris peace conference in 1919, Wilson had to recognize that some of his abstract sympathies for the peoples of Eastern Europe could not simply be mapped onto the postwar geopolitical settlement, and that the transformative moment of redesign included political compromises that not only contradicted the principle of self-determination but also ensured the instability of the peace. His sudden remembering of the mountaineers on June 28, 1919, brought back vividly the innocent—almost Rousseauist—commitment to discovering the political will of even primitive peoples and applying their own determinations to the new map. Without his intervention, he feared, the Tatra mountaineers were at risk of becoming members of a minority population, forsaken on the wrong side of the newly drawn borders. Here, as in so many other cases, the idea that the mapping of Eastern Europe was a matter of self-determination—of goatherds in shaggy fur caps giving voice to their political allegiances—was very much a sentimental matter of Wilsonian fantasy. Yet for Wilson himself, on the day that the peace treaty was signed at Versailles, it was reassuring to reflect on his own sentimental feelings of friendship and affinity as the foundation for the reimagining of Eastern Europe.

Notes

The sixty-nine volumes of *The Papers of Woodrow Wilson*, edited by Arthur S. Link (Princeton, NJ: Princeton University Press, 1966–94) are cited in the notes below as *Papers of Woodrow Wilson* followed by the relevant volume and page numbers.

INTRODUCTION

1. Paderewski to Wilson, October 4, 1917, *Papers of Woodrow Wilson*, 44:305.
2. Masaryk to Wilson, August 5, 1918, *Papers of Woodrow Wilson*, 49:185.
3. "First Inaugural Address," in *President Wilson's Addresses*, ed. George McLean Harper (New York: Henry Holt, 1918), 3–8
4. Harold Nicolson, *Peacemaking 1919* (1933; New York: Grosset & Dunlap, 1965), 196–200; Jill Lepore, "The Tug of War: Woodrow Wilson and the Power of the Presidency," *The New Yorker*, September 9, 2013, 83.
5. Alexander George and Juliette George, *Woodrow Wilson and Colonel House: A Personality Study* (New York: Dover Publications, 1964), 117; A. Scott Berg, *Wilson* (New York: Berkley Books, 2013), 294.
6. Norbert Götz and Janne Holmén. "Introduction to the Theme Issue: 'Mental Maps: Geographical and Historical Perspectives,'" *Journal of Cultural Geography* 25, no. 2 (2018): 157–61; Larry Wolff, *Mental Mapping and Eastern Europe*, vol. 12 of the Södertörn lectures, Södertörn University, 2016.
7. Nicole Phelps, *U.S.-Habsburg Relations from 1815 to the Paris Peace Conference* (Cambridge: Cambridge University Press, 2013), 248; Constantin Dumba, *Memoirs of a Diplomat*, trans. Ian Morrow (Boston: Little, Brown, 1932), 224; Gary Gerstle, "Race and Nation in the Thought and Politics of Woodrow Wilson," in *Reconsidering Woodrow Wilson: Progressivism, Internationalism, War, and Peace*, ed. John Milton Cooper Jr. (Washington, DC: Woodrow Wilson Center Press, 2008), 101.
8. Walter Lippmann, *The Political Scene: An Essay on the Victory of 1918* (New York: Henry Holt, 1919), 70.
9. Arthur Herman, *1917: Lenin, Wilson, and the Birth of the New World Disorder* (New York: HarperCollins, 2017), 300–305.
10. Maurice Hankey and Paul Mantoux, notes on Council of Four meeting, April 22, 1919, *Papers of Woodrow Wilson*, 57:614.
11. Sigmund Freud and William C. Bullitt, *Thomas Woodrow Wilson: Twenty-Eighth President of the United States: A Psychological Study* (Boston: Houghton Mifflin, 1966).
12. Charles Neu, *Colonel House: A Biography of Woodrow Wilson's Silent Partner* (Oxford: Oxford University Press, 2015), 331.
13. Larry Wolff, *Inventing Eastern Europe: The Map of Civilization on the Mind of the Enlightenment* (Stanford, CA: Stanford University Press, 1994), 356–74; Holly Case, *The Age of Questions, or, A First Attempt at an Aggregate History of the Eastern, Social, Woman, American, Jewish, Polish, Bullion, Tuberculosis, and Many Other Questions*

over the Nineteenth Century, and Beyond (Princeton, NJ: Princeton University Press, 2018), 8–18.

14. Victor Mamatey, *The United States and East Central Europe, 1914–1918: A Study in Wilsonian Diplomacy and Propaganda* (Princeton, NJ: Princeton University Press, 1957); Erez Manela, *The Wilsonian Moment: Self-Determination and the International Origins of Anticolonial Nationalism* (Oxford: Oxford University Press, 2007).

15. Lloyd Ambrosius, *Woodrow Wilson and American Internationalism* (Cambridge: Cambridge University Press, 2017); Trygve Throntveit, *Power without Victory: Woodrow Wilson and the American Internationalist Experiment* (Chicago: University of Chicago Press, 2017); Manfred Berg, *Woodrow Wilson: Amerika und die Neuordnung der Welt* (Munich: C. H. Beck, 2017); Patricia O'Toole, *The Moralist: Woodrow Wilson and the World He Made* (New York: Simon & Schuster, 2018). See also John Milton Cooper, Jr., *Woodrow Wilson: A Biography* (New York: Vintage Books, 2009).

16. Eckart Conze, *Die Große Illusion: Versailles 1919 und die Neuordnung der Welt* (Munich: Siedler, 2018); Jörn Leonhard, *Der überforderte Frieden: Versailles und die Welt, 1918–1923* (Munich: C. H. Beck, 2018); Leonard Smith, *Sovereignty at the Paris Peace Conference of 1919* (Oxford: Oxford University Press, 2018).

17. Eric Yellin, *Racism in the Nation's Service: Government Workers and the Color Line* (Chapel Hill: University of North Carolina Press, 2013).

18. Larry Wolff, "Woodrow Wilson's Name Has Come and Gone Before," *Washington Post*, December 3, 2015.

19. Ibid.

20. *The Diary of Vaslav Nijinsky*, ed. Joan Acocella, trans. Kyril Fitzlyon (Urbana: University of Illinois Press, 2006), 36–37.

21. Ibid., 62–65.

CHAPTER 1

1. Sigmund Freud and William C. Bullitt, *Thomas Woodrow Wilson: Twenty-Eighth President of the United States: A Psychological Study* (Boston: Houghton Mifflin, 1966), 82–85.

2. R. W. Seton Watson, *Disraeli, Gladstone, and the Eastern Question: A Study in Diplomacy and Party Politics* (New York: Macmillan, 1935); Richard Shannon, *Gladstone and the Bulgarian Agitation, 1876* (1963; 2nd ed., Hassocks, England: Harvester Press, 1975).

3. *The Papers of Woodrow Wilson*, ed. Arthur S. Link (Princeton, NJ: Princeton University Press, 1966–94), 1:412 (1876), 1:642 (1880), 2:6–7 (1881).

4. H. H. Asquith, "The Political Career of Mr. Disraeli," *British Quarterly Review* 64 (July 1876): 179; *Papers of Woodrow Wilson*, 1:187 (1876).

5. *Papers of Woodrow Wilson*, 2:43 (1881).

6. Wilson, "Fourteen Points Speech," January 8, 1918, Point 12.

7. Voltaire to the empress Catherine of Russia, November 15, 1768, cited in Larry Wolff, *Inventing Eastern Europe: The Map of Civilization on the Mind of the Enlightenment* (Stanford, CA: Stanford University Press, 1994), 211.

8. David Katz, *The Shaping of Turkey in the British Imagination, 1776–1923* (New York: Palgrave Macmillan, 2016), 162; William Ewart Gladstone, *Bulgarian Horrors and the Question of the East* (London: John Murray, 1876), 31.

9. Nevzat Uyanik, *Dismantling the Ottoman Empire: Britain, America and the*

Armenian Question (London: Routledge, 2015), 96.

10. Colonel House, diary, December 18, 1912, in *Papers of Woodrow Wilson*, 25:610.

11. Wilson Address in Cincinnati, October 26, 1916, *Papers of Woodrow Wilson*, 38:539.

12. H. H. Asquith, *Memories and Reflections, 1852–1927* (Boston: Little, Brown, 1928), 2:38–39.

13. Colonel House to Wilson, May 21, 1916, *Papers of Woodrow Wilson*, 37:89.

14. Wilson address in Cincinnati, October 26, 1916, *Papers of Woodrow Wilson*, 38, 539.

15. Ibid.

16. Ibid., 537–38.

17. William Graves Sharp to Lansing, translation from the French of Allied note, January 10, 1917, *Papers of Woodrow Wilson*, 40:441; *The Public: An International Journal of Fundamental Democracy* (New York) 20, no. 981, January 19, 1917, 63–64.

18. Balfour to Sir Cecil Arthur Spring Rice, January 13, 1917, *Papers of Woodrow Wilson*, 40:500.

19. Ibid., 501.

20. Diary of Colonel House, January 3, 1917, *Papers of Woodrow Wilson*, 40:404.

21. Ibid.

22. Wilson, speech to the Senate, January 22, 1917, *Papers of Woodrow Wilson*, 40:537.

23. Colonel House to Wilson, January 26, 1917, *Papers of Woodrow Wilson*, 41:24–25; Johann Heinrich von Bernstorff to Lansing, January 31, 1917, *Papers of Woodrow Wilson*, 41: 75–76.

24. Ludovic Moncheur to Charles de Broqueville, August 14, 1917, on meeting with Wilson on August 13, 1917, *Papers of Woodrow Wilson*, 43: 469.

25. Diary of Colonel House, October 13, 1917, *Papers of Woodrow Wilson*, 44: 378–79.

26. Ibid., 379.

27. Morgenthau to Wilson, November 26, 1917, *Papers of Woodrow Wilson*, 45: 123.

28. Ibid., 124.

29. Wilson, State of the Union address, December 4, 1917, *Papers of Woodrow Wilson*, 45: 197.

30. Ibid.

31. Papers of Archibald Cary Coolidge, Harvard University Archives, Writings ser., *Suleiman the Magnificent*, boxes 12 and 13; Harold Jefferson Coolidge and Robert Howard Lord, *Archibald Cary Coolidge: Life and Letters* (Boston: Houghton Mifflin, 1932), 36–37, 192–93; Robert Byrnes, *Awakening American Education to the World: The Role of Archibald Cary Coolidge, 1866–1928* (Notre Dame, IN: University of Notre Dame, 1982), 163–67. See also Lawrence Gelfand, *The Inquiry: American Preparations for Peace, 1917–1919* (New Haven, CT: Yale University Press, 1963).

32. Coolidge to H. Charles Woods, November 20, 1917; and Coolidge to S. E. Mezes, November 24, 1917, Papers of Archibald Cary Coolidge, Harvard University Archives, Life and Letters ser., box 7, The Inquiry folder.

33. Robert Howard Lord, "The Congress of Berlin," in *Three Peace Congresses of the Nineteenth Century and Claimants to Constantinople* (Cambridge, MA: Harvard University Press, 1917), 66-68.

34. Archibald Cary Coolidge, "Claimants to Constantinople," in *Three Peace Congresses of the Nineteenth Century and Claimants to Constantinople*, 77–78, 92–93.

35. Sidney Edward Mezes, David Hunter Miller, and Walter Lippmann, "The Present Situation: The War Aims and Peace Terms It Suggests," memorandum, December 1917, *Papers of Woodrow Wilson*, 45: 471–72.

36. Gelfand, *The Inquiry*, 144–45.

37. First drafts of Fourteen Points, January 5, 1918; transcript of shorthand draft, January 6. 1918; Fourteen Points address, January 8. 1918, *Papers of Woodrow Wilson*, 45: 481–85, 514–15, 536–37.

38. Wilson to the emperor Karl in message from Prince Karl Emil von Fürstenberg to Count Ottokar Czernin, March 5, 1918, *Papers of Woodrow Wilson*, 46: 552.

39. Ljubomir Mihailović to Lansing, April 23, 1918, *Papers of Woodrow Wilson*, 47: 416–17.

40. Sir Eric Drummond to Sir William Wiseman, September 12, 1918, *Papers of Woodrow Wilson*, 49: 537.

41. Lippmann-Cobb memorandum, October 29, 1918, *Papers of Woodrow Wilson*, 51: 501–3.

42. Wilson, address, Metropolitan Opera House, New York, March 4, 1919, *Papers of Woodrow Wilson*, 55:414–15.

43. United Kingdom, Imperial War Cabinet minutes, December 30, 1918, *Papers of Woodrow Wilson*, 53:561.

44. Perin Gürel, "Turkey and the United States after World War I: National Memory, Local Categories, and Provincializing the Transnational," *American Quarterly* 67, no. 2 (June 2015): 353–76; Uyanik, *Dismantling the Ottoman Empire*, 53.

45. Robert Lansing, *The Peace Negotiations: A Personal Narrative* (Scotts Valley, CA: CreateSpace, Jefferson Publication, 2016), 64.

46. Maurice Hankey, notes on Council of Four meeting, March 20, 1919, *Papers of Woodrow Wilson*, 56:114.

47. Memorandum on "Future Administration of Certain Portions of the Turkish Empire," drafted by Wilson or under his direction, March 25, 1919, *Papers of Woodrow Wilson*, 56: 273–74.

48. Hankey, notes on Council of Four meeting, May 5, 1919, *Papers of Woodrow Wilson*, 58: 442.

49. Hankey and Paul Mantoux, notes on Council of Four meeting, May 6, 1919, *Papers of Woodrow Wilson*, 58:475.

50. Hankey and Paul Mantoux, notes on Council of Four meeting, May 7, 1919, *Papers of Woodrow Wilson*, 58: 508.

51. Hankey, notes on Council of Four meeting, May 17, 1919, *Papers of Woodrow Wilson*, 59: 208; Erez Manela, *The Wilsonian Moment: Self-Determination and the International Origins of Anticolonial Nationalism* (Oxford: Oxford University Press, 2007), 97.

52. Edwin Samuel Montagu to Wilson, May 17, 1919, *Papers of Woodrow Wilson*, 59: 238.

53. Ibid.

54. Hankey and Mantoux, notes on Council of Four meeting, May 21, 1919, *Papers of Woodrow Wilson*, 59: 328–30.

55. Voltaire to the empress Catherine, November 15, 1768, cited in Wolff, *Inventing Eastern Europe*, 211.

56. Peace conference diary of William Linn Westermann, May 22, 1919, *Papers of Woodrow Wilson*, 59: 376.

57. Wilson to Henry White, May 23, 1919, *Papers of Woodrow Wilson*, 59: 444; diary of Roy Stannard Baker, May 28, 1919, *Papers of Woodrow Wilson*, 59: 575.

58. Margaret MacMillan, *Paris 1919: Six Months That Changed the World* (2001; New York: Random House, 2003), 434.

59. Hankey and Paul Mantoux, notes on Council of Four meeting, June 25, 1919, *Papers of Woodrow Wilson*, 61: 158–60.

60. Ibid.

61. Ibid.

62. Hankey, notes on Council of Four meeting, June 26, 1919, *Papers of Woodrow Wilson*, 61: 210.

63. Uyanik, *Dismantling the Ottoman Empire*, 96.

64. Hankey and Mantoux, notes on Council of Four meeting, June 25, 1919, *Papers of Woodrow Wilson*, 61: 156–57.

65. Hankey, notes on Council of Four meeting, June 26, 1919, *Papers of Woodrow Wilson*, 61: 210–11.

66. Ibid.

67. Ibid.

68. Treaty of London, Article 9, April 26, 1915, cited in Rodney Carlisle, *World War I* (New York: Facts on File, 2007), 331.

69. Mantoux's notes on meeting of Council of Four, June 26, 1919, *Papers of Woodrow Wilson*, 61: 219–20.

70. Ibid., 221.

71. Ibid., 221–22.

72. "Allies to Italy," June 28, 1919, *Papers of Woodrow Wilson*, 61: 343.

73. Ibid., 345.

74. Wilson, memorandum on future relations with Italy, June 28, 1919, *Papers of Woodrow Wilson*, 61: 346.

75. Notes of press conference, June 27, 1919, *Papers of Woodrow Wilson*, 61: 240.

76. Wilson, address to the Senate, July 10, 1919, *Papers of Woodrow Wilson*, 61: 430.

77. Covenant of the League of Nations, article 22, cited in Arthur Walworth, *Wilson and His Peacemakers: American Diplomacy at the Paris Peace Conference, 1919* (New York: Norton, 1986), 568.

78. Wilson to Lansing, August 8, 1919, *Papers of Woodrow Wilson*, 62: 235.

79. Robert Lansing, "The President's Feelings as to the Present European Situation," August 20, 1919, *Papers of Woodrow Wilson*, 62: 428–29.

80. Ibid.

81. Ibid.

82. Covenant of the League of Nations, article 22, cited in Walworth, *Wilson and his Peacemakers*, 568.

83. Frank Lyon Polk to Wilson and Lansing, August 25, 1919, *Papers of Woodrow Wilson*, 62: 511.

84. Wilson address in St. Louis, September 5, 1919, *Papers of Woodrow Wilson*, 63: 49.

85. Henry Morgenthau, "Mandates or War?" *New York Times Magazine*, November 9, 1919; Uyanik, *Dismantling the Ottoman Empire*, 97–98.

86. Uyanik, *Dismantling the Ottoman Empire*, 151.
87. Lansing to Wilson, January 8, 1920, *Papers of Woodrow Wilson*, 64: 261.
88. Commentator [Archibald Cary Coolidge], "Constantinople and the Straits," *New York Evening Post*, March 19, 1920, Papers of Archibald Cary Coolidge, Harvard University Archives, Biographical Materials ser., Scrapbook, Selections from *The Evening Post*, boxes 4 and 12.
89. Lloyd Ambrosius, *Woodrow Wilson and American Internationalism* (Cambridge: Cambridge University Press, 2017), 189.

CHAPTER 2

1. Frederic Penfield to Wilson, June 28, 1914; Wilson to the emperor Franz Joseph, June 28, 1914, *Papers of Woodrow Wilson*, 30:222.
2. Wilson address in Helena, September 11, 1919, *Papers of Woodrow Wilson*, 63:187.
3. Wayne Vucinich, *Memoirs of My Childhood in Yugoslavia*, ed. Larry Wolff (Palo Alto, CA: Society for the Promotion of Science and Scholarship, 2007), 1–8.
4. Nicole Phelps, *U.S.-Habsburg Relations from 1815 to the Paris Peace Conference* (Cambridge: Cambridge University Press, 2013), 219–57; Victor Mamatey, *The United States and East Central Europe, 1914–1918: A Study in Wilsonian Diplomacy and Propaganda* (Princeton, NJ: Princeton University Press, 1957), 233–317.
5. Johann Heinrich von Bernstorff to Lansing, memorandum, January 31, 2017, *Papers of Woodrow Wilson*, 41: 74–77.
6. Lansing to Walter Hines Page, February 8, 1917, *Papers of Woodrow Wilson*, 41:158–59.
7. Lansing to Penfield, February 22, 1917, *Papers of Woodrow Wilson*, 41:267.
8. Colonel House, diary, April 28, 1917, *Papers of Woodrow Wilson*, 42:156; Charles Neu, *Colonel House: A Biography of Woodrow Wilson's Silent Partner* (Oxford: Oxford University Press, 2015), 299–300.
9. Neu, *Colonel House*, 303.
10. Wilson, Flag Day address, June 14, 1917, *Papers of Woodrow Wilson*, 42:500.
11. Ibid., 501.
12. "Citizens of Foreign Birth to Demonstrate Loyalty in Fourth of July Celebration," *Official Bulletin*, May 25, 1917, 7.
13. Ludovic Moncheur to Charles de Broqueville, August 14, 1917, *Papers of Woodrow Wilson*, 43: 468.
14. Roman Dmowski to W. G. Sharp, November 13, 1917, *Papers of Woodrow Wilson*, 45:553n2.
15. Wilson, State of the Union address, December 4, 1917, *Papers of Woodrow Wilson*, 45:197–99.
16. Bohemian National Alliance of America to Wilson, December 5, 1917, *Papers of Woodrow Wilson*, 45:223–24.
17. Inquiry memorandum, "The Present Situation: The War Aims and Peace Terms It Suggests," memorandum by Sidney Edward Mezes, David Hunter Miller, and Walter Lippmann, December 1917, *Papers of Woodrow Wilson*, 45:460–61.
18. Ibid., 463.
19. Seppo Zetterberg, *Die Liga der Fremdvölker Russlands, 1916–1918: Ein Beitrag zu Deutschlands antirussischem Propagandakrieg unter den Fremdvölkern Russlands im Ersten Weltkrieg* (Helsinki: Suomen Historiallinen Seura, 1978).

20. Lawrence Gelfand, *The Inquiry: American Preparations for Peace, 1917–1919* (New Haven, CT: Yale University Press, 1963), 210–14.

21. R. W Seton-Watson to Intelligence Bureau, "Special Memorandum on the Question of a Separate Peace with Austria," May 1917, in *R. W. Seton-Watson and the Yugoslavs: Correspondence, 1906–1941*, vol. 1 (London: British Academy; Zagreb: University of Zagreb, 1976), 292–93.

22. Inquiry memorandum, "The Present Situation: The War Aims and Peace Terms It Suggests," December 1917, *Papers of Woodrow Wilson*, 45:466–67.

23. Ibid., 471.

24. First drafts of Fourteen Points, January 5, 1918, *Papers of Woodrow Wilson*, 45:481.

25. Frank Lyon Polk to Wilson, January 22, 1918, *Papers of Woodrow Wilson*, 46:78; see also Mamatey, *United States and East Central Europe*, 179–80.

26. Wilson to Frank Lyon Polk, January 23, 1918, *Papers of Woodrow Wilson*, 46:82–83.

27. Reply of Foreign Minister Czernin to the Fourteen Points, January 24, 1918, in *Official Statements of War Aims and Peace Proposals: December 1916 to November 1918*, ed. James Brown Scott (Washington, DC: Carnegie Endowment for International Peace, 1921), 259–60.

28. Ibid., 261; Mamatey, *United States and East Central Europe*, 213–14; Phelps, *U.S.-Habsburg Relations*, 238–39.

29. *New York Times*, November 23, 1916.

30. Phelps, *U.S.-Habsburg Relations*, 226–30; Rudolf Agstner, *Austria (-Hungary) and Its Consulates in the United States of America since 1820* (Zurich: LIT, 2012), 115–24.

31. George Talbot Odell to Lansing, November 10, 1917, *Papers of Woodrow Wilson*, 45:55–57.

32. Ibid., 56.

33. *Frank Leslie's Popular Monthly* 31 (January–June 1891): 749–50.

34. Hugh Robert Wilson to Lansing, January 31, 1918, *Papers of Woodrow Wilson*, 46:198–99; Mamatey, *United States and East Central Europe*, 138–39; Thomas G. Masaryk, *The Making of a State: Memories and Observations, 1914–1918* (1927; New York: Howard Fertig, 1969), 279–83.

35. George Herron, memorandum of conversation, February 3, 1918, *Papers of Woodrow Wilson*, 46:242–47.

36. Ibid., 244.

37. Ibid., 244–45.

38. Ibid., 245–46.

39. Ibid., 246.

40. Ibid., 246–47.

41. Ibid., 247.

42. Wilson, address to joint session of Congress ("Four Points" [Four Principles]), February 11, 1918, *Papers of Woodrow Wilson*, 46:319, 322.

43. Ibid., 320–21.

44. Ibid., 322–23.

45. Ibid., 323.

46. Sigmund Freud and William Bullitt, *Thomas Woodrow Wilson: Twenty-Eighth President of the United States: A Psychological Study* (Boston: Houghton Mifflin, 1966), 6.

47. Balfour to Colonel House, February 27, 1918, *Papers of Woodrow Wilson*, 46:483.

48. Ibid., 484.

49. Seton-Watson to Intelligence Bureau, February 1918, in *R. W. Seton-Watson and the Yugoslavs*, 1:315–16.
50. King Alfonso XIII of Spain to Wilson (message from Emperor Karl to Wilson), February 25, 1918, *Papers of Woodrow Wilson*, 46:440–42.
51. Ibid., 442.
52. Prince Karl Emil von Fürstenberg to Count Ottokar Czernin (reply from Wilson to Emperor Karl), March 5, 1918, *Papers of Woodrow Wilson*, 46:551–52.
53. Ibid., 552.
54. Mamatey, *United States and East Central Europe*, 228.
55. Count Ottokar Czernin to Prince Karl Emil von Fürstenberg (Emperor Karl's reply to Wilson), March 23, 1918, *Papers of Woodrow Wilson*, 47:124–26; Mamatey, *United States and East Central Europe*, 232.
56. Lansing to Wilson, May 10, 1918, *Papers of Woodrow Wilson*, 47:589–91.
57. Ibid., 591.
58. George Herron to Wilson, May 31, 1918, *Papers of Woodrow Wilson*, 48:210–13.
59. Ibid., 212–13.
60. Lansing, "Memorandum on the Policy of the United States in Relation to the Nationalities Included within the Austro-Hungarian Empire," June 24, 1918, *Papers of Woodrow Wilson*, 48:435–37.
61. Ibid., 437.
62. Lansing to Ljubomir Mihailović, June 24, 1918, *Papers of Woodrow Wilson*, 48:437.
63. Wilson to Lansing, June 26, 1918, *Papers of Woodrow Wilson*, 48:435.
64. Wilson, "Constitutional Government in the United States" (1908), *Papers of Woodrow Wilson*, 18: 72–73.
65. Lansing to Wilson, June 27, 1918, *Papers of Woodrow Wilson*, 48:447–48; Mamatey, *United States and East Central Europe*, 270.
66. *Address of President Wilson Delivered at Mount Vernon*, July 4, 1918 (Washington, DC: Government Printing Office, 1918), 3–5.
67. Lansing to Wilson, August 19, 1918, *Papers of Woodrow Wilson*, 49: 287–89.
68. Wilson to Lansing, August 22, 1918, *Papers of Woodrow Wilson*, 49:313.
69. Masaryk, memorandum on "The Recognition of the Czechoslovak National Council and of the Czechoslovak Army," August 31, 1918, cited in Mamatey, *United States and East Central Europe*, 306–7.
70. Mamatey, *United States and East Central Europe*, 309.
71. Masaryk to Wilson, September 7, 1918, *Papers of Woodrow Wilson*, 49:485.
72. Wilson to Masaryk, September 10, 1918, *Papers of Woodrow Wilson*, 49:511–12; A. Scott Berg, *Wilson* (New York: Berkley Books, 2013), 305.
73. Draft of a note to the Austro-Hungarian Government, October 19, 1918, *Papers of Woodrow Wilson*, 51:383; Mamatey, *United States and East Central Europe*, 330–31; Declaration of Independence of the Czechoslovak Nation, October 18, 1918, in David Armitage, *The Declaration of Independence: A Global History* (Cambridge, MA: Harvard University Press, 2007), 225–30.
74. Cardinal James Gibbons to Wilson, October 12, 1918, *Papers of Woodrow Wilson*, 51:309.
75. Wilson to Cardinal James Gibbons, October 18, 1918, *Papers of Woodrow Wilson*, 51:374.

76. August Ekengren to Lansing, October 29, 1918, *Papers of Woodrow Wilson*, 51:505.

77. Lippmann-Cobb Memorandum, October 29, 1918, *Papers of Woodrow Wilson*, 51:501.

78. Ibid., 501–3.

79. Franklin Knight Lane, memorandum, November 1, 1918, *Papers of Woodrow Wilson*, 51:548.

80. Ibid.

81. Joseph McAuley, "When Presidents and Popes Meet: Woodrow Wilson and Benedict XV," *America Magazine: The Jesuit Review*, September 4, 2015.

82. Thomas Nelson Page to Wilson, November 5, 1918, *Papers of Woodrow Wilson*, 51:602–3.

83. Wilson, appeal to peoples of Austria-Hungary, conveyed in telegram from Lansing to Pleasant Alexander Stovall, November 5, 1918, *Papers of Woodrow Wilson*, 51:603.

84. Harold Jefferson Coolidge and Robert Howard Lord, *Archibald Cary Coolidge: Life and Letters* (Boston: Houghton Mifflin, 1932), 195–96.

85. Ibid.

86. Ibid., 198, 204–5.

87. Ibid., 209–11.

88. Robert Byrnes, *Awakening American Education to the World: The Role of Archibald Cary Coolidge, 1866–1928* (Notre Dame, IN: University of Notre Dame Press, 1982), 173–74.

89. Draft of Covenant for League of Nations, January 8, 1919, *Papers of Woodrow Wilson*, 53:672

90. Wilson, address, Metropolitan Opera House, New York, March 4, 1919, *Papers of Woodrow Wilson*, 55:414–15.

91. Ibid.

92. Cary Grayson, diary, March 4, 1919, *Papers of Woodrow Wilson*, 55, 412.

93. Maurice Hankey, notes on Council of Four meeting, March 20, 1919, *Papers of Woodrow Wilson*, 56:114.

94. Archibald Cary Coolidge, "Memorandum: The New Frontiers in Former Austria-Hungary," March 10, 1919, in *Papers Relating to the Foreign Relations of the United States: The Paris Peace Conference, 1919*, 12:272–73.

95. Wilson, "Memorandum Concerning the Question of Italian Claims on the Adriatic," April 14, 1919, *Papers of Woodrow Wilson*, 57:343.

96. Ibid., 344–45.

97. Hankey and Mantoux, notes on Council of Four meeting, May 26, 1919, *Papers of Woodrow Wilson*, 59:496.

98. Ibid., 498.

99. Ibid.

100. Ibid., 499.

101. Hankey, notes on Council of Four meeting, May 31, 1919, *Papers of Woodrow Wilson*, 59: 631.

102. Mantoux, notes on Council of Four meeting, May 27, 1919, *Papers of Woodrow Wilson*, 59:536–37.

103. Hankey, notes on Council of Four meeting, 27 June 1919, *Papers of Woodrow Wilson*, 61, 256.

104. Coolidge and Lord, *Archibald Cary Coolidge: Life and Letters*, 218–19.

105. Mantoux, notes on Council of Four meeting, May 28, 1919, *Papers of Woodrow Wilson*, 59: 567.

106. Béla Kun, telegram to Georges Clemenceau, June 16, 1919, *Papers of Woodrow Wilson*, 60:598.

107. Vittorio Orlando, memorandum citing report from Budapest of Livio Borghese, March 25, 1919, *Papers of Woodrow Wilson*, 56:277.

108. Wilson, address, Columbus, Ohio, September 4, 1919, *Papers of Woodrow Wilson*, 63:10.

109. Ibid., 10–11.

110. Ibid., 13.

111. Wilson, address, San Diego, CA, September 19, 1919, *Papers of Woodrow Wilson*, 63:372–73.

112. Wilson, address, Omaha, Nebr., September 8, 1919, *Papers of Woodrow Wilson*, 63:98.

113. Wilson, address, San Diego, CA, September 19, 1919, *Papers of Woodrow Wilson*, 63:372.

114. Ibid.

CHAPTER 3

1. Wilson, "Memorandum Concerning the Question of Italian Claims on the Adriatic," April 14, 1919, *Papers of Woodrow Wilson*, 57:344.

2. Jörn Leonhard, *Der überforderte Frieden: Versailles und die Welt, 1918–1923* (Munich: C. H. Beck, 2018), 373; Leonard Smith, *Sovereignty at the Paris Peace Conference of 1919* (Oxford: Oxford University Press, 2018), 196–210.

3. Wilson, "Memorandum Concerning the Question of Italian Claims on the Adriatic," April 14, 1919, *Papers of Woodrow Wilson*, 57:344.

4. Wilson, speech at the White House to the Democratic National Committee, February 28, 1919, cited in Joseph Tumulty, *Woodrow Wilson as I Know Him* (Garden City, NY: Doubleday, 1921), 372; also cited in *Papers of Woodrow Wilson*, 55:317–18.

5. Wilson, speech at the White House to the Democratic National Committee, February 28, 1919, cited in n. 4 above.

6. Steven Seegel, *Map Men: Transnational Lives and Deaths of Geographers in the Making of East Central Europe* (Chicago: University of Chicago Press, 2018), 71–106; Robert Byrnes, *Awakening American Education to the World: The Role of Archibald Cary Coolidge, 1866–1928* (Notre Dame, IN: University of Notre Dame Press, 1982), 165–66.

7. Eugeniusz Romer, *Pamiętnik paryski (1918–1919)*, ed. Andrzej Garlicki and Ryszard Świętek (Wrocław: Zakład Narodowy imienia Ossolińskich, 1989), 108–9, 251.

8. Robert Howard Lord, *The Second Partition of Poland: A Study in Diplomatic History* (Cambridge, MA: Harvard University Press, 1915); based on his doctoral dissertation at Harvard, "Austrian Policy and the Second Partition of Poland" (1910).

9. Lawrence Gelfand, *The Inquiry: American Preparations for Peace, 1917–1919* (New Haven, CT: Yale University Press, 1963), 201, 219.

10. Ibid., 54–59, 168–69, 217–18.

11. David Glaser, *Robert Lansing: A Study in Statecraft* (Bloomington, IN: Xlibris, 2015), 34.

12. Gelfand, *The Inquiry*, 158.

13. Wilson, address, Des Moines, Iowa, September 6, 1919, *Papers of Woodrow Wilson*, 63:82.

14. Robert Lansing, *The Peace Negotiations: A Personal Narrative* (Scotts Valley, CA: CreateSpace, Jefferson Publication, 2016), 46.

15. Wilson, Remarks to a delegation from the National Race Congress, October 1, 1918, *Papers of Woodrow Wilson*, 51:168.

16. Alexander of Serbia to Wilson, October 24, 1917, *Papers of Woodrow Wilson*, 44:436–37.

17. Ibid.

18. Nicole Phelps, *U.S.-Habsburg Relations from 1815 to the Paris Peace Conference* (Cambridge: Cambridge University Press, 2013), 254.

19. George Jan Sosnowski to Wilson, August 8, 1917, *Papers of Woodrow Wilson*, 44:4–5; M. B. Biskupski, "Polonia's Ambassador to the United States: The Mystery of Jerzy Jan Sosnowski, 1917–1918," *Polish American Studies* 73, no. 1 (Spring 2016): 83–95.

20. Alexander Dębski and Bronisław Kulakowski to Wilson, August 8, 1917, *Papers of Woodrow Wilson*, 44:7.

21. Piotr Wandycz, *The United States and Poland* (Cambridge, MA: Harvard University Press, 1980), 111–13; Kay Lundgreen-Nielsen, *The Polish Problem at the Paris Peace Conference: A Study of the Policies of the Great Powers and the Poles, 1918–1919* (Odense, Denmark: Odense University Press, 1979), 40–44; Wilson, "Peace without Victory" speech, January 22, 1917, *Congressional Record*, 64th Cong., 2nd sess.

22. Colonel House to Wilson, April 4, 1917, *Papers of Woodrow Wilson*, 41:543–44; Wandycz, *United States and Poland*, 129; Charles Neu, *Colonel House: A Biography of Woodrow Wilson's Silent Partner* (Oxford: Oxford University Press, 2015), 302; Margaret MacMillan, *Paris 1919: Six Months That Changed the World* (2001; New York: Random House, 2003), 213; Michael Kunczik, "Forgotten Roots of International Public Relations: Attempts of Germany, Great Britain, Czechoslovakia, and Poland to Influence the United States during World War I," in *Pathways to Public Relations: Histories of Practice and Profession*, ed. Burton St. John III, Margot Opdycke Lamme, and Jacquie L'Etang (London: Routledge, 2014), 101.

23. Paderewski to Wilson, October 4, 1917, *Papers of Woodrow Wilson*, 44:303. See also Mirosław Frančić, *Komitet Obrony Narodowej w Ameryce 1912–1918* (Wrocław: Zakład Narodowy im. Ossolińskich, 1983); and Louis Gerson, *Woodrow Wilson and the Rebirth of Poland 1914–1920: A Study in the Influence on American Policy of Minority Groups of Foreign Origin* (New Haven: Yale University Press, 1953).

24. Lundgreen-Nielsen, *The Polish Problem at the Paris Peace Conference*, 41.

25. Gelfand, *The Inquiry*, 148.

26. Paderewski to Wilson, October 4, 1917, *Papers of Woodrow Wilson*, 44:305.

27. Norman Hapgood to Wilson, January 29, 1917, *Papers of Woodrow Wilson*, 41:56–57.

28. Charles Crane to Wilson and Wilson to John Sharp Williams, both May 8, 1918; Wilson to Joseph Tumulty, May 10, 1918, *Papers of Woodrow Wilson*, 47:561.

29. Wilson to Helena de Rosen Paderewska, May 9, 1918, *Papers of Woodrow Wilson*, 47:576.

30. Lithuanian National Council, petition, May 2, 1918, *Papers of Woodrow Wilson*, 47:492–94.

31. Gelfand, *The Inquiry*, 211.

32. George Herron to Wilson, May 31, 1918, *Papers of Woodrow Wilson*, 48:210–13.
33. Charles Crane, July 2, 1918, *Papers of Woodrow Wilson*, 48:485–86.
34. Neu, *Colonel House*, 341.
35. Harold Jefferson Coolidge and Robert Howard Lord, *Archibald Cary Coolidge: Life and Letters* (Boston: Houghton Mifflin, 1932), 24–25, 45–46, 178–79, 346; see also Byrnes, *Awakening American Education to the World*, 102–12.
36. Larry Wolff, *Inventing Eastern Europe: The Map of Civilization on the Mind of the Enlightenment* (Stanford, CA: Stanford University Press, 1994), 312–13.
37. Wilson to Senator Gilbert Hitchcock, July 11, 1918, *Papers of Woodrow Wilson*, 48:591.
38. Wilson to Lansing, June 19, 1918, *Papers of Woodrow Wilson*, 48:358; Victor Mamatey, *The United States and East Central Europe, 1914–1918: A Study in Wilsonian Diplomacy and Propaganda* (Princeton, NJ: Princeton University Press, 1957), 285–86.
39. Masaryk to Wilson, September 7, 1918, *Papers of Woodrow Wilson*, 49:485–86; Wilson to Masaryk, September 10, 1918, *Papers of Woodrow Wilson*, 49:511–12.
40. Wilson to Masaryk, October 21, 1918, *Papers of Woodrow Wilson*, 51:395.
41. "Declaration of Independence of the Czechoslovak Nation," October 18, 1918 (New York: Czechoslovak Arts Club of New York City, 1918), 6.
42. Neu, *Colonel House*, 356, 383.
43. Coolidge and Lord, *Archibald Cary Coolidge: Life and Letters*, 196–97, 200–201.
44. Masaryk to Wilson, January 2, 1919, *Papers of Woodrow Wilson*, 53:590; Andrea Orzoff, *Battle for the Castle: The Myth of Czechoslovakia in Europe, 1914–1948* (Oxford: Oxford University Press, 2009), 50–56.
45. Wilson to Masaryk, January 10, 1919, *Papers of Woodrow Wilson*, 53:711.
46. Archibald Cary Coolidge, "Memorandum: The New Frontiers in Former Austria-Hungary," March 10, 1919, in *Papers Relating to the Foreign Relations of the United States: The Paris Peace Conference, 1919*, 12:274–75.
47. Nicholas I of Montenegro to Wilson, January 7, 1919, *Papers of Woodrow Wilson*, 53:701.
48. Ibid., 702.
49. Pierre-Augustin Caron de Beaumarchais, *The Barber of Seville*, trans. John Wood (London: Penguin Classics, 1988), 61–62.
50. Nicholas I of Montenegro to Wilson, January 7, 1919, *Papers of Woodrow Wilson*, 53:702.
51. Ibid., 703.
52. Wilson to Lansing, January 9, 1919, *Papers of Woodrow Wilson*, 53:700.
53. Wilson to Nicholas I of Montenegro, January 9, 1919, *Papers of Woodrow Wilson*, 53:704.
54. Ibid.
55. Hankey, notes on Council of Ten meeting, January 12, 1919, *Papers of Woodrow Wilson*, 54:18–19
56. Ibid., 20.
57. Balfour to Colonel House, 28 March 1919, *Papers of Woodrow Wilson*, 56, 394–95.
58. Ibid.
59. "Winning the Peace," in *The Public: A Journal of Democracy* 21, no. 1077 (November 23, 1918): 1423.
60. Clive Day to Lansing, May 6, 1919, *Papers of Woodrow Wilson*, 59:178–79n2.

61. Harold Nicolson, *Peacemaking 1919* (1933; New York: Grosset & Dunlap, 1965), 151–52; Wayne Vucinich, "An American View of Conditions in Montenegro, 1918–1919," *Balcanica*, 13–14 (Belgrade, 1982–83):271–79.

62. Queen Marie of Romania to Wilson, July 3, 1917, *Papers of Woodrow Wilson*, 43:95.

63. Cary Grayson, diary, April 10, 1919, *Papers of Woodrow Wilson*, 57:190–91.

64. Ibid., 191.

65. Ibid., 192.

66. Ibid., 192–93.

67. Ibid., April 11, 1919, *Papers of Woodrow Wilson*, 57:238.

68. Ibid., 238–39.

69. Edith Benham, diary, April 11, 1919, *Papers of Woodrow Wilson*, 57:241–42.

70. Lansing, "Memorandum: The President's Feelings as to the Present European Situation," August 20, 1919, *Papers of Woodrow Wilson*, 62:428–29.

71. Diary of Ray Stannard Baker, 22 April 1919, *Papers of Woodrow Wilson*, 57: 585.

72. Ray Stannard Baker, memorandum for the President, December 18, 1918, *Papers of Woodrow Wilson*, 53:435.

73. Wilson, address to the Italian Parliament, January 3, 1919, *Papers of Woodrow Wilson*, 53:598.

74. Ibid.

75. Thomas Nelson Page to Wilson, January 7, 1919, *Papers of Woodrow Wilson*, 53:639–40.

76. Ibid., 641.

77. Colonel House to Wilson, telegram no. 120, November 18, 1918, *Papers of Woodrow Wilson*, 53:123–24.

78. Cary Grayson, diary, January 9, 1919, *Papers of Woodrow Wilson*, 53:697.

79. Ibid., 696–97.

80. Wilson to King Vittorio Emanuele III, January 9, 1919, *Papers of Woodrow Wilson*, 53:697.

81. Wilson to Prime Minister Vittorio Orlando, January 13, 1919, *Papers of Woodrow Wilson*, 54:50–51.

82. Wilson, address, Boston, Mass., February 24, 1919, *Papers of Woodrow Wilson*, 55:242–43.

83. Isaiah Bowman to Colonel House, April 11, 1919; Wilson, "Italy" memorandum, April 11, 1919, *Papers of Woodrow Wilson*, 57:270–71.

84. Hankey, notes on Council of Four meeting, April 19, 1919, *Papers of Woodrow Wilson*, 57:486–87; Neu, *Colonel House*, 416.

85. Hankey, notes on Council of Four meeting, April 19, 1919, *Papers of Woodrow Wilson*, 57:489.

86. Ibid., 486.

87. Hankey and Mantoux, notes on Council of Four meeting, April 21, 1919, *Papers of Woodrow Wilson*, 57:549.

88. Hankey and Mantoux, notes on Council of Four meeting, April 22, 1919, *Papers of Woodrow Wilson*, 57:614.

89. Hankey and Mantoux, notes on Council of Four meeting, April 23, 1919, *Papers of Woodrow Wilson*, 58:15.

90. Nicolson, *Peacemaking*, diary entry for April 25, 1919, 315–16.

91. Hankey and Mantoux, notes on Council of Four meeting, April 23, 1919, *Papers*

of Woodrow Wilson, 58:17.

92. Wilson, statement on the Adriatic question, April 23, 1919, *Papers of Woodrow Wilson*, 58:5–7.

93. Nikola Pašić to Wilson, April 23, 1919, *Papers of Woodrow Wilson*, 58:44.

94. "Orlando Makes Protest," *New York Times*, April 25, 1919, *Papers of Woodrow Wilson*, 58:98–99.

95. Mantoux, notes on Council of Four meeting, June 6, 1919, *Papers of Woodrow Wilson*, 60:215.

96. Ibid., 214.

97. Larry Wolff, *Venice and the Slavs: The Discovery of Dalmatia in the Age of Enlightenment* (Stanford, CA: Stanford University Press, 2001), 86–87.

98. Colonel House, diary, May 12, 1919, *Papers of Woodrow Wilson*, 59:68.

99. Mantoux, notes on conversation among Wilson, Clemenceau, and Lloyd George, May 26, 1919, *Papers of Woodrow Wilson*, 59:494.

100. Hankey and Mantoux, notes on Council of Four meeting, May 26, 1919, *Papers of Woodrow Wilson*, 59:506–7.

101. Mantoux, notes on Council of Four meeting, June 12, 1919, *Papers of Woodrow Wilson*, 60:478.

102. Mantoux, notes on Council of Four meeting, June 13, 1919, *Papers of Woodrow Wilson*, 60:530.

103. Mantoux, notes on Council of Four meeting, June 26, 1919, *Papers of Woodrow Wilson*, 61:219 & 223.

104. Wilson, memorandum on future relations with Italy, June 28, 1919, *Papers of Woodrow Wilson*, 61:346.

105. Report of press conference, July 10, 1919, *Papers of Woodrow Wilson*, 61:420.

106. Wilson, address in Columbus, Ohio, September 4, 1919, *Papers of Woodrow Wilson*, 63:11.

107. Ibid., 13.

108. Ibid., 14.

109. Aviva Taubenfeld, *Rough Writing: Ethnic Authorship in Theodore Roosevelt's America* (New York: New York University Press, 2008), 42–44.

110. Message from Peter Augustus Jay at U.S. Embassy in Rome, September 12, 1919, cited in telegram from William Philipps to Wilson, September 15, 1919, *Papers of Woodrow Wilson*, 63:297–98.

111. Instructions from the president to Peter Augustus Jay, cited in telegram from Wilson to William Phillips, September 28, 1919, *Papers of Woodrow Wilson*, 63:534.

112. Coolidge and Lord, *Archibald Cary Coolidge: Life and Letters*, 219–20.

113. Wilson to Lansing, with Enclosure, 7 February 1920, *Papers of Woodrow Wilson*, 64, 375–80.

114. Wilson to Bainbridge Colby, November 15, 1920, first of three letters, *Papers of Woodrow Wilson*, 66:367.

115. Wilson to Bainbridge Colby, November 15, 1920, second of three letters, *Papers of Woodrow Wilson*, 66:367.

116. Wilson to Francis Klapuš, January 3, 1923, *Papers of Woodrow Wilson*, 68:263.

117. Alice Garrigue Masaryk to Wilson, March 20, 1923, *Papers of Woodrow Wilson*, 68:296–97.

118. Wilson to Alice Garrigue Masaryk, April 18, 1923, *Papers of Woodrow Wilson*, 68:337.
119. Wilson to Tomáš Masaryk, May 19, 1923, *Papers of Woodrow Wilson*, 68:364.
120. Sylvester Beach to Wilson, May 1, 1923, *Papers of Woodrow Wilson*, 68:352.
121. Wilson to Masaryk, November 23, 1923, *Papers of Woodrow Wilson*, 68:481.
122. Venizélos, Pašić, Beneš, Nubar, and Sokolow to Wilson, July 7, 1919, *Papers of Woodrow Wilson*, 61:461.
123. Wilson to Frank Lyon Polk, July 12, 1919, *Papers of Woodrow Wilson*, 61:461.

CHAPTER 4

1. Wilson, address, Boston, Mass., February 24, 1919, *Papers of Woodrow Wilson*, 55:242–43; Venizélos, Pašić, Beneš, Nubar, and Sokolow to Wilson, July 7, 1919, *Papers of Woodrow Wilson*, 61:461.
2. Eugeniusz Romer, *Pamiętnik paryski (1918–1919)*, ed. Andrzej Garlicki and Ryszard Świętek (Wrocław: Zakład Narodowy imienia Ossolińskich, 1989), 49.
3. Lippmann-Cobb Memorandum, October 29, 1918, *Papers of Woodrow Wilson*, 51:501.
4. Sigmund Freud and William Bullitt, *Thomas Woodrow Wilson: Twenty-Eighth President of the United States: A Psychological Study* (Boston: Houghton Mifflin, 1966), 153–54.
5. Lippmann-Cobb Memorandum, October 29, 1918, *Papers of Woodrow Wilson*, 51:501.
6. Ibid., 503–4; Kay Lundgreen-Nielsen, *The Polish Problem at the Paris Peace Conference: A Study of the Policies of the Great Powers and the Poles, 1918–1919* (Odense, Denmark: Odense University Press, 1979), 84–86.
7. Paderewski to Wilson, October 4, 1917, *Papers of Woodrow Wilson*, 44:305.
8. Louis Marshall to Wilson, November 7, 1918, *Papers of Woodrow Wilson*, 51:625; Carole Fink, "Louis Marshall: An American Jewish Diplomat in Paris, 1919," *American Jewish History*, 94, no. 1–2 (March–June 2008): 21–40.
9. Piotr Wandycz, *The United States and Poland* (Cambridge MA: Harvard University Press, 1980), 121–22.
10. Louis Marshall to Wilson, November 7, 1918, *Papers of Woodrow Wilson*, 51:625–27; Wandycz, *United States and Poland*, 159.
11. Lundgreen-Nielsen, *The Polish Problem at the Paris Peace Conference*, 42–44.
12. Louis Marshall to Wilson, November 16, 1918, *Papers of Woodrow Wilson*, 53:104; Wandycz, *United States and Poland*, 159.
13. Marshall to Wilson, November 16, 1918, *Papers of Woodrow Wilson*, 53:105.
14. Paderewski to Colonel House, January 12, 1919, *Papers of Woodrow Wilson*, 54:32; Larry Wolff, *The Idea of Galicia: History and Fantasy in Habsburg Political Culture* (Stanford. CA: Stanford University Press, 2010), 367–74.
15. Paderewski to Colonel House, January 12, 1919, *Papers of Woodrow Wilson*, 54:33.
16. Paderewski to Lansing, January 21, 1919, *Papers of Woodrow Wilson*, 54:195.
17. Maurice Hankey, notes on Supreme War Council meeting, January 22, 1919, *Papers of Woodrow Wilson*, 54:201.
18. Ibid., 202.

19. Ibid., 203.
20. Lansing to Paderewski, January 22, 1919, *Papers of Woodrow Wilson*, 54:217.
21. Cary Grayson, diary, February 8, 1919, *Papers of Woodrow Wilson*, 55:3.
22. Wilson, address, Boston, Mass., February 24, 1919, *Papers of Woodrow Wilson*, 55:243.
23. American Jewish Congress (Julian Mack, Louis Marshall, Stephen Wise, Bernard Richards), memorandum on East European Jews, March 1, 1919, *Papers of Woodrow Wilson*, 55:368–85.
24. Charles Neu, *Colonel House: A Biography of Woodrow Wilson's Silent Partner* (Oxford: Oxford University Press, 2015), 338; Freud and Bullitt, *Thomas Woodrow Wilson*, 154.
25. American Jewish Congress (Julian Mack, Louis Marshall, Stephen Wise, Bernard Richards), memorandum on East European Jews, March 1, 1919, *Papers of Woodrow Wilson*, 55:369.
26. Ibid., 370–71.
27. Ibid., 373–76.
28. Ibid., 376–77.
29. Ibid., 378–79.
30. Ibid., 380
31. American Jewish Congress (Julian Mack, Louis Marshall, Stephen Wise, Bernard Richard), memorandum on Palestine, March 1, 1919, *Papers of Woodrow Wilson*, 55:382.
32. Chaim Weizmann to Wilson, January 23, 1919; Zionist Organizations for Poland, telegram, January 21, 1919, *Papers of Woodrow Wilson*, 54:231–32.
33. American Jewish Congress (Julian Mack, Louis Marshall, Stephen Wise, Bernard Richards), memorandum on East European Jews, March 1, 1919, *Papers of Woodrow Wilson*, 55;381.
34. Lansing, House, Tasker Bliss, and Henry White to Wilson, March 20, 1919, *Papers of Woodrow Wilson*, 56:122–24.
35. Hankey, notes on Council of Ten meeting, March 19, 1919, *Papers of Woodrow Wilson*, 56:94.
36. Gilbert Fairchild Close to Lansing, March 19, 1919, *Papers of Woodrow Wilson*, 56:96.
37. Alexander Comstock Kirk to Gilbert Fairchild Close, March 19, 1919, *Papers of Woodrow Wilson*, 56:97.
38. Wilson to Lansing, March 20, 1919, *Papers of Woodrow Wilson*, 56:119; Larry Wolff, *The Idea of Galicia*, 374–79.
39. Tasker Bliss to Wilson, March 31, 1919, *Papers of Woodrow Wilson*, 56:468–69.
40. Paul Mantoux, notes on meeting of Council of Four, April 2, 1919, *Papers of Woodrow Wilson*, 56:529. See also Mieczysław Biskupski, "The Wilsonian View of Poland: Idealism and Geopolitical Traditionalism," in *Wilsonian East Central Europe: Current Perspectives*, 123–45.
41. Mantoux, notes on meeting of Council of Four, April 1, 1919, *Papers of Woodrow Wilson*, 56:508.
42. Ibid., 508–9.
43. Archibald Cary Coolidge, "Memorandum: The New Frontiers in Former Austria-Hungary," March 10, 1919, in *Papers Relating to the Foreign Relations of the United States: The Paris Peace Conference, 1919*, 12:273–74.
44. Archibald Cary Coolidge, memorandum on the rights of national minorities, April 1, 1919, *Papers of Woodrow Wilson*, 56:511–12; Harold Jefferson Coolidge and

Robert Howard Lord, *Archibald Cary Coolidge: Life and Letters* (Boston: Houghton Mifflin, 1932), 231–32.

45. Coolidge, memorandum on the rights of national minorities, cited in n. 48 above.

46. Wilson, "Memorandum Concerning the Question of Italian Claims on the Adriatic," April 14, 1919, *Papers of Woodrow Wilson*, 57:345.

47. Ray Stannard Baker, diary, March 31, 1919, *Papers of Woodrow Wilson*, 56:442.

48. Ibid.

49. Waldemar Ireneusz Oszczęda, "Polskie postaci historyczne Orawy i Spiszu," *Almanach Muszyny 2011*, 185–90; Thaddeus Gromada, "Woodrow Wilson and Self-Determination for Spisz and Orawa," in *Wilsonian East Central Europe: Current Perspectives*, ed. John Micgiel (New York: Piłsudski Institute, 1995), 25–39.

50. Gromada, "Woodrow Wilson and Self-Determination," 34.

51. Cary Grayson, diary, April 11, 1919, *Papers of Woodrow Wilson*, 57: 237–38.

52. Paul Mantoux, notes on Council of Four meeting, April 12, 1919, *Papers of Woodrow Wilson*, 57: 290.

53. Ibid., 289–90.

54. Lansing to Wilson, April 13, 1919, *Papers of Woodrow Wilson*, 57:326–27.

55. R. H. Lord, memorandum on Polish-Ukrainian conflict, *Papers of Woodrow Wilson*, 57:327–29.

56. Ibid.

57. R. H. Lord to Joseph Clark Grew, April 8, 1919; Lord, memorandum on Baltic countries, *Papers of Woodrow Wilson*, 57: 137–39.

58. Hankey, notes on Council of Four meeting, May 1, 1919, *Papers of Woodrow Wilson*, 58: 284–85.

59. Ibid.

60. Ibid., 285; Wiesław Śladkowski, "Clemenceau et la Pologne," *Annales Universitatis Mariae Curie-Skłodowska, Sectio F, Historia* 41–42 (1986–87): 9–12; Georges Clemenceau, *Au pied du Sinaï* (Paris: Henri Floury, 1898); Larry Wolff, *The Idea of Galicia*, 311–26.

61. Mantoux, notes on Council of Four meeting, "Protection of National and Religious Minorities," May 1, 1919, *Papers of Woodrow Wilson*, 58: 287.

62. David Hunter Miller, memorandum, May 3, 1919, *Papers of Woodrow Wilson*, 58:383.

63. Hankey and Mantoux, notes on Council of Four meeting, May 3, 1919, *Papers of Woodrow Wilson*, 58: 385–86.

64. David Hunter Miller, diary, May 3, 1919, *Papers of Woodrow Wilson*, 58:381.

65. Hankey and Mantoux, notes on Council of Four meeting, May 8, 1919, *Papers of Woodrow Wilson*, 58:537–38.

66. Colonel House, diary, May 7, 1919, *Papers of Woodrow Wilson*, 58:520.

67. Grayson, diary, May 7, 1919, *Papers of Woodrow Wilson*, 58:502.

68. Harold Nicolson, *Peacemaking 1919* (1933; New York: Grosset & Dunlap, 1965), April 16, 1919, 314.

69. Hankey, notes on Council of Four meeting, May 17, 1919, *Papers of Woodrow Wilson*, 59:215–17; Paderewski to Wilson, October 4, 1917, *Papers of Woodrow Wilson*, 44:305.

70. Committee on New States, second report, May 13, 1919, *Papers of Woodrow Wilson*, 59:180–83.

71. David Hunter Miller to Wilson, May 15, 1919, *Papers of Woodrow Wilson*, 59:179.
72. Hankey, notes on Council of Four meeting, May 17, 1919, *Papers of Woodrow Wilson*, 59:218–20.
73. Ibid., 220.
74. Felix Frankfurter to Gilbert Fairchild Close, May 22, 1919, with enclosure dated May 12, 1919, from an unnamed Warsaw correspondent, *Papers of Woodrow Wilson*, 59:411–13.
75. Louis Marshall to Wilson, May 23, 1919, *Papers of Woodrow Wilson*, 59:445–46; Larry Wolff, *The Idea of Galicia*, 370–74.
76. Louis Marshall to Wilson, May 26, 1919, *Papers of Woodrow Wilson*, 59:515.
77. Hankey and Mantoux, notes on Council of Four meeting, May 26, 1919, *Papers of Woodrow Wilson*, 59:507.
78. Nicolson, *Peacemaking*, April 4, 1919, 298.
79. Paderewski to Wilson, May 31, 1919, *Papers of Woodrow Wilson*, 59:638.
80. Ibid.
81. Romer, *Pamiętnik paryski*, 150.
82. Committee on New States, report on method of appeal to the League of Nations, June 6, 1919, *Papers of Woodrow Wilson*, 60:223.
83. Hankey and Mantoux, notes on Council of Four meeting, June 6, 1919, *Papers of Woodrow Wilson*, 60:221–22.
84. Inter-Allied Conference on the Preliminaries of Peace, minutes of plenary session of meeting, May 31, 1919, *Papers of Woodrow Wilson*, 59:628–29.
85. Ibid., 629–30.
86. Ibid., 630.
87. Mantoux, notes on Council of Four meeting, June 9, 1919, *Papers of Woodrow Wilson*, 60:314.
88. Ibid.
89. Ibid.
90. Ibid., 315.
91. Mantoux, notes on Council of Four meeting, June 10, 1919, *Papers of Woodrow Wilson*, 60:351–53.
92. Committee on New States, report on Paderewski memorandum, June 17, 1919, *Papers of Woodrow Wilson*, 60:629–31.
93. Hankey, notes on Council of Four meeting, June 23, 1919, *Papers of Woodrow Wilson*, 61:88–92.
94. Deborah Moore, *At Home in America: Second Generation New York Jews* (New York: Columbia University Press, 1981), 104.
95. Henry Morgenthau to Wilson, June 20, 1919, *Papers of Woodrow Wilson*, 61:43.
96. Hankey, notes on Council of Four meeting, May 17, 1919, *Papers of Woodrow Wilson*, 59:215–17.
97. Hugh Gibson, American minister in Warsaw, to the American Commission to Negotiate Peace, confidential message from Paderewski to Wilson, May 14, 1919, *Papers of Woodrow Wilson*, 59:261–63.
98. Ibid.
99. R. H. Lord to Wilson enclosing May 25 report from Reginald Foster, May 29, 1919, *Papers of Woodrow Wilson*, 59:596–99.

100. Ibid., 598–99; see also Alison Fleig Frank, *Oil Empire: Visions of Prosperity in Austrian Galicia* (Cambridge MA: Harvard University Press, 2005), 205–36.

101. Lord to Wilson with Foster's report, cited in n. 99 above, *Papers of Woodrow Wilson*, 59:599.

102. Charles Swem, transcript of Council of Four meeting, June 5, 1919, *Papers of Woodrow Wilson*, 60:160–61.

103. Ibid., 161–62.

104. Ibid., 163–64.

105. Ibid., 164.

106. Ibid., 164.

107. Ibid., 160.

108. Ibid., 165.

109. Ibid., 165–66; Larry Wolff, *The Idea of Galicia*, 374–79.

110. Wilson, press conference remarks, June 27, 1919, *Papers of Woodrow Wilson*, 61:243.

111. Tomasz Kamusella, *Silesia and Central European Nationalisms: The Emergence of National and Ethnic Groups in Prussian Silesia and Austria Silesia, 1848–1918* (West Lafayette, IN: Purdue University Press, 2007), 238–71.

112. Hankey, notes on Council of Four meeting, May 21, 1919, *Papers of Woodrow Wilson*, 59:329.

113. Ibid.

114. Sherman Miles, memorandum for the president, May 22, 1919, *Papers of Woodrow Wilson*, 59:403.

115. Ibid., 404.

116. Mantoux, notes on Council of Four meeting, June 3, 1919, *Papers of Woodrow Wilson*, 60:86.

117. Ibid., 87.

118. Ibid. 87.

119. Ibid. 88.

120. Swem, transcript of Council of Four meeting, June 5, 1919, *Papers of Woodrow Wilson*, 60:157.

121. Ibid., 158.

122. Ibid. 158.

123. Ibid., 159.

124. Ibid., 167.

125. R. H. Lord, "Remarks on the Observations of the German Delegation on the Conditions of Peace: 'Eastern Question' (Poland and Lithuania)," June 5 1919, *Papers of Woodrow Wilson*, 60:182.

126. R. H. Lord, "Considerations on a Plebiscite in Upper Silesia," June 5 1919, *Papers of Woodrow Wilson*, 60:189–90.

127. Ibid.

128. Hankey, notes on Council of Four meeting, June 17, 1919, *Papers of Woodrow Wilson*, 60:628.

129. Mantoux, notes on Council of Four meeting, June 11, 1919, *Papers of Woodrow Wilson*, 60:426; see also James Bjork, *Neither German nor Pole: Catholicism and National Indifference in a Central European Borderland* (Ann Arbor: University of

Michigan Press, 2008), 214–66; Brendan Karch, *Nation and Loyalty in a German-Polish Borderland: Upper Silesia 1848–1960* (Cambridge: Cambridge University Press, 2018), 96–147.

130. Hankey and Mantoux, notes on Council of Four meeting, June 14, 1919, *Papers of Woodrow Wilson*, 60:558.

131. Ibid., 559–60.

132. Ibid., 562–63.

133. Wilson, address, Omaha, Nebr., September 8, 1919, *Papers of Woodrow Wilson*, 63:98.

134. Wilson, address, Tacoma, Wash., National Guard Armory, September 13, 1919, *Papers of Woodrow Wilson*, 63:249–50.

135. Ibid., 250.

CONCLUSION

1. Colonel House, diary, December 18, 1912, in *Papers of Woodrow Wilson*, 25:610; Wilson, address, St. Louis, Mo., September 5, 1919, *Papers of Woodrow Wilson*, 63:49.

2. Wilson, draft of note to the Austro-Hungarian Government, October 19, 1918, *Papers of Woodrow Wilson*, 51:383; Victor Mamatey, *The United States and East Central Europe, 1914–1918: A Study in Wilsonian Diplomacy and Propaganda* (Princeton, NJ: Princeton University Press, 1957), 330–31.

3. Ludovic Moncheur to Charles de Broqueville, August 14, 1917, *Papers of Woodrow Wilson*, 43:468.

4. Wilson, address, Metropolitan Opera House, New York, March 4, 1919, *Papers of Woodrow Wilson*, 55:414–15.

5. Wilson, address, San Diego, CA, September 19, 1919, *Papers of Woodrow Wilson*, 63:372.

6. Bohemian National Alliance of America to Wilson, December 5, 1917, *Papers of Woodrow Wilson*, 45:223–24.

7. Maurice Hankey, notes on Council of Four meeting, March 20, 1919, *Papers of Woodrow Wilson*, 56:114.

8. Norman Davies, "Lloyd George and Poland," in *Contemporary History* 6, no. 3 (1971): 132–54; Wiesław Śladkowski, "Clemenceau et la Pologne," *Annales Universitatis Mariae Curie-Skłodowska, Sectio F, Historia* 41–42 (1986–87): 9–12; Georges Clemenceau, *Au pied du Sinaï* (Paris: Henri Floury, 1898).

9. Wilson to Francis Klapuš, January 3, 1923, *Papers of Woodrow Wilson*, 68:263; Alexander George and Juliette George, *Woodrow Wilson and Colonel House: A Personality Study* (New York: Dover Publications, 1964), 30–31.

10. Cary Grayson, diary, April 11, 1919, *Papers of Woodrow Wilson*, 57: 237–38.

11. Wilson, address, Cincinnati, Ohio, October 26, 1916, *Papers of Woodrow Wilson*, 38:539.

12. Sigmund Freud and William Bullitt, *Thomas Woodrow Wilson: Twenty-Eighth President of the United States: A Psychological Study* (Boston: Houghton Mifflin, 1966), 128.

13. Hankey, notes on Council of Four meeting, March 20, 1919, *Papers of Woodrow Wilson*, 56:114.

14. Wilson, address, Des Moines, Iowa, September 6, 1919, *Papers of Woodrow Wilson*, 63: 82.

15. Wilson, speech to Democratic National Committee, February 28, 1919, cited in Joseph Tumulty, *Woodrow Wilson as I Know Him* (Garden City, NY: Doubleday, 1921), 372; *Papers of Woodrow Wilson*, 55:317–18.

16. Edith Benham, diary, April 11, 1919, *Papers of Woodrow Wilson*, 57:241–42.

17. Wilson to Bainbridge Colby, November 15, 1920, second of three letters, *Papers of Woodrow Wilson*, 66:367.

18. Freud and Bullitt, *Thomas Woodrow Wilson*, 153–54.

19. Mantoux, notes on Council of Four meeting, April 1, 1919, *Papers of Woodrow Wilson*, 56: 508–9.

20. Isaiah Bowman to Colonel House, April 11, 1919; Wilson, "Italy" memorandum, April 11, 1919, *Papers of Woodrow Wilson*, 57:270–71; Steven Seegel, *Mapping Europe's Borderlands: Russian Cartography in the Age of Empire* (Chicago: University of Chicago Press, 2012), 267–68.

21. Mantoux, notes on Council of Four meeting, June 6, 1919, *Papers of Woodrow Wilson*, 60:214–15.

22. Harold Nicolson, *Peacemaking 1919* (1933; New York: Grosset & Dunlap, 1965), May 29, 1919, 351.

23. Wilson, address, Columbus, Ohio, September 4, 1919, *Papers of Woodrow Wilson*, 63:13.

24. Wilson, press conference remarks, June 27, 1919, *Papers of Woodrow Wilson*, 61:243..

25. Hankey and Mantoux, notes on Council of Four meeting, April 22, 1919, *Papers of Woodrow Wilson*, 57:614.

26. Charles Swem, transcript of Council of Four meeting, June 5, 1919, *Papers of Woodrow Wilson*, 60:158.

27. Mantoux, notes on Council of Four meeting, June 11, 1919, *Papers of Woodrow Wilson*, 60:426.

28. Paderewski to Wilson, October 4, 1917, *Papers of Woodrow Wilson*, 44:305.

29. Hugh Simons Gibson to Bainbridge Colby, July 17, 1920, *Papers of Woodrow Wilson*, 65:527–28.

30. Wilson to Bainbridge Colby, July 20, 1919, *Papers of Woodrow Wilson*, 65:531.

31. Ambassador Kazimierz Lubomirski to Bainbridge Colby, cable from Wincenty Witos to Wilson, July 31, 1920, *Papers of Woodrow Wilson*, 66:9–10.

32. Wilson to Bainbridge Colby, August 5, 1920, *Papers of Woodrow Wilson*, 66:11.

33. Stephen Wise to Joseph Patrick Tumulty, September 9, 1919, *Papers of Woodrow Wilson*, 66: 109–10.

34. Enclosure, from Wise to Tumulty, September 9, 1919, *Papers of Woodrow Wilson*, 66: 110; Wilson, "President Urges Justice for Jews," *New York Times*, September 12, 1920, E3.

35. Wilson, "President Urges Justice for Jews."

36. Stephen Wise to Wilson, November 12, 1920; S. Litovtzeff-Polyakoff (S. L. Poliakoff-Litovtzeff), *Jewish Tribune*, October 15, 1920, *Papers of Woodrow Wilson*, 66:356–57.

37. Wilson to Lloyd George, November 3, 1920, *Papers of Woodrow Wilson*, 66:307–8.

38. Eugeniusz Romer, *Pamiętnik paryski (1918–1919)*, ed. Andrzej Garlicki and Ryszard Świętek (Wrocław: Zakład Narodowy imienia Ossolińskich, 1989), 164–65.

39. Kazimierz Lubomirski, September 16, 1921, *Papers of Woodrow Wilson*, 67:392.

40. Wilson to Kazimierz Lubomirski, October 3, 1921, *Papers of Woodrow Wilson*, 67:400.
41. Wilson to Michał Kwapiszewski, November 5, 1922, *Papers of Woodrow Wilson*, 68:177.
42. Paderewski to Wilson, December 27, 1923, *Papers of Woodrow Wilson*, 68:507–8.
43. Ray Stannard Baker, diary, June 26, 1919, *Papers of Woodrow Wilson*, 61:231.
44. Wilson, press conference report, June 27, 1919, *Papers of Woodrow Wilson*, 61:250; Lansing, memorandum, June 28, 1919, *Papers of Woodrow Wilson*, 61:324.
45. Wilson to Beneš, June 28, 1919, *Papers of Woodrow Wilson*, 61:347.
46. Wilson to Lansing, June 28, 1919, *Papers of Woodrow Wilson*, 61:347.

Index

Abduction from the Seraglio (Mozart), 22
Adriatic dispute, *see* Dalmatia, Italian claims; Fiume; South Slavs; Treaty of London (1915); Yugoslavia
African Americans: Emancipation Proclamation, 81, 82, 114; federal government segregation, 8, 119–20; Jim Crow laws, 82; rights, 8, 81–82, 119–20, 151, 199
Albania: independence, 28, 228; Italian protectorate, 45, 158, 162; post-Ottoman mandates, 36–37; Wilson on, 243
Alexander, Crown Prince of Serbia, 120–21, 134
Alfonso XIII, King of Spain, 84, 85
Allied Supreme War Council, 174, 239
Alsace-Lorraine, 22, 87
Ambrosius, Lloyd, 10
American Geographical Society, 117
American Historical Association, 27
American Hungarian Loyalty League, 61
American Jewish Committee, 170, 176, 178, 190–91
American Jewish Congress, 176–80, 190–91, 199
American Relief Administration, 124, 197
Anatolia: ethnographic map, 38, 39, 55, 215, 237; Greek population, 31, 39, 47, 54, 215; Greek troops in, 37, 41, 54; Italian troops in, 37, 41, 45, 46–47, 158; mandate discussed, 37, 39, 43; plebiscite proposal, 215; possible Italian territories, 45–46
Anti-Semitism: of Dmowski, 170, 171, 177, 193, 198, 236; of Harold Nicolson, 201; in Poland, 170–73, 177, 193, 198, 199–200, 241; of Robert Kerner, 117–18; Wilson on, 202–3, 241–42. *See also* Jews
Armenia: mandate proposal, 31, 33–36, 37, 39, 40, 43, 48–49, 53, 230; Soviet, 54
Armenians: in Anatolia, 47; in Constantinople, 39; massacres, genocide, 18–19, 21–22, 25, 30–31, 36, 52; at Paris Peace Conference, 166
Asquith, Herbert H., 16, 19
Atatürk, Mustafa Kemal Pasha, 17, 41, 54
Austria: new state or old state, 108; potential union with Germany, 98; territorial disputes with Yugoslavia, 101, 216
Austria-Hungary (Habsburg monarchy): ambassadors to United States, 4, 71–72; assassination of Archduke Franz Ferdinand, 56–58, 112, 246; autonomous development of nationalities, 62–64, 68–71, 75–78, 80, 81, 96–97, 229–30; constitutional law, 70, 83; democracy in, 70, 72–74, 83; immigrants in United States from, 61–62, 63–64; interpretation of Fourteen Points, 69–70, 77–78, 79; military defeats, 97, 98; peace treaty, 17, 107–10, 111, 112, 114, 194; Reichsrat, 83, 86; relations with United States, 71–78, 98; reparations, 109; rights of nationalities, 70, 83; separate peace discussions with United States, 29–30, 58, 66, 72, 74–78, 84–87, 96–97, 98, 105; sovereignty issue, 72, 79, 81, 85, 93; subject peoples, 29–30, 36, 39, 83–84, 97–98, 111–14, 119, 151; U.S. ambassadors to, 56, 59, 72; U.S. declaration of war on, 60, 73; war debts to Germany, 67–68; Wilson

INDEX

on illegitimacy, 93–94; Wilson's Point Ten, 29–30, 58, 66, 67–71, 80, 96, 229–30. *See also* Franz Joseph, Emperor; Karl, Emperor
Austria-Hungary (Habsburg monarchy), breakup of: as allied war aim, 25, 26, 31, 32, 58–59, 90–91, 93–94; border drawing, 104–10; collapse, 98, 99–100, 101, 107, 110, 113, 115, 148; Coolidge's memorandum on, 104–05, 133, 184; emancipation of subject peoples, 81–82, 89, 95–98, 104, 111–14, 151, 154, 230; evolution of Wilson's thought on, 58–60, 62–64, 70–71, 79–82, 86, 91–96, 105–7, 229–30; federalism proposal, 75–77; Four Principles speech on, 79–82, 84–86, 87, 88; independence groups, 56, 57–58, 64–65; Inquiry memorandum on, 64, 67, 70–71, 86; Lansing presses Wilson on, 87–94; parallels to Ottoman empire, 30, 31–32, 54–55, 103–4, 229–30; in peace settlement, 34, 36, 43, 47, 51, 58, 110; successor states, 58, 103, 105–10, 106 (fig.), 111–14, 116; territories promised to Italy by Entente, 45, 47, 59, 83, 103, 107, 115; vacuum left by, 99–100, 107, 115, 132, 133, 148; as Wilson's aim, 23, 96–98, 230; Wilson's message to liberated peoples, 99–100
Autonomy as national aim, 17, 28–29, 31, 58, 66, 68–71, 80, 81, 96, 97, 229–30. *See also* National self-determination

Baker, Ray Stannard, 143, 144, 185–86, 245, 246
Balfour, Arthur, 21–22, 30, 33, 46–47, 59–60, 82–84, 138, 158
Balfour Declaration, 22, 179
Balkan states (Southeastern Europe): American experts (The Inquiry), 27, 117–18, 138–39, 144, 162; mental mapping of, 86, 116, 137–38, 238; national self-determination, 19, 29–30, 144–45; Wilson's Point Eleven on, 17, 29. *See also* Albania; Bosnia; Croatia; Montenegro; Romania; Serbia; South Slavs; Yugoslavia
Balkan Wars, 21, 28, 53, 228
Baltic states, 2, 66, 127, 190, 200. *See also* Estonia; Latvia; Lithuania
Beach, Sylvester, 165
Beach, Sylvia, 165–66
Beaumarchais, Pierre Augustin Caron de, *The Barber of Seville*, 135
Beethoven, Ludwig von, 74
Belgium, 22, 23, 62
Benedict XV, Pope, 76, 96, 98–99
Beneš, Edvard, 70, 109, 166, 205, 246
Benham, Edith, 142
Berg, A. Scott, 95
Berg, Manfred, 10
Bernstorff, Johann Heinrich von, Count, 23, 58
Bessarabia, 140
Bismarck, Otto von, 140
Black Hand, 56, 113
Bliss, Tasker H., 180–81, 182
Bohemia, 105, 111–12. *See also* Czechoslovakia; Prague; Sudeten Germans
Bohemian Americans, 61, 63–64, 126
Bohemian National Alliance of America, 63–64, 82
Bolshevik Revolution, 6, 40, 65, 128. *See also* Russia
Borglum, Gutzon, 12, 13 (fig.)
Borowy, Piotr, 186, 246–48
Bosnia: Allied plans for, 59; annexation by Austria-Hungary, 27, 59; assassination of Archduke Franz Ferdinand, 56–58, 112, 246; in Eastern Crisis (1870s), 7, 18, 228; Young Bosnia, 56. *See also* Balkan states; Yugoslavia
Bowman, Isaiah, 117, 149, 156, 237
Brandeis, Louis, 177
Brătianu, Ion, 141, 203–5
Bratislava, 10, 12
Breslau (Wrocław), archbishop of, 219–20

INDEX

Britain: Foreign Office, 30–31; Intelligence Bureau, 30, 66, 84; Jews, 192, 193, 198, 202–3; Paris Peace Conference delegation, 3, 139, 153; relations with Ottoman empire, 16, 21–22; Royal Navy, 16; supporters of breakup of Austria-Hungary, 66; Wales, 204, 205, 211, 212, 218, 231; Wilson's visit, 4, 33. *See also* Balfour, Arthur; Gladstone, William; Lloyd George, David; World War I

Broqueville, Charles de, Count, 23

Bryan, William Jennings, 88

Budapest, 101–2, 201. *See also* Hungary

Bukovina, 140

Bulgaria: American expert, 118; Dobruja dispute, 142, 164; Ottoman atrocities in, 15, 16, 18, 32; Wilson on, 163–64, 235–36

The Bulgarian Horrors and the Question of the East (Gladstone), 15, 17–18, 32, 42, 53, 229

Bullitt, William C., 9, 15, 234

Carinthia, 101, 216, 221

Carpatho-Ruthenia, 213

Cartography, 117, 237–38. *See also* Maps

Catherine II (the Great), empress and tsarina, 17, 40

Charles University, Prague, 246

Christian missionaries in Ottoman empire, 30–31, 43

Civil War, Russian, 128–29

Civil War, U.S., 8, 12, 81, 82, 95, 131

Clemenceau, Georges: knowledge of Galicia, 191, 231; at Paris Peace Conference, 34, 42, 44, 46–47, 49, 150, 158, 183, 191, 196, 205, 220, 223; on reparations, 223; on Silesia, 220; Sixtus affair, 86–87;

Cobb, Frank, 31, 97–98, 169–70

Colby, Bainbridge, 163–64, 239, 240, 241

Cold War, 2, 229, 233

Comintern (Communist International), 7, 238

Committee on New States, 198

Committee on the Rights of Minorities, 193

Communism: Comintern, 7, 238; in Hungary, 101–2; as threat to Eastern Europe, 119, 152–53, 173–74, 199, 208. *See also* Bolshevik Revolution; Hungarian Soviet Republic; Soviet Union

Confederacy, 8, 12, 81

Congress, U.S.: bill on Polish independence, 130; Senate rejection of Treaty of Versailles, 3, 50, 53, 162, 230; Wilson's speeches to, 22, 25–26, 49–50, 63, 122, 123–24

Congress of Berlin, 27, 140, 194, 228

Congress of Vienna, 79

Constantinople (Istanbul): mixed population, 39, 44; Ottoman conquest, 27, 44, 49; possible American mandate, 17, 33–40, 42, 43, 45, 48–49, 52–54, 230–31; postwar status discussions, 27, 31, 43, 44–45; rival claims, 27; Russian claim, 6, 40; separation from Turkey discussed, 27, 48–49, 52–54; sultan's residence, 39, 40, 43. *See also* Ottoman empire; Turkey

Constitution, U.S., Fourteenth Amendment, 81–82

Conze, Eckart, 11

Coolidge, Archibald Cary: on Constantinople, 27, 53–54; Inquiry team led by, 5, 26–27, 233; interest in Ottoman empire, 26–27; "Memorandum on the Rights of National Minorities," 184, 191; "The New Frontiers in Former Austria-Hungary," 104–5, 133, 184; at Paris Peace Conference, 109–10, 162; roles in postwar Eastern Europe, 100–102, 104–5, 129, 132; in Russia, 129

Crane, Charles, 126, 127–28, 129

Crimean War, 31, 228

Croatians: appreciation of Wilson, 12, 155 (fig.), 229; fighting against Entente, 151. *See also* South Slavs; Yugoslavia; Zagreb

Czechoslovakia: appreciation of Wilson,

1, 11–12, 166, 229, 231, 232 (fig.); border conflict with Hungary, 204–6; Carpatho-Ruthenia included in, 213; declaration of independence, 95–96, 131, 169, 230; establishment, 66, 95, 132–33; immigrants in United States, Czech and Slovak, 61–62, 63–64, 95, 146; inclusion of Slovakia, 105, 133; independence objective, 66–67, 70, 80, 82, 92–93, 94, 95–96; Inquiry expertise, 117, 233; national minority issues, 191, 193–94; Nazi occupation, 11; Paris Peace Conference delegation, 204–5; Sudeten German population, 97, 100, 105, 133, 169, 184, 236, 247; territorial disputes with Poland, 101, 185–88, 189, 246–48; U.S. recognition of independent government, 94–95; Velvet Revolution, 11; Wilson's friendship for, 4, 164–66, 233, 246. *See also* Masaryk, Tomáš Garrigue; Slovakia
Czechoslovak Legion, 128, 131
Czecho-Slovak National Council, 61, 92–93, 94, 130, 131, 169
Czernin, Ottokar, Count, 29, 59, 69–70, 72, 75, 79

Dalmatia: American troops in, 146–47; ethnography, 45, 99, 107, 156, 160, 215; islands, 145–46, 151, 156–57, 215; maps, 149, 156, 237; plebiscite proposal, 215, 218
Dalmatia, Italian claims: based on Treaty of London, 45, 59, 83; discussed in Paris, 45–46, 47, 149, 150–52, 155–58, 162–63, 215; Herron on, 157; Orlando and Sonnino on, 145–46, 154–55; plebiscite proposed, 215, 218; settlement with Yugoslavia, 163; troops sent in, 146–47; Vittorio Emanuele on, 161; Wilson's memorandum to Italian government, 148, 184–85; Wilson's opposition to, 45–46, 107, 143, 149, 150–52, 153–54, 156–63, 238
Damat Ferid Pasha, 41, 54

D'Annunzio, Gabriele, 161
Danzig (Gdańsk), 173, 183, 188–89, 218, 223, 236
Day, Clive, 138–39
Declaration of Independence, U.S., 92, 94, 191
De Salis, Sir John Francis Charles, 139
Disraeli, Benjamin, 15, 16, 27
Dmowski, Roman: anti-Semitism, 170, 171, 177, 193, 198, 236; on Bohemia, 125; on emancipation of peoples, 82; Paderewski and, 171, 172; Wilson and, 171, 183, 237
Dobruja, 140, 142, 164, 188
Dreyfus Affair, 231
Drummond, Eric, 30–31
Dumba, Konstantin, 4, 71

Eastern Europe: American experts, 5, 26, 100–01, 117–18, 189–90, 218, 233; appreciation of Wilson, 1, 11–12, 13 (fig.), 155 (fig.), 166, 176, 229, 231, 232 (fig.), 240, 243–44; Bolshevik/communist threat, 119, 152–53, 173–74, 199, 208; borders redrawn by peace settlement, 104–5, 111, 112, 116; ethnographic complexity, 236–37; immigrants to United States from, 5, 234; use of term, 100; Wilson's knowledge of, 3, 4, 8–9, 10, 160, 191, 228, 231. *See also* Mental maps of Eastern Europe; *and specific countries and territories*
Eastern Galicia: attached to postwar Poland, 210, 216–17; discussed in Paris, 117, 197, 207–8, 210–14, 216–17; Lemberg (Lwów; Lviv), 172, 173, 182, 190, 212–13; military observer report, 209–10; mixed population, 97, 168–70, 207–10; plebiscite requirement, 216–17; Polish claim, 117, 181–82, 189–90, 210; Polish-Ukrainian hostilities, 100, 173, 182, 189, 197, 207–10, 212–13; Ukrainian claim, 182, 189–90. *See also* Galicia
Eastern Question, 26–27, 31, 32, 42, 43, 44–45, 53, 55

INDEX

East Prussia, 221
Edib, Halide, 33
Ekengren, August, 96–98
Elkus, Abram Isaac, 22, 31
Emancipation: from Habsburg rule, 81–82, 89, 95–98, 104, 111–14, 151, 154, 230; from Ottoman rule, 26, 81–82; as Wilson's war aim, 8, 62–64, 81–82, 230
Emancipation Proclamation, 81, 82, 114
Enslaved peoples, *see* Emancipation; Slavery
Estonia, 2, 66, 127, 190. *See also* Baltic states
Ethnographic maps: of Anatolia, 38, 39, 55, 215, 237; of Adriatic territories, 149, 152, 156–57, 159–60; of Silesia, 238–39
Ethnography: in mental maps of Eastern Europe, 130, 168–73, 236–37, 238, 247; mixed populations, 97–98, 159–60, 179, 184–85, 220, 236, 238; plebiscites and, 238–39. *See also specific groups and regions*

Ferdinand, King of Romania, 140, 141–42
Finland, 66
Fiume (Rijeka), 143, 149, 150, 153, 158, 159, 161, 218
Fortis, Alberto, 157
Foster, Reginald, 209–10
Four Principles speech, 79–82, 84–86, 87, 88
Fourteen Points speech: on Austria-Hungary (Point Ten), 29–30, 58, 66, 67–71, 80, 96, 229–30; autonomous development principle, 17, 28–29, 31, 58, 66, 68–71, 80, 81, 96, 97, 229–30; on Balkan states (Point Eleven), 17, 29; influence of Inquiry memorandum, 67–68; Lippmann-Cobb memorandum on, 31, 97–98, 169–70; on Ottoman empire (Point Twelve), 17, 28–30, 31–32, 80; on Poland (Point Thirteen), 1, 22, 90, 124, 168, 175, 224, 226; on Russia (Point Six), 6–7, 66
Fourteenth Amendment, 81–82
France: ambassador to United States, 69; claim to Syria, 31, 51; interest in Eastern Europe, 189; Dreyfus Affair, 231; Jews, 192, 193, 202–3, 231; recovery of Alsace-Lorraine, 22, 87. *See also* Clemenceau, Georges; Paris Peace Conference; World War I
Frankfurter, Felix, 199–200
Frank Leslie's Popular Monthly, 74
Franz Ferdinand, Archduke, assassination of, 56–58, 112, 246
Franz Joseph, Emperor, 56, 71, 73, 166
Frederick the Great, 214, 220
Freud, Sigmund, 9, 15, 234
Friendship in international relations: competition for U.S. favor, 126–27, 130, 236; cultivating, 116, 120–21; politics of sympathy, 120–21, 143, 144–48, 151, 153–54, 233–34, 247–48; Wilson's frictions and antipathies, 141–43, 158–59, 164, 182, 183, 190, 196, 212, 235–37
Friendships of Wilson: claims on, 132–34, 139–42, 146; cultivated by others for political reasons, 120–27; for Czechoslovakia, 1, 4, 164–66, 233, 246; with European leaders, 5, 116, 120–21, 147–48, 161, 166, 233–34, 246; with Herron, 157; importance and dependence, 233; interactions with individual foreigners, 143–44, 149–50, 185–88, 234, 246–48; with Masaryk, 1, 4, 5, 8, 124–26, 131, 132–33, 165, 166, 169, 173, 233; with Paderewski, 1, 5, 8, 122, 173, 197, 214, 233, 244; for Poland, 125 (fig.), 239–41, 243–44; with small nations, 4, 166–67. *See also* House, Edward
Furlong, Charles, 139
Fürstenberg, Karl Emil von, Prince, 29

Galicia: annexation by Habsburgs, 59; appropriation by Poland, 169; Clemenceau's knowledge of, 191, 231; ethnography, 169, 210, 213; Jews,

199, 231; Paderewski on, 210, 212–13; Polish claim, 97, 123, 210; rival claims, 182. *See also* Eastern Galicia
Gdańsk, *see* Danzig
Gelfand, Lawrence, 118
German Americans, 160
Germans: Catholic clergy, 219–21; in Polish territory, 170, 188–89, 192, 219–21; Sudeten, 97, 100, 105, 133, 169, 184, 236, 247
Germany: ambassador to United States, 23; border with Poland, 170, 192, 214, 220, 221–22; Eastern Europe and, 24, 60–61, 62, 116; Nazi period, 6, 11, 98, 105, 169, 247; potential union with Austria, 98; relations with Ottoman empire, 25, 26, 27, 28; relations with Russia, 65–66, 88; reparations, 222–25; Treaty of Brest-Litovsk, 40, 66, 86; unification (1871), 140; U.S. declaration of war on, 23, 60; Weimar Republic, 239; Wilson on, 25, 60–61, 62; Zimmerman Telegram, 60. *See also* Treaty of Versailles; World War I
Gettysburg battlefield, 95, 131
Gibbons, James, Archbishop 96
Gibson, Hugh, 181, 239–40
Gilbert and Sullivan, *The Mikado*, 22
Gladstone, William: *The Bulgarian Horrors and the Question of the East*, 15, 17–18, 32, 42, 53, 229; as Wilson's role model, 15–16, 20
Goatherds, from Tatra Mountains, 185–88, 234, 246–48
Grayson, Cary, 139–42, 146–47, 186–87, 196, 244–45, 246
Greece: military forces in Anatolia, 37, 41, 54; territorial claims, 51, 164; Thessaloniki, 28, 120
Greeks: in Anatolia, 31, 39, 47, 54, 215; in Constantinople, 39
Gürel, Perin, 33

Habsburg monarchy, *see* Austria-Hungary; Franz Joseph, Emperor; Karl, Emperor

Halczyn, Wojciech, 186, 246–48
Handman, Max, 118
Hapgood, Norman, 125–26
Harding, Warren, 163, 164, 243
Harvard University, 5, 26, 53, 100, 117, 129, 182, 199. *See also* Coolidge, Archibald Cary
Havel, Václav, 11
Headlam-Morley, James Wycliffe, 108
Herder, Johann Gottfried, 129
Herman, Arthur, 7
Herron, George, 74–78, 82–83, 89, 127, 150, 157
Herzl, Theodor, 72
History of the American People (Wilson), 4–5, 234
Hitchcock, Gilbert, Senator, 130
Hitler, Adolf, *see* Nazi Germany
Hofmannsthal, Hugo von, *Die Frau ohne Schatten*, 73
Hoover, Herbert, 124, 181, 197
House, Edward: Asquith and, 19; Balfour and, 59–60, 82–84, 138; closeness to Wilson, 24, 131–32, 233; diary, 18, 22, 24; discussions with Wilson, 22–23, 24–25, 27–28, 30, 64; formula for mandates, 51; Paderewski and, 122–23, 173–74; at Paris Peace Conference, 9–10, 110, 131–32, 149, 157, 195, 237; Poland and, 123, 180–81; Warsaw statue of, 123; Yugoslavia and, 146. *See also* The Inquiry
Howe, Irving, 207
Hungarians: immigrants to United States, 61, 91; as postwar minorities, 111; in Transylvania, 194
Hungarian Soviet Republic, 111, 143, 158, 204, 205
Hungary: borders, 105; communist revolution, 101–2, 111; Coolidge's visit, 101–2; historical, 91, 105; hopes for Wilson's help, 102; Jews, 201; territorial disputes, 101, 102, 142, 204–6; Treaty of Trianon, 102, 111, 194; Wilson's sympathy for, 91. *See also* Austria-Hungary; Transylvania

INDEX

Immigrants in United States: anti-immigrant sentiments, 160–61; from Austria-Hungary, 61–62, 63–64; from Czechoslovakia, 61–62, 63–64, 95, 146; demonstrations of loyalty, 61–62, 63–64, 126–27; from Eastern Europe, 5, 234; Hungarians, 61, 91; Italians, 154, 159–60; Jews, 176, 180, 193, 207; from Polish lands, 5, 61, 186, 225–26; from Romania, 61; from Serbia, 57; South Slavs, 57, 61, 146; sympathies with home countries, 20; Wilson on, 4–5, 20–21, 160–61, 234

Imperialism, 36, 37, 45, 50–51, 113, 211–12, 231.

India, Muslim population, 38–39, 40

The Inquiry: on Austria-Hungary, 64–65, 66–68, 70–71, 86; on Eastern Europe, 28, 31, 64–66, 97–98, 117–18, 169–70; establishment of, 5; geography and ethnography experts, 5, 117–18, 121, 138–39, 149, 209, 216, 233, 237; information provided to Wilson, 42, 228–29, 231–33; Lippmann-Cobb memorandum, 31, 97–98, 169–70; maps, 117, 118, 149, 231, 237; members, 6, 26–27, 117–18; on Ottoman empire, 27–28; on Poland, 124. *See also* Coolidge, Archibald Cary

International relations: new postwar order, 115–16; Wilson's rejection of old diplomacy, 40, 45, 79–81, 144, 150. *See also* Friendship in international relations; National self-determination; League of Nations

Islamic world, reactions to breakup of Ottoman empire, 38–39, 40

Istria, 45, 162

Italian Americans, 154, 159–60

Italy: American troops in, 146–47; battle of Vittorio Veneto, 97, 98; entry into World War I, 45, 46; Fiume, 143, 149, 150, 153, 158, 159, 161, 218; friendship with United States, 153–54, 158–59; immigrants to United States from, 154, 159–60; military forces in Anatolia, 37, 41, 45, 46–47, 158; Ottoman territory claimed, 45, 48; parliament, 144–45; protectorate of Albania, 158, 162; representation at peace conference, 137–38; territorial ambitions, 45–47, 103, 107, 109; Treaty of London, 45–47, 59, 83, 103, 107, 115, 143, 148, 150; U.S. ambassadors to, 99, 145–46; Wilson's memorandum to government, 105–7, 115–16; Wilson's popularity, 144, 147; Wilson's views of, 156–60, 163; Wilson's visit to Rome, 4, 99, 144–45, 146–48. *See also* Dalmatia, Italian claims; Orlando, Vittorio Emanuele

Jagiellonian University, 176, 243–44

Jay, Peter Augustus, 161

Jewish Tribune, 242–43

Jews: American, 170–73, 176–80, 190–91, 193, 198, 199–201, 202–3, 206–7, 236; Balfour Declaration, 22, 179; and Bolsheviks, 199, 201; in Constantinople, 39; cultural identity, 178; discrimination against, 177–78, 191; in Eastern Europe, 176–80, 190–91, 199–203, 241–43; languages, 171, 178, 206–7; as loyal citizens, 192–93, 206; minority rights, 178–80, 190–91, 198–202, 206–7; pogroms, 172–73, 199–201; in Poland, 168–69, 170–73, 180, 198–202, 206, 214, 231, 241–42; Polish attitudes toward, 191–93, 198, 199–202, 206; sabbath, 198–99; U.S. ambassadors to Ottoman empire, 18–19, 22; in Western Europe, 192, 193, 198, 202–3, 231; Wilson's views of, 177, 192, 199; world population, 177; Zionist movement, 179–80, 200. *See also* Anti-Semitism

Joseph August, Archduke, 102

Joseph II, Emperor, Josephine era, 74

Jusserand, Jean Jules, 69

INDEX

Karl, Emperor, 29, 71, 72–78, 84–86, 87, 107
Károlyi, Mihály, 102
Kemal, Mustafa, *see* Atatürk, Mustafa Kemal Pasha
Kerensky, Alexander, 6
Kerner, Robert, 26, 117–18, 216, 233
Keynes, John Maynard, 223
King, Leroy, 101
King, William Henry, 30
Kingdom of Serbs, Croats, and Slovenes, 134, 154. *See also* Yugoslavia
Kipling, Rudyard, 33
Korošec, Anton, 146
Kun, Béla, 111, 143, 158, 201, 204

Lammasch, Heinrich, 74–78, 82–83, 86
Lane, Franklin Knight, 98
Lansing, Robert: on Austria-Hungary policy, 87–88, 89–94; communications with Austria, 72–73, 97; communications with Germany, 58; Coolidge and, 100, 101; German ambassador and, 23; at Paris Peace Conference, 119, 131–32, 136, 245; Poland and, 174, 175, 180–82, 189; on possible American mandates, 33–34, 50–51; on Romania, 142; Serbia and, 30; on Turkish peace negotiations, 53; on volatility of Eastern Europe, 119; Wilson and, 34, 50–51, 87–94, 119, 131, 162–63, 239
Latvia, 2, 66, 127, 190. *See also* Baltic states
League of Nations: authority in former Habsburg territories, 103–4; Covenant, 50, 51, 102–3, 119; enforcement of treaties, 202; Lenin on, 7; protection of minority rights, 103, 198, 202, 206; as support for newly independent countries, 116; trusteeships proposed, 102–4. *See also* Mandates; Treaty of Versailles
Lemberg (Lwów; Lviv), 172, 173, 182, 190, 212–13
Lenin, Vladimir, 6, 7, 66, 80, 238
Leonhard, Jörn, 11, 115
Lepore, Jill, 3
Lincoln, Abraham, 63, 64, 81, 82, 95, 114, 230
Lincoln Memorial, 82
Lippmann, Walter, 6, 26, 31, 64, 67
Lippmann-Cobb memorandum (October 1918), 31, 97–98, 169–70
Lithuania: compared to Wales by Lloyd George, 212; independence, 66, 127, 190; pogroms, 200; territorial disputes with Poland, 190. *See also* Baltic states; Polish-Lithuanian Commonwealth
Lithuanian Americans, 126–27
Lithuanian National Council, 126–27
Lithuanians: in Poland, 121, 168–70, 212; Paderewski on, 211–12
Lloyd George, David: on Austria-Hungary issues, 108, 109, 110, on "brigand peoples," 205, 208; on Czechoslovakia, 205; on Hungarian borders, 158; on Italian war effort, 46; on Italy and the South Slavs, 149–52, 155–56; on Jewish minority issues, 191–94, 199, 206; on Ottoman issues, 37, 38, 39, 41–42, 44; in Paris among Big Four, 34; on Poland, 183, 188, 196, 197, 210–13; on reparations, 222–25; on Silesia and plebiscite, 215, 217–19, 223–25; as Welshman, 41, 204, 205, 211, 212, 218, 231; with Wilson in London, 33
Lord, Robert Howard: on Baltic countries, 190; on Congress of Berlin, 27; Eastern Galicia issue and, 182, 189–90, 209; as expert on Poland, 117, 182, 189, 190, 220, 221, 222, 233; influence on Wilson, 117, 218; at Paris Peace Conference, 117, 118; as part of The Inquiry, 26, 233; on Polish-German border, 220; on Silesian plebiscite, 220–21, 222
Lower Silesia, 214, 222. *See also* Silesia
Lubomirski, Kazimierz, 243–44
Lybyer, Albert, 118

278

Macedonia, 118
Machay, Ferdynand, 186
Mamatey, Victor, 10, 58, 70, 86, 94
Mandates: for Albania, 36–37; for Anatolia, 37, 39, 43; for Armenia, 33–36, 37, 39, 40, 43, 48–49, 53, 230; for Constantinople, 17, 33–40, 42, 43, 45, 48–49, 52–54, 230–31; discussion at Paris Peace Conference, 32–43, 47; distinction from partition, 47; in former Ottoman territories, 31–32, 36, 50–51, 103; justification, 36, 49–50; in League of Nations Covenant, 50, 51; for Palestine, 31, 36; possible American role, 32–36, 37–40, 42, 43, 45, 48–49, 52–54; seen as imperialist, 36, 37, 45, 50–51; Turkish opposition, 41–42
Manela, Erez, 10
Maps: of Bohemia and Poland, 125–26; of Eastern Europe, 118–19, 195 (fig.); historical and cultural influences, 157, 237; in peace process, 118, 195 (fig.); studied by Wilson, 117, 118, 149, 152, 156–57, 222, 237–39. *See also* Ethnographic maps; Mental maps of Eastern Europe
Marie, Queen of Romania, 5, 139–42, 143, 164, 187, 235
Marienwerder region, 188–89
Marinelli, Olinto, 149, 156
Marshall, Louis, 170–73, 176, 190–91, 200–201, 207, 236
Masaryk, Alice, 164–65
Masaryk, Charlotte, 165
Masaryk, Tomáš Garrigue: Coolidge and, 101; declaration of Czech independence, 95–96, 131; friendship with Wilson, 1, 4, 5, 124–26, 131, 132–33, 165, 166, 169, 173, 233; on Habsburg monarchy, 94, 98; postcard image with Wilson, 134 (fig.); as president of Czechoslovakia, 133, 164; School of Slavonic Studies and, 233; lecture on "The Problem of Small Nations," 4, 80
McKinley, William, 56

Mehmed VI, sultan, 40–41, 54
Mental mapping, defined, 4
Mental maps of Eastern Europe: attempts to influence Wilson's mental mapping, 121, 129–30, 152, 168–70, 172–73, 176–80, 208–10; of Balkan region, 86, 116, 137–38, 238; building a new Europe, 150, 234–35; component parts, 194, 204, 235; described in speeches, 116, 119, 235; Enlightenment, 4, 10, 129, 157; ethnographic complexity, 130, 168–73, 236–37, 238, 247; Germany and German influence, 24–25, 60–61, 62, 116; Herron on, 89, 127; Hungary in, 91, 105; Jewish minorities in, 202–3, 242; legacy of redrawn borders, 6, 228–33, 245; of Lithuania, 127; new borders and states, 9–10, 100, 116, 119, 127, 204, 231, 235, 238; personal factors influencing Wilson, 5, 9, 142–43, 233–36, 247–48; of Poland, 130, 170, 199–200, 236–37; of post-Habsburg lands, 99–100, 107, 115–16, 148; Russia and the Slavs, 128, 152–53; of Ruthenia, 213–14; vision of peaceful postwar Europe, 29–30, 115–16, 150; vacuum left by breakup of Austria-Hungary, 99–100, 107, 115, 132, 133, 148; volatility, 152–53, 205
Mezes, Sidney Edward, 26–27, 64
Mihailović, Ljubomir, 30, 90–91
The Mikado (Gilbert and Sullivan), 22
Miles, Sherman, 101, 216
Miller, David Hunter, 26, 64, 193, 194, 198
Miller, Herbert, 95
Minority protection, at Paris Peace Conference, 170–73, 177–80, 190–94, 198, 202, 203, 206, 220
Minority rights: Coolidge memorandum on, 184, 191; in newly-formed states, 9, 170, 172, 178–80, 184–85, 190–94, 198–204, 207, 210. *See also* Jews
Mitteleuropa (Naumann), 24–25, 62, 64, 93

279

Moncheur, Ludovic, Baron, 23, 62
Montagu, Edwin Samuel, 38
Montenegro: merger with Serbia, 133–39, 143, 145–46; representation at peace conference, 137. *See also* Nicholas, King of Montenegro
Morgenthau, Henry, 18–19, 25, 31, 52–53, 207
Morgenthau commission, 202
Mozart, Wolfgang Amadeus, 74; *Abduction from the Seraglio*, 22
Munich crisis (1938), 105, 169, 247
Muslims, in India, 38–39, 40. *See also* Islamic world; Ottoman empire

Namier, Lewis, 198
National Democracy (ND; Endecja), 170, 171
National minorities: in Czechoslovakia, 191, 193–94; in Eastern Europe, 97–98; Greeks in Ottoman empire, 31, 39, 47, 54, 215; Hungarians, 111, 194; in Poland, 168–73, 181–82, 191–94, 198–202, 206–7, 214, 227, 236; in Romania, 191, 193–94, 203–4; in Russia, 7, 65–66, 88; Sudeten Germans, 97, 100, 105, 133, 169, 184, 236, 247; in Yugoslavia, 185. *See also* Armenians
National self-determination: Asquith on, 19; of Balkan states, 19, 29–30, 144–45; borders based on, 104–5; challenges of determining will of population, 135–37, 138–39, 216, 220; challenges of drawing borders in areas of mixed populations, 159–60, 179, 181, 184–85, 220; Coolidge on, 104–5; Lansing on, 89–90; Lenin on, 7, 80, 238; of small nationalities, 3–4, 19–21, 57, 79–81, 89–90, 190, 204, 211; Wilson on, 3–4, 20–21, 22, 57, 79–81, 144–45, 148, 150–51, 157; as Wilson's aim in peace settlement, 24–26, 150–51. *See also* Fourteen Points speech; Plebiscites
Naumann, Friedrich, *Mitteleuropa*, 24–25, 62, 64, 93

Nazi Germany, 6, 11, 98, 105, 169, 247
Neu, Charles, 60
New York City: City College, 26; Delmonico's, 122; Italian Americans, 160–61; Metropolitan Opera House, 32, 103–4, 230; *New York Evening Mail*, 72; *New York Evening Post*, 54; *New York Times*, 52, 71, 242; Paderewski in, 122, 244; schools, 206–7
New York Times, 52, 71, 242
Nicholas, King of Montenegro, 133–37, 138, 139, 143
Nicolson, Harold, 3, 139, 153, 196, 201, 237
Nijinsky, Vaslav, 12–14
Nubar Pasha, Boghos, 166

Odell, George Talbot, 72–73, 74
Oedipus complex, 15
Orawa (Orava), 185–86, 234
Orlando, Vittorio Emanuele: on Dalmatia, 154–55, 157, 218; at Paris Peace Conference, 34, 108–9, 149, 201; resignation, 46; Wilson and, 148, 154, 157
O'Toole, Patricia, 10–11
Ottoman Eastern Crisis (1870s), 15–16, 19, 43, 140
Ottoman empire: American missionaries, 30–31, 43; Armenian massacres, genocide, 18–19, 21–22, 25, 30–31, 36, 52; Balkan Wars, 21, 28, 228; Christian hatred of, 17–18, 32, 37–38; Congress of Berlin and, 27; Eastern Question, 26–27, 31, 32, 42, 43, 44–45, 53, 55; European territories, 21–22, 27, 28, 33, 36–37, 43–44, 228; Gladstone's denunciation of "Bulgarian Horrors," 15–16, 18, 32, 42; operatic portrayals, 22, 42; representation at peace conference, 41–43; subject peoples, 17, 19, 23, 26, 27–30, 34; sultans, sultanate, 26, 33, 38, 39, 40, 43, 54, 82, 118, 230; Treaty of Sèvres, 17, 54; U.S. ambassadors to, 18–19, 22, 31, 52;

war not declared by U.S., 30–31;
Wilsonian Principles League, 33;
Wilson's antipathy toward, 18, 19,
22–26, 42–43, 54–55, 229, 230;
Wilson's Point Twelve, 17, 28–
30, 31–32, 80. *See also* Anatolia;
Armenians; Constantinople
(Istanbul); Palestine; Turkey
Ottoman empire, dissolution of:
abdication of sultan, 54; as allied war
aim, 21–22; discussions in Paris, 34–
49, 104; as emancipation of peoples,
26, 81–82; parallels to Austria-
Hungary, 30, 31–32, 54–55, 103–4,
229–30; reactions in Islamic world,
38–39, 40; recommendations by The
Inquiry, 27–28, 31–32; renunciation
of sovereignty, 51; vacuum left by,
115, 132; Wilson on, 34, 49–50; as
Wilson's aim, 18, 22–23, 24–26,
28–29, 54–55. *See also* Mandates

Paderewska, Helena, 126
Paderewski, Ignacy Jan: Dmowski and,
171, 172; friendship with Wilson,
122–24, 172, 175, 183, 196, 197,
208–9, 214, 233, 239, 244; House
and, 122–23, 173–74; on Jews, 191,
192–93, 201–2, 206; late entrance
at Versailles, 195–97; at League of
Nations, 244; on Lemberg conflict,
172, 212–13; letters to Wilson, 1,
120, 124, 170, 239, 244; meetings
with Wilson, 5, 122, 237; musical
career, 122, 195, 196, 244; in Paris,
189, 195–98, 206, 210–13, 219–20;
postcard image, 125 (fig.); as prime
minister, 174, 188–89, 207–9; on
Silesia, 219–20; on Ukrainians
and Galicia, 208–9, 210, 212–
13; in Washington, 122, 237
Page, Thomas Nelson, 99, 145–46
Palestine: Balfour Declaration,
22, 179; mandate, 31, 36. *See
also* Zionist movement
Pan-Slavism, 129, 152, 153, 238
Papacy, Vatican, *see* Benedict XV, Pope

Paris Peace Conference: discussion of
Austria-Hungary, 104, 107–09;
discussion of Hungarian borders,
205; discussion of Italians and
South Slavs, 150–52, 215; discussion
of mandates, 32–43; discussion
of minorities, 198–99, 202–04,
206–07; discussion of Montenegro,
137–38; discussion of plebiscites,
215, 217–19, 222–25; discussion
of Polish borders, 183, 188–89,
210–13; discussion of reparations,
109, 222–25; farewell letter to
Wilson, 168; final months, 162–64;
Ottoman negotiations, 53; Ottoman
representatives, 41–43; treaty with
Austria, 107–10, 111, 112, 114, 194;
Wilson on new European order,
149–50; Wilson's arrival, 32–33.
See also Treaty of Versailles; *and
specific individuals and issues*
Pašic, Nikola, 154, 166
Penfield, Frederic, 56, 59, 72
Persia, 38
Petliura, Symon, 182
Phelps, Nicole, 58, 72
Philippines, 33
Piłsudski, Józef, 197–98, 209, 216
Pittsburgh, 95, 122, 218
Plebiscites: in Anatolia, 215; in Dalmatia,
215, 218; in Eastern Galicia, 216–17;
potential influences on, 216–21, 222,
223–25; reparations issue and, 222–
25; in Silesia, 214, 215, 217–22, 223–
26, 238–39; in United States, 214–15
Podgorica Assembly (Montenegro), 137
Poland: American relations with, 124,
180–81, 239–41; appreciation of
Wilson, 12, 13 (fig.), 176, 240, 243–
44; food relief, 124, 197; immigrants
to United States from, 5, 61, 186,
225–26; independence leaders
and supporters, 82, 121–24, 130;
independence supported by Wilson,
22, 90, 122, 123–24, 168, 175–76;
Jews, 168–69, 170–73, 177, 180,
198–202, 206–07, 214, 231, 241–42;

Lord as American expert, 117, 182, 189, 190, 220, 221, 222, 223; mental map, 170, 199–200, 236–37; military forces, 174–75, 189, 212–13, 214; national minorities, 191–94, 198–202, 206–7, 236; partitions, 112, 114, 117, 123, 206; pogroms, 172, 199–200; provisional government, 174, 175, 180–81, 189–90, 197–98; representation at peace conference, 177–78, 197, 207–8; U.S. minister to, 180–81; war with Soviet Union, 173–74, 182, 239–40, 241; Wilson's friendship for, 125 (fig.), 239–41, 243–44; Wilson's Point Thirteen, 1, 22, 90, 124, 168, 175, 224, 226; Wilson's views of, 181, 182–83, 188–89, 196–97, 207–8, 223–24, 225–27, 236–37, 239, 240–41. *See also* Paderewski, Ignacy Jan; Polish-Lithuanian Commonwealth

Poland, territorial issues: American experts, 117; border with Czechoslovakia, 101, 185–88, 189, 246–48; border with Germany, 170, 192, 214, 220, 221–22; discussed in Paris, 181–83, 188–89, 210–14; disputes with Lithuania, 190; "indisputably Polish populations" criterion, 1–2, 168–69, 210, 226; Marienwerder region, 188–89; national minorities, 168–70, 181–82, 202–04, 206–07, 214, 227; Polish claims, 123, 174–75, 183, 210–14, 237; Romer on, 117,168–69. *See also* Eastern Galicia; Galicia; Silesia

Polasek, Albin, statue of Wilson, 232 (fig.)

Polish Americans, 19, 121, 122, 123, 225–26

Polish-Lithuanian Commonwealth, 123, 190, 201

Polish National Committee, 170–71, 178

Polish National Defense Committee, 122

Polish National Department, 61

Polk, Frank Lyon, 51, 69

Posen (Poznań), 170

Prague: Charles University, 246; royal castle, 133, 173; statue of Wilson at train station, 11, 166, 229, 231, 232 (fig.). *See also* Czechoslovakia

Princeton University, 2, 11, 15, 140, 228, 237

Princip, Gavrilo, 56, 57, 58

Progressive movement, 2, 3, 214–15, 239

Prussia, 1, 25, 75, 188, 214, 220–21

Psychoanalytic study of Wilson (Freud and Bullitt), 9, 15, 234

The Public: A Journal of Democracy, 138

Punch, 35 (fig.)

Pupin, Mihajlo, 143, 144, 152, 153

Reagan, Ronald, 229

Reconstruction, American, 81–82

Religious minorities, 31, 191, 198. *See also* Armenians; Jews

Reparations, 109, 222–25

Rhodes, 158

Roman Catholic Church: in Germany, 98; in Poland, 172–73, 201; in Silesia, 219–21. *See also* Benedict XV, Pope

Romania: Bessarabia, 140; boundaries drawn in Paris, 158; Brătianu as prime minister, 141, 203–05; Bukovina, 140; Dobruja, 140, 142, 164, 188; Handman as American expert, 118; immigrants to United States from, 61; independence in nineteenth century, 140, 228; Jews, 177–78, 193–94; Lansing's support, 90; Marie, Queen, 5, 139–42, 143, 164, 187, 235; monarchy, 139–42, 143; national minority protections, 191, 193–94, 203–4; Paris Peace Conference delegation, 141, 203–5; seen as new state, 194, 203–4; territorial claims, 140–41, 142, 163–64; territories added by treaty, 204; Wilson's antipathy toward, 142–43, 236; in World War I, 140. *See also* Transylvania

Rome, Wilson's visit to, 4, 99, 144–45, 146–48. *See also* Benedict XV, Pope; Italy

Romer, Eugeniusz, 117, 168–69, 190, 202, 243
Roosevelt, Theodore, 2, 3, 56–57, 131, 160–61
Roumanian National League, 61
Rousseau, Jean-Jacques, 4, 247
Russia: affinity with other Slavic groups, 7, 151–53, 155–56, 238; backwardness, 156; Bolshevik Revolution, 6, 40, 65, 128, 152; Catherine the Great, 17, 40; Civil War, 128–29; claim to Constantinople, 6, 40; Crimean War, 228; Jews, 199; national minorities, 7, 65–66, 88; Ottoman empire and, 15, 16, 17, 27, 40; Treaty of Brest-Litovsk, 40, 66, 86; Wilson's Point Six, 6–7, 66; Wilson's view of, 6–7, 128, 152–53, 156, 238. *See also* Soviet Union.
Ruthenians, 97, 117, 121, 168, 169, 178, 209, 210, 212, 213–14, 236. *See also* Carpatho-Ruthenia; Eastern Galicia; Ukrainians

Sarajevo, assassination of Archduke Franz Ferdinand, 56–58, 112, 246. *See also* Bosnia
Schleswig, 221
School of Slavonic Studies (London), 233
Seegel, Steven, 117
Self-determination, *see* National self-determination
Serbia: ambassador to United States, 30; Black Hand, 56, 113; and Bosnia, 59; Crown Prince Alexander, 120–21, 134; formation of Yugoslav kingdom (of Serbs, Croats, and Slovenes), 134, 154; immigrants to United States from, 57, 61; merger with Montenegro, 133–39, 143, 145–46; Wilson's popularity, 143–44. *See also* South Slavs; Yugoslavia
Serbian Americans, 57, 61, 144. *See also* Pupin, Mihajlo
Seton-Watson, R. W., 66, 83, 84, 125, 233
Silberer, Geza "Sil-Vara," 72–73, 74

Silesia: Coolidge on, 105; division between Germany and Poland, 214, 221–22; Lower, 214, 222; mineral wealth, 214, 223; mixed population, 214, 217, 219–21, 222; occupation troops, 221–22, 225–26; paramilitary forces, 221–22; plebiscite, 214, 215, 217–22, 223–26, 238–39; Teschen region, 101, 185, 189, 214, 247; Upper, 214, 217–22, 223–26, 238–39
Sixtus, Prince of Bourbon-Parma, 86–87
Slavery: conception of subject peoples in Eastern Europe, 8, 83, 112, 113–14, 154, 180, 221, 230; in United States, 81, 82, 114. *See also* Emancipation
Slavic studies, 117, 129, 233
Slavs: divisions among, 127–28, 130; emancipation from Habsburg rule, 151, 154; Lloyd George on, 155–56; pan-Slavism, 129, 152, 153, 238; Polish leadership of; 121; Russian influence, 7, 151–53, 155–56, 238; Wilson's view of group, 121, 151–53, 199, 238. *See also* Czechoslovakia; Poland; Russia; South Slavs
Slovakia, 12, 61, 105, 133, 185, 204–5, 247. *See also* Czechoslovakia
Slovenia, 61, 101, 146, 216. *See also* Carinthia; South Slavs; Yugoslavia
Small nations, 4, 20, 80, 204, 205, 211, 212, 218, 231. *See also* National self-determination; *and specific nations*
Smith, Leonard, 11, 115
Sokolow, Nahum, 166
Sonnichsen, Albert, 118
Sonnino, Sidney, 137–38, 145, 149, 206, 223
Sosnowski, George (Jerzy) Jan, 121–22
South Slavic National Council, 61, 121, 130
South Slavs: in Dalmatia, 45, 107, 156, 160, 215; discontent in Austria-Hungary, 64–65; friendship for Wilson, 120–21; Italians and, 144–48, 156–57, 185; immigrants to United States, 57, 61, 146; independent state proposed by

Lansing, 90; Kingdom of Serbs, Croats, and Slovenes, 134, 154; political leaders, 66–67; unification, 56, 75, 117, 144. *See also* Bosnia; Croatia; Montenegro; Serbia; Slovenia; Yugoslavia
Soviet Union: Armenia, 54; Eastern Europe and, 2, 6; war with Poland, 173–74, 182, 239–40, 241. *See also* Comintern; Russia
Spa conference, 239, 247
Spain, as intermediary between Washington and Vienna, 84–85
Spisz (Spiš), 185–86, 234
Stalin, Josef, 2
Steed, Henry Wickham, 83
Strauss, Richard, 73
Sudeten Germans, 97, 100, 105, 133, 169, 184, 236, 247
Sweden, as intermediary between Washington and Vienna, 96–97, 98
Sydorenko, Grigory, 182
Syria, 21, 28, 31, 36, 43, 51

Taft, William Howard, 2, 56, 131
Tarnowski, Adam, 71–72
Tatra Mountains region, 185–88, 246–48. *See also* Goatherds; Orawa; Spisz
Tetmajer, Kazimierz, 186
Thanksgiving, 52, 53, 54, 229
Thrace, 21, 36, 51, 164
Throntveit, Trygve, 10
Transylvania: discussed in Paris, 158; Hungarian-Romanian conflict, 100, 102, 158, 164, 189, 204–6; in Lammasch proposal, 75; mixed population, 97–98, 194; Romanian claim, 50, 140, 142
Treaty of Brest-Litovsk, 40, 66, 86
Treaty of Lausanne, 17, 54
Treaty of London (1915), 45–47, 59, 83, 103, 107, 115, 143, 148, 150
Treaty of Paris (1856), 228
Treaty of Saint-Germain, 17, 110
Treaty of Sèvres, 17, 54
Treaty of Trianon, 102, 111, 194
Treaty of Versailles: presentation to Germany, 194–97; rejection by U.S. Senate, 3, 50, 53, 162, 230; signing, 194, 245, 246, 247; Wilson's campaign for public support, 32, 52, 103–4, 111–14, 116, 119, 148–49, 159–60, 225–27. *See also* Germany; League of Nations
Trieste, 45, 59, 75
Troeltsch, Ernst, 115
Tumulty, Joseph, 241
Turkey: exchange of populations with Greece, 54; Treaty of Lausanne, 17, 54; Wilson's Thanksgiving joke, 52, 54, 229. *See also* Atatürk; Ottoman empire

Ukraine, 182, 200–201
Ukrainians: in Eastern Galicia, 97, 168–70, 181–82, 207–10; as minority in Poland, 170, 178, 193, 214; Paderewski on, 208–9, 210, 212–13; representative in Paris, 182, 212, 213. *See also* Ruthenians
United States: American Relief Administration, 124, 197; Civil War, 8, 81, 82, 95; Declaration of Independence, 92, 94, 191; Emancipation Proclamation, 81, 82, 114; entry into World War I, 23, 60, 71–72; Fourteenth Amendment, 81–82; Jewish organizations, 170, 176–80, 190–91, 199; neutrality, 20, 21, 23, 88. *See also* African Americans; American Jewish Committee; American Jewish Congress; Congress, U.S.; Immigrants in United States
Upper Silesia, 214, 217–22, 223–26, 238–39. *See also* Silesia
Uyanik, Nevzat, 18, 43

Venizélos, Elefthérios, 166
Versailles, *see* Treaty of Versailles
Vilnius (Wilno), 190, 200
Vittorio Emanuele III, King of Italy, 147–48, 161
Vittorio Veneto, battle of, 97, 98

INDEX

Voltaire, 4, 17, 40

Wales, 204, 205, 211, 212, 218, 231
Warsaw: American minister in, 181, 239-40; Plac Wilsona, 12; statue of House in, 123. *See also* Poland
Weimar Republic, 239
Weizmann, Chaim, 180
Westermann, William Linn, 40
White, Henry, 180-81
White, William Allen, 118
Wilhelm II, Kaiser, 71, 133
Williams, John Sharp, 126
Wilson, Edith, 8, 139-40, 142, 143, 177
Wilson, Ellen, 8
Wilson, Hugh, 74
Wilson, Margaret, 122
Wilson, Woodrow: academic career, 2, 11, 237; central role in remapping Europe, 129-30, 149-50, 157-58, 204, 219, 247; as charismatic figure, 132-33, 134, 147, 162; condolences for Franz Ferdinand, 56-57, 58; condolences for Franz Joseph, 71; education, 2, 15, 140, 228; gradualism, 119-20; idealism, 2, 16, 34, 144; as lame duck, 163-64; meeting with goatherds, 186-88, 234, 246-48; as messianic figure, 9, 12-13, 76, 89, 127, 234; on monarchies, 141-42; moral sense, 18, 19, 34, 49, 51; on national aspirations, 79-80, 81, 86, 88, 116, 148-49, 175; at Paris Peace Conference, 32-33, 34-49, 119, 132-42, 143-44, 147, 149-53, 155-56, 190-94, 196, 245; previous scholarship on, 10-11; Protestantism, 98, 198-99, 224, 242-43; psychoanalytic study, 9, 15, 234; *Punch* cartoon, 35 (fig.); reelection campaign (1916), 19-21, 122; righteousness, 2-3, 20; stroke, 14, 162-63, 244; Vatican visit, 99; Virginia background, 8, 62, 81-82, 198-99. *See also* Mental maps of Eastern Europe; National self-determination

Wilson, Woodrow, speeches of: on Adriatic question, 153-55; in Boston, 148-49, 168, 176; campaign for public support of Treaty of Versailles, 32, 52, 103-4, 111-14, 116, 119, 148-49, 159-60, 225-27; in Cincinnati, 20-21; in Columbus, 111-12, 159-60; to Congress, 22, 25-29, 49-50, 63, 67-70, 122, 123-24; in Des Moines, 119; first inaugural address, 2; Flag Day (1917), 60-61, 62; Four Principles, 79-82, 84-86, 87, 88; Fourth of July (1918), 92; in Helena, 57; at Metropolitan Opera House, 32, 103-4, 230; in Omaha, 113, 225-26; in San Diego, 112-14, 230; in St. Louis, 52, 229; in Tacoma, 226-27. *See also* Fourteen Points speech
Wilson Square (Wilsonov Trg), Zagreb, 12, 155 (fig.), 229
Wise, Stephen, Rabbi, 176, 190-91, 236, 241-42
Wiseman, William, 30
Witos, Wincenty, 241
World War I: battle of Vittorio Veneto, 97, 98; beginning, 56-58, 112; Gallipoli campaign, 22; Italian entry, 45, 46; separate peace negotiations with Austria-Hungary, 72, 74-78, 86-87, 108; U.S. entry, 23, 60, 71-72; U.S. neutrality, 20-23, 88; war relief from United States, 19, 20; Wilson's mediation efforts, 21. *See also* Paris Peace Conference

Yellin, Eric, 11
Young Bosnia, 56
Yugoslavia: Adriatic dispute with Italy, 146-48, 149, 150-52, 153-55, 162-63; American experts, 117-18; appreciation of Wilson and America, 12, 143-44, 146-47, 154, 155 (fig.), 229; disintegration, 229; establishment, 66, 120, 143; Montenegro, 133-39, 143, 145-46; Paris Peace Conference

delegation, 204–5; territorial disputes with Austria, 101, 216. *See also* Balkan states; Bosnia; Croatia; Dalmatia, Italian claims; Serbia; Slovenia; South Slavs

Zagreb, Wilson Square (Wilsonov Trg), 12, 155 (fig.), 229
Zimmerman Telegram, 60
Zionist movement, 166, 179–80, 200
Zita, Empress, 74–75

The authorized representative in the EU for product safety and compliance is:
Mare Nostrum Group
B.V Doelen 72
4831 GR Breda
The Netherlands

www.ingramcontent.com/pod-product-compliance
Lightning Source LLC
Chambersburg PA
CBHW031759220426
43662CB00007B/466